IN MY SHOES
A WRITER IS BORN

BASED ON A TRUE STORY

IN MY SHOES
A WRITER IS BORN

BASED ON A TRUE STORY

BRENDA HAMPTON

www.brendamhampton.com

Voices Books & Publishing
P.O. Box 3007
Bridgeton, MO 63044

First Trade Paperback Printing May 2012
Printed in the United States of America

ISBN 13: 978-1470160449
ISBN 10: 1470160447

To God be the glory...

Prologue

September 12, 1984

My frizzy long hair was scattered all over my head and my skin was pale as ever. Tears streamed down my face as I watched the round clock on the wall tick away. After lying in the hospital bed at St. Louis County Hospital for seventeen hours, I knew exactly when the next contraction was coming.

The minute hand hit the twelve, causing me to brace myself. I squeezed the sheets on the bed, balling them up in my hands so tight that they turned red. I squeezed my eyes together and took quick breaths that I was advised to do. My legs flopped around like fishes. I did my best to cease the excruciating pain from the ongoing contractions.

"Somebody...anybody, please help me," I shouted, as the rigorous pain took over my entire body. It lasted for a few minutes, and then it went away. I sighed from relief, recognizing that I would only remain this calm for the next twelve minutes. It was time to beg for help again, but the nurses and doctors were delayed with their response.

As I screamed out again, the nurse came into the room, smiling at me as if there was something to smile about. She reached for my arm to take my blood pressure. I was mad as hell by the way things were progressing, and the twisted look on my face showed it.

"Brenda, you must keep the oxygen over your mouth so the babies can get oxygen and breathe too. If you keep removing it, you'll put their lives at risk and yours."

She placed the oxygen mask over my mouth, again, but it was sure to come off. At this point, I didn't give a damn. How long did this have to go on? As the nurse took my blood pressure, the doctor entered the room. He was grinning from ear-to-ear, too, and I didn't understand what the fuck was so funny. Maybe they were trying to make me suffer; after all, I was a seventeen year old pregnant with twins. Through their eyes, I should have known better than to put myself into a predicament like this one. Basically, I was getting what I deserved and they were doing nothing to help me ease the situation at hand.

The doctor eyeballed the clock, knowing that my outburst was coming soon. He massaged my arms, before wiggling his fingers into a pair of sterile white gloves. Walking to the end of the bed, he stood in front of it. He ordered me to bend my knees and widen my legs. I frowned. Exposing myself to him was very uncomfortable. But at this point, I was willing to do whatever was necessary to get this over and done with.

The nurse held my shaky legs apart, while he inserted his fingers inside of me. *Nasty*, I thought. *Just nasty*. And for making me wait this long, I hoped he got a whiff of my pee since I had already peed on myself.

"I can feel one of the baby's heads, but we're still not quite there yet. Relax," he said, patting my leg. "We're almost there."

That was so easy for him to say, and as soon as those thoughts left my head, it was that time again. The oxygen mask was driving me nuts, so I snatched it off and reached for the nurses red long hair, yanking it.

"Can't you see that I need some damn help?" I said through gritted teeth. "When does this shit stop?! Why can't y'all do nothing for me? Damn!" I pounded my other fist on the bed, displaying my frustrations.

The nurse did her best to remove her hair from my fingers, but the grip was so tight that the doctor had to come over to assist.

"Calm down," he said, pulling my fingers away from the nurse's hair.

"I can't go on like this," I cried out. "Make this stop, please!"

He tried to calm me, but the nurse had given up and walked out. I guess she'd thought I was one crazy bitch, and under these conditions, yes, I was.

"Deep breaths," the doctor repeated. "Take deep breaths and keep the oxygen over your mouth."

He waited until I calmed down, and then he left the room. The deep breaths weren't working and he knew they weren't. I swear, if I could've left, I would have. This was ridiculous and did it take all of this, just to bring a child...children into the world?

As my raging anger ceased, I listened to another lady who was in the same room as I was. A dingy white curtain separated us, and even though her contractions weren't as rapid as mine, she was going through as well.

"I swear to God that I'm never fucking again!" she shouted. "This shit is for the birds! No more pussy for you, man. Do you hear that, Jake? No more pussy for you!"

For a second, I couldn't help but laugh. I felt what the White woman had said, but my thoughts had turned to that deadbeat Negro who had gotten me knocked up. If he only knew what I was going through. *Damn him*, I thought. What a lowlife bastard to make me experience something of this magnitude alone. I didn't realize how much I'd hated him, up until I sat in my bed, watching the clock and waiting as the minute hand struck twelve. I braced myself again, thinking of ways I could kill him.

At 7:53 a.m. the next day, twin A was born and twin B followed at 8:03 a.m. Completely exhausted, I barely had enough strength to look at the babies in the nurses' arms. All I could see was him, and hating him so much gave me something I could look at every single day. I turned my head, wiping a slow tear that had rolled from the corner of my eye. My only thought was... *where in the hell do me and my babies go from here?*

Chapter One

Seven years earlier...

Just who did we think we were moving, from Wellston, a rough part of St. Louis, to Black Jack, Missouri where the uppity Black folks and rich White folks lived? We didn't have the dollars, the look...not even a car to keep up with the elite people who lived in Black Jack, but Mama had her faith and pride to keep our family together and moving.

My sisters, Jesse, Rita and I were teased at school about being *different*; poor, according to many of the other children who had been born with silver spoons in their mouths. For us, the finer things in life didn't exist and we were forced to make a way out of no way. There were rarely any birthday celebrations and Christmas was just another day. Money was hard to come by and Mama often sent us to the grocery store with food-stamps; food-stamps that many people in the suburbs hadn't seen before, until they'd seen them in our hands. We could hear the whispers and giggles while standing in line at the grocery store.

"What is she doing with those," one snobby lady said to the other. "Get a job."

Mama wasn't the one to mess with; after all, she did have a job. It just didn't pay much, but for the time being, it was enough to upgrade our status. Mama turned to the Black lady, as she and her friend pursed their lips as if their shit didn't stink.

"Mind your own damn business, heifer," Mama spat with venom in her eyes. "And one more word from you, in front of my kids or not, I will tear into your ass!"

Both women's eyes bugged, nearly breaking from their sockets. They were shocked, and quickly tightened their lips like kids who had just been scolded. Little did they know, Mama could light a fire with some of the words that spilled from her mouth. Her hard stare could break you down and leave you in fear. She was so mad that day at the grocery store, she could have hurt somebody. She ranted all the way home, and since we didn't have a car, we piled the groceries in a shopping cart, taking turns pushing it down Old Halls Ferry Road, until we got home.

I was so embarrassed as people drove by in cars, looking at us as if we were hillbillies. More so, I feared seeing some of those cruel kids who made fun of us while walking to and from school. We were teased about every little thing the kids could find. From the light color of our skin, to the hand-me-down clothes we wore. Our nappy thick hair wasn't a hit, and I'd been officially granted the name "Musty Mama" by a fat boy in my classroom who chanted that name every single day. I remember crying so hard about being made fun of, Mama would say, "Brenda, I thought you were stronger than that. Just because we don't live up to other people's expectations, and I get government assistance, it doesn't make us poor. Things will get better."

She must have told me that a million times, but it still didn't stop anyone from teasing us. And as I looked around at our nearly empty house that had an echo, and compared it to our neighbors' lavishly furnished houses, I thought Mama didn't know what she was talking about. To me, we didn't have much to brag about. The ranch style home on Burchard Drive that we lived in was just a rectangle that kept a roof over our heads. The house had three bedrooms, a spacious kitchen and living room, two bathrooms and a finished basement. Much of the furniture was from the Goodwill and was tacky as hell. It was all that Mama could afford, though, and was a definite improvement from the matchbox house we'd lived in, in Wellston where there were many killings in the neighborhood, theft and plenty of robberies.

To make matters worse, we didn't even have a daddy. Many of the other kids in the neighborhood had one, but yet again, we were shit out of luck. I didn't understand why our family had to be so different from the other families in Black Jack, and there was no secret that we just didn't fit in.

I never asked Mama about our daddy, because, somehow, I believed she made us all by herself. She was the sole provider, so I figured daddies weren't needed. I often thought that maybe things would be different if daddy was around, and maybe, just maybe, we could afford to have some of the finer things in life. Again, that was just a thought, but over the years, I learned to put the thoughts of having a father behind me. Mama had everything under control, and financially, things took a slight turn for the better when she started working as an assembly line worker for Emerson Electric Company on West Florissant Ave. It seemed as if she was barely around, though. And when she was, she was bitching about cleaning the house or doing the yard work. She came home from work one day, fussing about the dishes in the sink not being washed.

"Didn't I tell y'all to clean up that kitchen before y'all went to bed," she said, standing in the doorway to me and Jesse's bedroom with her hands on her curvy hips. "Get up and go get those dishes out of the sink!"

It was after midnight—Mama was tripping. I remembered washing the dishes earlier, and Jesse confirmed it as we both tossed our covers aside and sluggishly got out of bed. "We did wash those dishes, Mama," Jesse whined. "Daaang."

Mama trailed us down the narrow hallway and into the kitchen. I stood in front of the stainless steel sink in total disbelief that Mama had caused all this ruckus over a fork that was left in the sink and hadn't been washed. She pointed to it.

"When you wash the dishes, you need to make sure every last thing is clean. Get that fork out of there and wash down my sink with bleach and hot water."

Mama cut her eyes like a razor-sharp knife and stormed away, leaving Jesse and me standing there shaking our heads. It couldn't be that serious, but for Mama, it was. Her house had to be spotless and Pine-sol infused the air around us every day.

Upon turning twelve, I felt like a lost child and was utterly bitter about so many things. My grades suffered; I was constantly being bullied at school. I tried to make friends with the other students, but many of the girls hated me. The boys were cruel, and after what had happened to me in a supply closet one day, it left me devastated.

I was excited that my teacher, Mrs. Brooks, had chosen me to go to the supply closet to get pencils and paper. Dressed in a dingy pink shirt, a flowered skirt and rundown white shoes, I skipped to the closet. My hair was in a nappy Afro puff that two boys made fun of as I skipped by them.

"Why don't you go comb yo hair, ole nappy head girl?" Barry said, as him and Martin giggled. "Wit yo ugly, dumb self."

My face fell flat and feelings were hurt by their harsh words. I swallowed the huge lump in my throat, ignoring what they had said about me. But as I was inside of the closet, looking for the pencil box, they came inside. They giggled and closed the door behind them.

"What you doin' in this closet?" Martin asked, as he hit the light switch.

I widened my eyes in the dark, trying to see but couldn't. "Stop playing," I yelled out. "Turn the lights back on!"

My voice sent the two boys in my direction, and before I knew it, one of them placed his hand over my mouth.

"If you scream, we gon' beat yo butt. Now, shut up!"

I didn't know what was going to happen and I surely didn't want to get beat up by any boys. I did, however, attempt to rush out of the closet, but one of the boys grabbed my arms and held them from behind. His grip was tight, and almost twice my size, he was very strong. I wiggled my shoulders, hoping to break his grip.

"Let me go," I shouted. "I'm telling on both of y'all!"

They laughed and the one behind me kept a grip on my arms. The other boy stood in front of me and raised my shirt over my head, exposing my tiny breasts. As my shirt was tightened on my face, both boys rubbed their hands all over my breasts. The touch of their grimy hands made my flesh crawl and I stood with tears in my eyes, shivering and afraid of what else they would do to me.

"She got some tiny ass tiddays," Barry said. "And she probably ain't got no hair on her pussy."

Next thing I knew, Barry shoved me away. He pushed me so hard that I fell against a shelf, knocking it down. The loud crash caused them to rush out of the closet, but I remained there wounded. I pulled my shirt down and wiped the flowing tears from my face. One of my scuff-marked shoes had come off, so I hurried to put it back on. Needless to say, I returned to the classroom, without supplies. Mrs. Brooks was livid. I told her I couldn't find the pencils and paper, so she sent another student to go look. So hurt by what Martin and Barry had done to me, I laid my head on the desk so no one would see my unstoppable tears. I told no one about the incident, and every time I saw Barry and Martin, they held up their fists as a warning for me to keep quiet.

The torture didn't stop there. On a regular basis, I'd hear those famous words from classmates: "Didn't your sister wear that yesterday? Uggh, that's nasty!" Jesse probably did have it on yesterday, but at least we didn't have to wear the same underclothes. It surprised me as to how many kids noticed us wearing the same clothes, but for whatever reason, many of them did. I guess Jesse and I thought we could get away with it, because we looked so much alike. She was only a year older than me, and we were all mello-yello with dark brown eyes. Jesse's hair was a long dusty brown, and because I was a bit thicker than she was, that's how some people recognized our differences.

As for my eldest sister, Rita, she was five years older than I was. She had moved on to junior high school and things had gotten better for her. Appearance wise, she had it going on. Tresses of long curls hung down her back, and according to many of the boys in our neighborhood, she was known for having one of the most voluptuous bodies they'd ever seen. Rita took good care of herself, and going to school didn't seem to be an issue for her. She easily made new friends in school, and Jesse and I hoped that once we got to junior high school, things would change in our favor as well. But before we ever made it to junior high school, something happened. Daddy came into the picture and it sure as hell was no picnic.

Jesse and I were walking home from Black Jack Elementary School that day. We had just gotten into a heated confrontation with some rude girls in the neighborhood who wanted to fight Jesse because a boy named Chuck liked her. Chuck put it all to rest, when he pushed one of the girls on the ground, causing her to fall hard.

"Leave them alone," he said with tightened fists as he evil-eyed the girls who had formed a circle around us. "If you want to fight them, you gon' have to fight me first!"

Chuck was pretty thick and none of the girls were about to challenge him. He also had a brother, Darrell, who had Chuck's back and he was right there beside him. Jesse and I were relieved. These two brothers had saved the day. We ran off laughing and talking about how brave they were, but forgot to thank them for having our backs. As we neared the corner of Burchard Dr., a putting smoking mini-van started trailing behind us. Inside was a man with golden brown smooth skin, a shoulder length dripping-wet jerry curl and a rugged goatee. He called out our names, causing Jesse and I to stop in our tracks. We frowned at the unknown man, and I narrowed my eyes to get another look, before running up the hill to our house. "I'm yo daddy," the man yelled out the window, causing me to halt my steps again.

I turned to take another look, but Jesse tugged at my arm. "Come on, Brenda! We don't really know who that man is." My book bag hit the ground. I shot off like a rocket, trying to get as far away from him as I could.

When we got home, Mama wasn't there. She worked from three in the afternoon, until midnight. We didn't know what to do and had hoped Daddy wouldn't come to the door.

Mama was adamant about us not talking to strangers, and as far as I was concerned, Daddy or not, he was a stranger. Jesse and I never knew what Daddy looked like, but Rita did. When she was a little girl, he was always around. That was until him and Mama got divorced. It was finalized a year after I was born.

That night, we stayed up until Mama came home and couldn't wait to tell her about the man in the van, claiming to be our father. Like always, she looked tired and yawned as she made her way down the long hallway to her bedroom. We followed closely behind, while Rita was asleep. She didn't see it as a big deal, but said she was anxious to see Daddy again. I wasn't.

"Mama," I said, plopping down next to her on a full-sized mattress without a fitted sheet. The mattress was pushed against the lime green painted wall, as green was one of Mama's favorite colors. "A man followed Jesse and me home today. We were kind of scared."

Mama squinted and removed her shoes to rub her aching feet. "Scared for what, Brenda? Who was he and what did he say? I told y'all about talking to strangers and—"

"He said he was our daddy," Jesse blurted out. "We didn't know whether to believe him or not."

Silence fell over the room. Mama's lips were clipped tight. She changed into her nightgown, and made us go into our room to go to bed. Before we did, we told Mama that we were afraid, and that we didn't want to see him again. She nodded, so we *thought* she understood.

Within the next few weeks, Daddy showed up time and time again. Simply put...I hated him. Mama was trying to make everything okay between us, and she seemed perky when he was around. She was always a pretty woman, but it seemed as if she jazzed herself up to look even prettier for him. Her long pressed hair was feathered and it lay on her shoulders. Her face was round like mine, and even though her flawless skin didn't need any make-up, she wore plum lipstick and blush to brighten up her high cheekbones. Her brown eyes shone for Daddy, and as happy as Mama appeared to be, I was crushed. The only thing I could think about was where in the fuck had he been for all these years? Did she forget how he'd left us? What was wrong with her for allowing him to come back into our lives? At this point, I was beginning to despise her, too.

Rita was also enthused about Daddy being around, and even though he'd abandoned us, their previous relationship allowed her to develop love for him. As for Jesse, she often kept her thoughts to herself. Still, I knew she felt the same way I did. I could see the hurtful look in her eyes, and she was the only one who hadn't said much to Daddy at all.

Less than a few months after being introduced to Daddy, he managed to move in with us. We started to connect with him, and that's when we discovered another family we didn't know existed. We met my grandparents, who we often referred to as Mu and Granddaddy. We also met a bunch of cousins, aunts and uncles. Daddy seemed so proud to have us around his family, it made me wonder...if he was so proud, why did he leave us to begin with?

I remember how sharp he used to look on holidays with his white, black and brown leather suits, wide-brim hats to match, and Stacy Adams. He stood about six-two, and made me think of Billy Dee Williams every time I'd see him. He had swagger in his walk and was granted respect when he came into a room. Frankly, after two months of being around him, he'd earned my respect. I had high hopes of marrying a man like him, and to say he was fine would be an understatement.

There did, however, become a time when I noticed Daddy drinking excessively. He would always stop by the liquor store and come out with a bottle of something wrapped in a brown paper bag.

He'd often hide his bottle of liquor underneath the seat of his silver Deuce-And-A-Quarter so Mama wouldn't see it. I didn't quite understand his reasoning for hiding it, because you could smell the liquor on his breath a mile away.

At first, Mama and Daddy seemed to get along well. So well, that I wondered why they ever got divorced. I began to think our family was finally coming together. And even though Mama and Rita seemed enthused about Daddy's presence, there was still a little doubt in me that this would all work out. You see, Rita was Daddy's favorite. It was so obvious that Jesse and I started to develop a little coldness towards Daddy because of it. If anything, I felt that since he didn't know Jesse and me that well, his connection with us should have been greater. I'd guessed since Rita was his first child, that could have been his reasoning for showing favoritism. Still, it wasn't a good feeling, but we all tried to make the best of it.

As Mama and Daddy managed to work through their differences, Mama and Rita weren't getting along at all. Rita was being the typical teenager, staying out late, sometimes, because she had to work at Happy Joe's Pizza. But Mama wasn't down with late hours, no matter what. When she set the rules, it was smart to follow them. She was known for being very strict and not following her rules always meant trouble.

"Rita, you can get your shit and get the hell out of here," Mama yelled, while smoking a Kool cigarette, pacing the hallway.

Rita yelled from inside of her bedroom. "I hate this house! You don't let me do nothing, and I can't help it if I got off work late! I can't wait to go away to college!"

From our bedroom, Jesse and I listened to the bickering with tears welled in our eyes. We hated to hear Mama and Rita yell at each other, but staying out of it was the best we could do. They were going at it, and for the first time, Daddy intervened, adding his two cents.

"Don't talk to yo mama like that," he shouted. "If you don't like the rules, then maybe you should pack yo shit up and go."

"Maybe I should!" Rita yelled back. "I'm sick of being in this house and I'm tired of Mama always trying to tell me what I can and can't do! I buy my own clothes, my own food...what else in the hell does she want!"

After that, all Jesse and me heard was tussling, then a bunch of name calling. Mama and Rita were known for going to blows with each other, and pulling each other's hair was nothing new. This time, however, we heard a loud thud, and Rita's voice screeched so loudly that we jumped up from our beds. We rushed to see what had happened, only to find Rita crouched down on the floor with her hands covering her face. Daddy stood over her with a tightened fist and a mean mug on his face.

"I told you to shut yo mouth, didn't I?" he spat. "And don't you ever put your hands on yo mama in front of me again!"

I stood in disbelief about what had just happened. My mouth hung open and my body felt as if cement had been poured over it—I couldn't move. Mama had turned to walk away, and Daddy bumped my shoulder as he went into Mama's bedroom and slammed the door. Rita slowly got off the floor, face dripping wet with tears and her right eye closed shut. My stomach tightened in knots, and without saying a word, Rita also returned to her bedroom, closing the door.

I didn't know what to say or what to think about Daddy, but when I returned to my bedroom, I picked up a spiral notebook on my dresser and started to scribble. Hateful words were being written about Daddy and Mama, too: *Why must I have the worst parents in the world! Poor Rita didn't deserve this and why did Mama let Daddy go there? I am so disappointed in her and none of this mess ever happened before Daddy got here. He hadn't been around to teach none of us wrong from right. A spanking may have done Rita just fine, but to blacken her eye was a bunch of bullshit. He lucky it wasn't me, because I would have blackened his eye right back. Mama's too, if she tried to jump in it. Yep, Mama too, because she deserved it for letting him get away with this stuff...*

As Daddy's true colors had started to show, that same week, he stood tall and shameful for what he had done. He continuously apologized to everyone in the family, and Rita was rewarded a fancy white wicker bedroom set with a round mirror.

"Every teenage girl's room should look like this," Mama said, obviously feeling guilty. She proudly stood next to Daddy, as he, too, agreed with Mama.

"I hope this makes you feel better, baby. I'm sorry about what happened and yo mama and me picked out the bedroom set for you."

Daddy embraced Rita, and needless to say, she was ecstatic. She seemed pleased to put this incident behind her. I wasn't pleased, and yet again, Jesse and I felt left out. Did we have to get a black-eye in order for somebody to do something for us? Our bedroom was crappy as fuck! We had twin beds that were made of wood, with slats underneath the bottom to hold up the springy mattress. Mama said that when she was a little girl, her daddy would take the slats off the beds and whip their asses. The dresser was old as dirt, too, and two of the drawers were missing. As a newborn baby, I used to sleep in the top drawer because I didn't have a baby bed. So, no, I wasn't being ungrateful about the situation. We were just being left the hell out. I was kind of glad that we weren't allowed to have visitors. I was sure they'd make fun of the place Jesse and I called a bedroom.

After that one incident, it took less than three months for our home to turn into a hellhole. There was so much arguing, I could hardly stand it. All I knew was, before my daddy moved in, all this mess wasn't happening. Most of the time he was drunk and he and Mama were arguing just as much as Mama and Rita. I wished that Rita would just listen to Mama and come in at a decent time. But night after night, the fighting continued.

Mama really didn't have a beef with Jesse and me, but she stayed on us about the housework. Considering the fact that Daddy sat around all day doing nothing, I didn't understand why he wasn't asked to do anything? He was getting away with murder, coming and going as he pleased, and I was in disbelief that Mama had allowed this to go on. Basically, he had it made, but we weren't even allowed to go outside and play with the other kids. If we did go outside, we had to sneak out, making sure we got home before Mama got off work.

As for visitors, no one was allowed to step one foot on our property. If anybody called for us or stopped by, they were cursed out by Mama, who yelled profanities at them through the door. It was the most embarrassing thing ever, and as soon as we'd go to school, the neighborhood kids had something else to tease us about. "Y'all's Mama is out of control!" Yes, she was, but it was her way of protecting us.

At fourteen, I was glad to leave Kirby Junior High School, where the bullying had continued. Riding the school bus was horrible and some of the boys, particularly a pudgy boy named,

Timmy, who obviously had his own insecurities, he didn't know when to cut it off. He and another boy who were best friends, used to stand up in the back of the bus, yelling, "Who in the neighborhood ain't got no car, they poor as hell, get free lunch and wear the same clothes every day!" Some of the other students would fall out laughing and point to me. I would just sit there, looking out the window to ignore them, and feeling humiliated with tears at the brim of my eyes. The "Who" game was played every single day. From a simple pimple on my face, to my tiny breasts, I was laughed at. I used to repeat to myself, "Mama said ignore them, Mama said ignore them...," but a person could only ignore so much. I started to say insulting things back to them, but that prompted their eagerness to fight. I definitely didn't want to go there with boys, but by high school, that shit changed. Boys were fair game and so were girls.

I spent the summer getting ready to start my freshman year at Hazelwood East High School and Jesse was going to be a sophomore. Rita was on her way to college and couldn't wait to leave home. I was sad to see Rita go, but I was also glad that all the fighting, at least between her and Mama, would be over.

A few weeks before Rita was set to leave, Mama had finally gotten a car. She didn't know how to drive, and Rita and Daddy were the only drivers in the house. Using his car wasn't an option. Mama said that he couldn't be relied upon to get her back and forth to work, so therefore, Jesse or I had to quickly learn how to drive. The car was an old blue beat-up Ford Pinto. It got us from point A to B, and with limited time, Rita did her best to teach me the basics. I wasn't supposed to be driving at all, but learning how to was imperative.

Certainly, having a car had benefits, and Mama working nights enabled us to hit the streets. Along with some girls from the neighborhood, Jesse and I hung out at the Halls Ferry Cinema and chilled out with gangs of teenagers on the White Castles' parking lot. We returned home at almost midnight one night, shocked to see nearly every light on inside. Daddy wasn't there, but Mama was.

"You know we about to get in hella trouble," I said to Jesse, putting the car in park as it sat in the driveway. My heart raced. Mama had eased up on letting us leave the house, but our 8:00 p.m. curfew was set in stone. Midnight was a no-no.

"What we gon' say?" Jesse whispered, as she got out of the car and followed behind me. I shrugged, figuring that we were about to catch a beat-down from Mama, or get cussed out and thrown out of the house. Afraid to go inside, Jesse and I tip-toed through the squeaking front door that was cracked open, only to find Mama curled up behind it. Her face was beet red and tears poured from her eyes. She could barely speak any words.

"Mama, what's wrong!" I yelled in a panic, dropping down beside her to see how badly she was hurt.

"Ya...y'all Daddy jumped on me," she stuttered. The harder she cried, the madder I got.

I smacked away a tear that had rolled down my cheek and stood up. Jesse had already gone to call the police, and once the dispatcher said the police were on the way, I called my grandparents' house, looking for Daddy so I could tell him what I really thought of him. How any man could treat a woman this way, I didn't understand. I wanted some answers, and if he ever came back here again, he'd have to fight all of us. My grandmother answered the phone, and the sound of her soft, sweet voice calmed me.

"What's the matter, Brenda?" she asked.

I sighed and pouted with fury in my eyes. "Please tell my daddy to call us. It's important that I speak to him right away."

I hung up, not knowing if my grandmother knew what her own son was capable of doing. I mean, damn! First Rita and now this. It was time for Mama to stand up. The police came, questioned Mama and issued a warrant for Daddy's arrest. That night, all I remembered thinking was...I hoped that when they caught up with him, they beat his ass like he did Mama's.

For the next few weeks, things were quiet around the house. Daddy was gone and Rita was gathering her belongings to take to college. We were all so miserable; she was moving away to Nashville, Tennessee. We didn't know if we would ever see her again. The day Rita left, I felt empty. She seemed delighted to go, but at the same time, I knew she was going to miss us too. With Mama and Jesse in the car, I drove Rita to her friend Micky's house because she was attending TSU as well. And after a bunch of hugs and kisses were exchanged, Rita moved on to experience a new way of life, and Jesse and I were stuck with the same ole, same ole shit!

Chapter Two

Mama started giving Jesse and me some breathing room. We didn't understand why, until we came home from a friend's house one day and Daddy was resting comfortably on the long green tweed couch in the living room with his legs propped up on the table.

"Hello, girls," he said, blowing smoke into the air from the cigarette he was smoking.

I rolled my eyes at him, and so did Jesse. We stormed toward Mama's bedroom and stood in the doorway, watching as she looked in the mirror and brushed her long hair.

"What is he doing here?" I hissed in a vicious tone. "Did you let him in here?"

"She had to," Jesse said, folding her arms.

Mama ignored us, but as we began to walk away from the door, she called our names. We turned, only to see her point the hairbrush in our direction. "Mind your business and stay the hell out of mine. This is my house, and there will be no explanation given for who I decide to have in it!"

Case closed. Nothing else needed to be said. Hurt by her actions, I went to our bedroom and lay across my bed. Jesse laid on hers.

"Is she stupid or something?" I asked Jesse in a whisper. "How could she let him beat her ass, and then let him come back over here? I ain't gon' never let nobody treat me like that, and I'll bust a mofo upside his head if he ever put his hands on me. Mama must be crazy."

"She got to be crazy and it don't make no sense to me either." Jesse removed the rubber-band from her thick ponytail. She sat up against the headboard, placing a pillow on top of her lap. "Tell me an imaginary dream, Brenda," she said. "I need to go to sleep and your stories be sooo good."

I laughed, because there were times that I would read Jesse some of the entries I'd written in my spiral notebooks. She would eventually fall asleep, either from boredom or from being tired. I reached underneath my mattress where I kept most of my notebooks and sat Indian style on my bed. I smiled at the first sentence I'd written, knowing that I had no business doing so much cursing. Instead of reading what I'd written, I dropped the notebook on my lap and used my imagination to create a story that I felt would put Jesse to sleep. It was a story about a Black girl who experienced her first kiss. Jesse giggled as I described it, but once I was almost finished with my story, I could hear her snoring. I fell back on the bed, held the notebook up high and turned it in half circles. I spoke softly to myself, as I looked at my name, Brenda Hampton, that I'd sketched with an eraser on front of the notebook.

"If I keep writing and telling stories like this, maybe one day I'll be a writer. Do you think I can be a writer, Jesse? Huh?"

I thought Jesse was asleep, but in a whisper I heard her say, "I think you can be whatever you want to be. Now, go to bed."

I smiled at the thought, and then closed my eyes. I went into deep thought, making up a fairytale story in my head about the way I wished our lives were. No matter what, I remained hopeful that things would get better.

***

Eventually, there became a plus side to Daddy being around. Mama became less overprotective of us, and Jesse and I took advantage of her sudden kindness. One night, we stayed out past midnight, again, thinking that Mama wouldn't mind. Maybe, not even notice, since she was so occupied with Daddy. We knocked on the door, and it flew wide open. "Where in the hell have y'all heifers been?!" she yelled, looking like a madwoman.

"We...we fell asleep at Dana's house," I lied. "School hasn't started back yet, Mama, so what's the big deal?" Truth of the matter was, we were having so much fun joy riding in the streets and going home to listen to Mama and Daddy argue was the last thing on our minds.

Mama snatched both of us into the house, yelling with fury in her eyes, "Get y'all asses in here, get your clothes and get out! I will not raise no street runners, running in and out of my house when y'all get good and ready to! This ain't no damn whore house over here!"

Out of respect, Jesse was one to always do what she was told, but I had to challenge Mama. "Dang, you gon' throw us out for coming in late? Why you always yelling so much?"

Mama pointed her finger at my face, touching the tip of my pointed nose. "Brenda, shut your damn mouth, girl, and get out of my house! Now!"

I backed away from her aggressiveness and went into the bedroom where Jesse was.

"She just wants to be here alone with Daddy," I whispered. "Where in the hell are we supposed to go?"

Jesse shrugged, shaking her head with disgust. We listened to Mama tell Daddy how tired she was of us. "I put up with all that backtalk and coming in late mess from Rita! I'll be damned if I go there with them! I be worried about them fools, and until they have kids, they will never understand!"

It didn't take Jesse and me long to pack up a few things and leave. On our way out, I peeked in the kitchen and saw Daddy sitting at the kitchen table. There was a whisky bottle in front of him, and with a glassy film over his eyes, he looked dazed. He took a few puffs from his cigarette, not saying a word. Obviously drunk, I don't think he knew or even understood what was going on.

At nearly two o'clock in the morning, Jesse and I walked up Burchard Drive with our clothes stuffed into a few grocery bags and no place to go. In a few days, we knew Mama was going to Nashville to see Rita and wished we could go along to stay. Rita's life had to be better than this, and from occasionally talking to her over the phone, moving away seemed to be the best thing she could have done.

Since our friend, Dana, stayed only a few blocks away, we stopped at her house first to see if we could stay the night. We tapped on her window to ask, but was told we'd have to ask her mother. Dana let us in and we entered her mother's bedroom to wake her.

"What is it, Dana?" she said in a groggy and tired voice.

"Brenda and Jesse need a favor."

Dana's mother turned on her lamp and slowly sat up in bed. Her head was wrapped in a flowered scarf, and by the frown on her face, I could tell she wasn't pleased about her sleep being interrupted.

"Ms. Lloyd," I said, hoping and praying that she wouldn't turn us away. "Do you mind if my sister and me stay at your house for a few days? My mother put us out and we don't have anywhere to go."

Her face scrunched and she gasped. "Put y'all out? Out for what?"

"Because we missed our curfew. My aunt said she'd come get us in a couple of days but..."

I lied about my aunt, because Ms. Lloyd seemed reluctant to let us stay. She removed her scarf, straightening her curly wig on her head and clearing her throat.

"No more than a couple of days," she said. "After that, make sure you and Jesse find somewhere else to go."

We nodded and headed for Dana's room. She spread out some thick blankets on the floor and we were glad to have a place to sleep. That night, my heart was heavy. I was angry with Mama for how she betrayed us and words couldn't express my hatred for Daddy. Even more, I wished he'd never come back into our lives. Shame on me for thinking that having him around would make our lives better.

Over the next few days, Jesse and I had to decide where to go. We didn't have many friends and going to live with someone in our family wasn't an option. Out of all the aunts, uncles and cousins we had, we weren't close to anyone. Many of them lived in the city, and we had no way to reach them. Our other friends' parents weren't getting involved and Ms. Lloyd was starting to catch an attitude. The only solution seemed to be the Greyhound Bus Station, because it was the only place we knew of that stayed open all night. We could easily mix in with the homeless people, so we saw it as an option.

Mama was expected to have left for Nashville to see Rita, and if Daddy wasn't going to be at the house, we had planned to sneak back in until Mama returned.

Up until then, though, we hit the streets with Dana, Shantell and Loretta. Dana seemed to be the only one who had a stable home, but Shantell and Loretta were just as lost as we were. We all made good friends and seemed to have so much in common. Shantell, Dana and Loretta were a year younger than me, and Jesse was the oldest of the bunch. To pass the days away, we stole food from an Overland Diary Market on Dunn Road, and walked the streets, looking for trouble in our subdivision known as Hathaway Manor. Shantell and Loretta hipped us to stealing merchandise from Target and Venture, and then we'd return the items to get money. At the time, it was called surviving and shoplifting had become a way to get by.

The night we planned to sneak back into the house, we walked by it, seeing Daddy's car parked outside with two other unfamiliar cars.

"Maybe Mama didn't go to Nashville," I said, looking over at Jesse as we continued to keep a close look-out on our house. "What do you think we should do?"

"Let's stay at Dana's house for one more night. Mama should definitely be gone by tomorrow."

We looked at Dana, as she hiked up the street with her short bowlegs. Shaking her head, she lit up a cigarette and inhaled the smoke. "Don't look at me. Y'all better go talk to my mother about that shit. I don't have nothing to do with it."

I hoped for a back-up plan, so I turned to Loretta and Shantell who were snacking on some chocolate chip cookies we'd just stolen. "Do you think either of your moms will let us stay the night? It would only be for one night."

"Hell, naw," Shantell said. "You can forget about asking my mother."

"Me too," Loretta said. "Y'all know damn well that my stepfather ain't going for it."

Having no other choice, we all walked to Dana's house and her mother was sitting at the kitchen table while reading the newspaper. I begged Dana to ask her for us and I was grateful when she did.

"I guess so, Dana," her mother said, sighing. "But I thought your aunt was coming to pick y'all up?"

"We couldn't get in touch with her," I lied again. "Hopefully, tomorrow."

The next morning, we crept by our house, noticing that the coast was clear. I climbed through the basement window, and then opened the basement door for Jesse to come inside. As I went up the stairs, I could smell marijuana smoke and the aroma of alcohol was potent. The kitchen was a disaster. Dishes were piled high, leftover food was scattered on the table, and beer cans and whisky bottles were all over the place. Upon entering the living room, I noticed a burn hole in Mama's couch. A thin white wrinkled sheet was on the couch and smoked blunts were in an ashtray that was on the floor.

As I headed for my bedroom, I saw the door closed, but I could hear someone inside. I placed my hand on the knob, and when I pushed on the door to open it, my Daddy's friend was lying on my bed with a light-skinned woman that had thick fat rolls bouncing up and down on her back. They were screwing so hard, neither heard me open the door. The loose headboard banged against the wall, damn near putting a hole in it.

"Give it to me Big Daddy," the heavyset woman shouted, as she pounded down hard on the skinny man underneath her. "This dick is guuuuud!"

I stood with my lips pursed, folding my arms with attitude. Once I cleared my throat, my father's friend lifted his head over the woman's shoulder. She snapped her head to the side, smiling, but kept on riding.

"Close the damn door," he yelled.

"I ain't closing shit! Y'all need to get off my bed," I shouted.

Jesse rushed back to where I was and looked into the room. "I'm calling Mama," she said, then made her way to the other room.

Daddy's friend shot daggers at me with his beady eyes, and he lifted the covers to hide the mass of mess on top of him. "I said close the door!" he said, again.

Without closing it, I walked away from the door to help Jesse look for Mama's phone book so we could call Rita's place and tell Mama what was going on.

By the time we found Rita's number, through the living room picture window, I saw Daddy staggering out of his car with a bottle of liquor in his hand. When he came inside, his eyes bugged; he was shocked to see us. His friend rushed out of our bedroom, griping about us being there.

"I thought you said you had the place to yourself, man. You didn't mention nothing about no kids being here."

"That's because they ain't supposed to be here," Daddy said. "Y'all need to get out, until y'all Mama come back."

I threw my hand back at him. "We're not going anywhere. This is my mama's house, and if she knew all of this was going on, she'd throw y'all out of here."

As I argued with Daddy and his friend, Jesse finally reached Mama. She advised Jesse to call the police and told me to get Daddy and his friend out of her house. Wasn't sure how I was supposed to do that, but when the police arrived, they asked for the Deed to the house. I didn't know what a Deed was, but Mama said they were papers that showed she was sole owner of her property and she told me where to find them. I gave the papers to the police officer, and after he looked the papers over, he asked Daddy, his friend, and the fat tramp who stood with an attitude because her sex session had been interrupted, to leave.

"This is my muthafuckin' house too," Daddy shouted while darting his finger at the police officer. "I help pay the bills here and I'm not goin' no damn where!"

It was evident that Daddy had had too much to drink. He was slurring and could barely stand up to talk. He started cursing at the police officers, acting a complete fool. The alcohol had him wound up, and as the officers tried to arrest him, he began to wrestle with them. We all moved out of the way, as the fighting became intense. One officer had his knee in Daddy's back and the other had his foot on his face. They handcuffed him, but the cuffs made him more aggressive.

"What?" he yelled while squirming around on the floor, kicking. "Y'all gon' kill me? Go ahead and kill me! Show everybody how the White man will do a Black man!"

The officers lifted Daddy to his feet. "No, this is how we will do any man who doesn't do as he's told. Now, shut the hell up! You have the right to remain silent…"

The officers escorted Daddy out of the house and shoved him in the back seat of the police car. For whatever reason, I watched from the window feeling sorry for Daddy. *Why didn't he just cooperate?* I thought. And after all that he'd done, how could I feel anything for a man who had done Mama so wrong?

The police told us they were going to take Daddy to the police station and book him—whatever that meant. And by the time Mama called back, everything was cool. She asked us to clean up the house and told us to stay there until she got home. No doubt, Jesse and I were delighted because we definitely had no other place to go.

When Mama came home, the house was sparkling clean and in tiptop condition. We couldn't do much about the cigarette burn hole in her couch, but Mama said she was going to make Daddy pay for it. I felt bad for Mama. From what I could see, she had really been through a lot with Daddy—probably more than I would ever know.

That night, we talked to her about him, and about her trip to Nashville. And even though Mama never apologized to us, I knew she was sorry for what had happened. If anything, I hoped Daddy was just a memory to us and maybe, just maybe, Mama had had enough. My wish came true. It would be a while before we ever saw Daddy again.

Chapter Three

High school was a bore. Hazelwood East was a predominately White school, with African American students sprinkled throughout. The school was laid out, had everything from an Olympic-sized swimming pool, to elevators. Circular stairs led to colorful lockers shaped like cubes on the second and third floors, and the cafeteria was humongous. The school grounds were well manicured and the immaculate football field made the school proud. Burgundy and Gold were the school colors and the mascot was a Spartan. Jesse had already been at East for a year, but this would be my first year.

By now, I had an attitude with everybody and carried a chip on my shoulder from being bullied for years. It was hard to make friends, and the ones we did have seemed to have issues like we did. One thing for sure, though, I was no follower—had become a leader. I was kind of on the rough side...kept my hair in ponytails and wore baggy jeans and sporty t-shirts. I had a reputation for being the tough-girl of the bunch, and for that, the friends I did have respected me. Jesse, on the other hand, was more laid back. She was mature than I was, and her appearance started to become a key factor for her. She'd always press and roll her hair, and before going to school in the morning, she made sure the clothes Mama could afford, or a few hand-me-downs from Rita, were neatly ironed. Her make-up was caked on heavy, but the Fashion Fair foundation made her skin look flawless. Me, I didn't give a damn about nothing or no one. I wasn't trying to impress anyone, nor did I care who was there to impress me.

As Jesse and I started to show our differences, we still hung tight. Wherever I was, she was. Wherever she was, I was. Her classmates used to gripe about her about always hanging around the underclassmen, but she didn't care because throughout my entire freshman year, we were inseparable.

By the time my sophomore year came, many things changed about me. Surprisingly, my appearance had taken priority and I started to care what others felt about me. My setback was when I'd gotten my period. I didn't know what the hell was going on with my body, and I was too scared to tell Mama. She didn't talk about those kinds of things and we were basically on our own when that time of the month came. Instead of using a maxi-pad, I used a sock to catch my blood flow and would always bleed through my clothes. The smell was horrible, and I knew if I could smell it, other people could too. I had finally gotten to the point where I would go into Mama's bathroom to steal maxi-pads, in hopes that she wouldn't notice they were missing and start asking questions.

I didn't know what Jesse had done when her time of the month came. As close as we were, a few things we never talked about were menstruation and sex. Sex was never discussed in our household and what little we knew about it was discovered through our friends. Shantell and Dana often shared their experiences with sex, and they'd tell us stories about a few boys in the neighborhood. Sex sounded pretty nasty to me; however, it didn't stop my curiosity from being sparked. And as nasty as sex may have sounded, when I set my eyes on a boy in one of my classrooms named Winston, I had a desire to see what was up. I didn't know, however, that he would be the first boy to teach me a very valuable lesson.

Winston was the young man that nearly every chick in my class wanted. From what I'd heard, he was giving it away and giving it away good. He was fine as ever...had a light mustache and trimmed hair on his chin. He was popular and smart as a whip. For a high school student, his voice was masculine and he seemed very mature. He always dressed preppy, and being on the sophomore football team, and playing on the basketball team, his muscles had an effect on many.

Thing is, I didn't stand a chance with Winston. I wasn't popular enough, and rumors had it that he liked not only pretty girls, but also smart girls. Pretty, I could do, but smart I was not. My grades were sinking by the day and I hadn't put forth much effort to make them any better.

During second semester, things started to look up for me. I signed up for a History class and Winston walked through the door. The teacher had assigned seats, and when she moved us right next to each other, I wanted to hug her. Every day, I couldn't wait for fifth hour to come, just so I could get a peek at Winston. At first, he didn't seem to notice me, but once I enhanced my outfits by showing more skin, yeah...that got his attention. Not only did my new look get his attention, but it had gotten the attention of other boys, too. None of which I was interested in, other than a boy named Darrell. He was attractive and was the same one who had taken up for me when those girls confronted Jesse and me in grade school.

As the year went on, Winston showed more interest, but Darrell showed major interest. He always walked with me to my classes, and since his brother, Chuck, still had a thing for Jesse, we all had gotten pretty close. So close, that when Mama would go to work, we'd walk to Darrell and Chuck's house to hang out. Their mother, Miss T, was down to earth and we couldn't believe how a mother could have such a close relationship with her sons and their friends. I mean, this lady would cook for us, watch TV with us and talk to us about anything that was on our minds. She was cool like that, and I started writing in my notebooks about Darrell being my future husband and Miss T being my mother-in-law. They were like the family I wished we'd had, and Darrell and Chuck were lucky to have a mother so down to earth.

It wasn't long before Darrell spoke about kissing and doing the nasty. I didn't know how to kiss anybody and I sure as hell wasn't ready to have sex. My fear was letting any of the boys know that I was still a virgin, especially Winston, who I, eventually, chose to be my first.

So luckily for me, Winston's advances picked up. While in class one day, he observed my well-endowed breasts that busted through the v-neck, low-cut shirt I wore to entice him. He licked across his thick lips, and I finally got up enough courage to say something to him.

"I...I hope you like what you see," I said, blushing.

He smiled, and hit me with his masculine voice that always gave me chills. "If I didn't like it, I wouldn't be lookin'."

I was in shock and his words clipped my mouth shut. The shyness in me came out, and I kept taking peeks at Winston as he sucked a Blow-Pop in and out of his mouth.

"Awww, this is good," he said, showing his tongue that I wanted to taste. He pulled the Blow-Pop out of his mouth and tried to hand it to me. "You want some?"

I cocked my head back and frowned. "Uh, I don't think so, especially since your mouth has been all over it."

He laughed, but deep inside, I had never wanted to suck on a Blow-Pop so bad. The teacher told us to hush, and ordered us to get back to work. Shortly thereafter, the bell rang, and Winston brushed up against my breasts on his way out the door.

"Excuse me," he said, killing me with his snow-white teeth and cute dimples. "Your melons were in the way."

I playfully rolled my eyes, leaving the classroom that day overly excited and giddy about the *attention* he'd given me.

That day led to many more days that Winston showed interest. The school year, however, was coming to an end, and time was running out for us to hook up. I was barely passing. My grades were downright awful. But to be honest, all I had on my mind was trying to impress Winston, and watching my back from the girls who were upset because he had made his move. While leaned against my locker, we talked.

"What's this I've been hearin' 'bout you likin' me, Brenda?" he asked.

I denied my attraction and shyly looked away. "Boy, who told you that? I…I don't think so."

After waiting all semester to hook up with him, those were the only words that left my mouth. Obviously, he knew I was lying and his confidence was a turn on.

"Well, if what I heard is true, my parents will be out of town this weekend. I'm havin' a party. Why don't you and some of your friends roll by and see what's up?"

I shrugged, feeling happy inside, but not letting it show. "We'll see. If we don't have nothing else to do, we'll definitely stop by and see what's up."

I'd already known where Winston lived because we often drove by his house to see if he was outside. I couldn't wait to tell

Jesse and my friends about his party, and as far as I was concerned, it was on.

The party was on a Friday night, so we knew Mama would be working until midnight. We were thrilled about that, knowing there wasn't a chance in hell that if we'd ask, she'd let us go. Instead, my friends and I arrived at Winston's house around seven o'clock that night. When he opened the door, my heart slammed against my chest. I didn't want to show just how eager I was to see him, but the wide smile on my face was a dead giveaway. Winston wore a white muscle t-shirt, revealing his biceps and wheat colored skin. His loose fitting sports shorts with white stripes down the sides gave a clear view of his thick toned calves. Showing how clean-cut he was, his faded cut was neatly lined and his long eyelashes and thick brows enhanced his handsome face.

"What's up," he said, pulling the door open so we could come in. As we walked inside, I observed a bunch of football players walking around. Many of them I'd known from school; some I didn't know at all. Winston introduced us, and then led us to the basement where more people were. Mostly everybody was listening to music, playing video games, or was indulged in a card game that was taking place in the middle of the basement floor.

By looking around, it was obvious that Winston's parents had money because the house was unlike anything I'd seen. The spacious L-shaped living room had a brown suede square pit couch and African art covered the walls. Round gold vases stuffed with decorative flowers were throughout the room and a huge black and brown shag rug lay over the shiny hardwood floors. The atrium was decked out with black spindles on the stairs, which led to the lower level of the house. The basement had a wet bar, a full-sized bathroom, and a sliding glass door that opened to the outside patio. The entire house was fit to be in a magazine, and it was no surprise that Winston seemed to have it going on all the way round. Still, I wasn't sure why he was interested...or seemed interested in someone like me.

As I mingled with the partygoers, Winston got my attention and suggested that we go upstairs. My heart skipped a beat, as I followed him upstairs to his bedroom. I wasn't sure what to expect, but I definitely knew what Winston wanted.

"You can sit down," he said, offering me a seat on his queen-sized oak bed. His room had posters on the walls and a shelf with many trophies.

I inched back on the bed, and since I was dressed to impress in a white and red striped short mini-dress that I sported twice a week, I quickly crossed my legs. I wore a pair of clean white tennis shoes Mama had just gotten me, and most of my hair was neatly pressed and pulled back into a sleek long ponytail. Several tresses of curls dangled along each side of my face, hiding the corners of my slanted eyes. A bit nervous, I nibbled on my short fingernails. I gazed at the 19 inch colored TV in front of me, waiting for Winston to make the next move. He could see how nervous I was, so he sat next to me, clinching my hand together with his.

"Are you all right?" he asked.

I shrugged. "Yeah, why wouldn't I be?"

"I don't know. You seem kind of nervous."

I moved my head from side to side, implying no. Wasting no time, Winston inched forward, barely touching his lips with mine. I had very little experience with kissing, so I didn't know if the kiss was doing the job it needed to do or not. His lips felt soft as melting butter as they touched mine, and when his tongue slipped into my mouth, I was lost. I was embarrassed by my inexperience, but I hoped that Winston didn't notice that the rhythm of my slow tongue could not keep up with his. Seconds later, his hands crept up my legs and he took several squeezes on my thighs. My mini-dress gave him easy access up my skirt, and when he touched my crotch, my stomach tightened. I held my breath as he massaged my pussy lips through my panties, feeling a slight tingle that I had never felt before. I couldn't believe how a simple touch could arouse me, so I opened my legs wider to show him I was pleased. Winston, however, backed away from me and stood to remove his clothes. Having no shame in his game, he stood naked, exposing every single muscle in his stallion-like frame. I shyly blinked away, but could feel the water forming in my mouth and stickiness fill my panties. I guess Winston figured I'd stand and get naked too, but I was nowhere near as brave as he was. Instead, I scooted back on the bed, and watched him make his way to a closet. He pulled out a box of something that looked like candy. He then tore open the package and put a piece of plastic over his dick. *Why was he putting candy wrapper on his dick?* I thought. *Did he want me to suck the candy off?*

"You don't mind if I use a condom, do you?" he asked, continuing to slide it on.

I shrugged, clueless and not knowing what a condom was used for. "No...no, I don't mind," I said. *Was I supposed to put on one too?*

Winston stepped forward, causing me to lay further back on the bed. Once again, his soft lips touched mine and all I could do was close my eyes and savor the moment. His body felt perfect on top of mine, and as we clothes burned, I felt his hardness pressing into my tight hole. That tingling feeling happened again and my pussy was thumping with eagerness. My legs had gotten even wider, and Winston stretched the crotch of my panties over to the side. He fondled my sticky insides with his cold fingers and I felt more moistness building between my legs. I gave him a gentle kiss for making me feel this way, but as he positioned himself to go inside of me, I quickly broke our kiss.

I placed my hand on his solid chest, slightly pushing it back. The feel of him splitting my insides was unbearable. "Wai...that, that hurts," I strained to say.

"What's wrong?" Winston asked. "I'm not even inside of you yet." I lay silently, looking into the eyes of a boy I wanted so badly. He looked upset. "Damn, Brenda, are you a virgin? I didn't know you were a virgin. I'll take my time, I promise, okay?"

I nodded, but this time, Winston removed my panties. He positioned himself again, and gave it everything he had to be gentle. No matter how hard he tried, though, I just couldn't get with it. My insides felt as if they were being ripped apart, and quite frankly, nothing about this shit felt good. I squeezed my eyes tightly together, forcing him backwards.

"This is too, too painful. I can't—"

"Just cool out and let me finish. You ain't even givin' me a chance."

"I did and I can't handle this. Would you mind getting up?"

Winston cut his eyes at me and sighed. He lifted his body off mine and lay next to me. He placed his arm across his forehead, glaring up at the ceiling. I eased out of bed and hurried into the bathroom. In so much pain, I wiped myself and blood was on the toilet paper. Whoever said that sex felt good was out of their minds! As much as I liked Winston, partial sex with him felt nothing like what I had imagined.

When I came out of the bathroom and looked into Winston's room, he was still lying on the bed with no clothes on. I think it was the first time he didn't appeal to me. He asked if we could continue, and even promising to be gentle, I declined. I walked off to join in with the rest of his company and with my girlfriends I had come to the party with.

It was getting close to midnight and we had to get home before Mama got there. She had been getting rides to and from work with a friend that she'd met at work, and that helped cut back on the late nights I had to get out of bed to go get her. In this case, it really helped that we didn't have to leave, but since it was getting late, we all said our goodbyes and jetted.

We managed to beat Mama home, and that night, I could hardly sleep as I thought about Winston the entire night. Jesse didn't ask me anything about what had taken place in Winston's room, and I wasn't about to tell her either. I wasn't sure how she'd feel about me "giving it up" and I wasn't taking any chances on Mama finding out. I knew she'd kill me, but a big part of me didn't care about what anybody thought of me. All I wanted to do was see Winston again. I wondered if he was up all night thinking about me, too. Did he still like me, or was he really upset that I'd made him stop? I had his phone number, but I thought it would be better to wait until morning to call.

The next day, Mama had us up early washing dishes, cleaning the bathrooms, and mopping floors. For some reason, I kept thinking that she'd known what I'd done. I felt so different, so adult-like...and so whorish? Why couldn't I get Winston off my mind? Damn, was it that good and I didn't realize it? Our encounter didn't last five minutes, and all he'd done was hurt me. So, why was I visualizing my experience like it was the best thing that ever happened to me? Crazy I guess. Pure deep, down right, crazy.

Around 3:30 p.m., Mama was done giving us chores around the house. I decided to sneak into the basement to call Winston. When he answered, the sound of his voice brought a pleasing smile to my face.

"Hello," he said for a second time.

"Hi, Winston, what's up?" I asked. My stomach felt queasy. I wasn't sure if he wanted to talk to me or not.

"Nothin', just sittin' here watchin' the game and thinkin' about us last night." Now, that news made me blush. It was good to know that he had been thinking about me. "What are you and your friends doin' tonight?" he asked.

I rushed to answer. "Nothing. Why ya asking?"

"Because, I thought you might want to see me again."

"Is that another invitation?"

"Yeah. My parents are still away and we had a cool time last night, didn't we?"

"Uh-huh. I'll see what's up with my friends, and if everything is cool, I'll see you later."

"Cool, Brenda. I'll see you later."

I rushed upstairs to tell Jesse that Winston wanted us to come over again. I was so glad he wasn't upset with me, and this time, I would do whatever to make it work. But with it being Saturday, how in the hell were we going to get out of the house on a Saturday night? Mama didn't work on Saturdays, so convincing her to let us go anywhere was going to be difficult. We contemplated the rest of the afternoon on what lie we could tell Mama. Somehow, though, I knew I was definitely going to see Winston that night. I even called up more of our friends to see if they wanted to go with us. I could feel it; this night was going to be a night I'd never forget.

By the time eight o'clock rolled around, Jesse and I had thought of a spectacular lie to tell Mama. We told her that Shantell's mother had a heart attack, and Shantell wanted us to take her to the hospital and stay with her. When Mama told us it was okay to leave, I was all smiles. Before she changed her mind, which she often did, we quickly jetted. On the way to Winston's house, we packed the blue Ford Pinto with our girlfriends: Shantell, Carlease, Dana and Tina. We arrived at Winston's house around 8:45 p.m., but this time, one of his friends opened the door.

"Is Winston here?" I asked.

"Yeah, come in," his friend said, opening the door and tossing out compliments. "Daaaaamn, y'all look good."

We all laughed and I felt good in my brown halter dress and high-heeled wooden clogs that used to be Rita's. Like often, my hair was in a sleek ponytail and my smile could be seen a mile away.

I could see Winston in the kitchen on the phone and he appeared to be indulged with his caller. *It betta not be no other girl he was talking to,* I thought. But who was I trying to call the shots after one night of...he-barely-put-it-in-me sex?

Winston spent about twenty minutes on the phone, and after he ended his call, he came into the living room where everyone was sitting.

He nudged his head towards the stairs. "I don't want everybody crowding up my parents' living room, so we need to take this downstairs."

Everybody got up, heading for the basement. Winston stood at the top of the atrium, watching us go down one by one. Instantly, I noticed him checking out my friend Carlease. She was a cute petite girl with slightly bowlegs. Had a shapely body and a bubbly personality to go with it. *What boy wouldn't give her a second look?* I thought.

Since I was the last one down the steps, I figured Winston would stop me to ask if I wanted to continue what we started last night. He didn't. Instead, I moseyed on down the steps just like everyone else did.

The fellas had everybody cracking up as they told jokes, talking about each other's mamas and blurting out other stomach-grabbing jokes. And even though the jokes kept me tuned in, I couldn't keep my eyes off Winston. Seemed to me, though, as if he couldn't keep his eyes off Carlease. My stomach turned; I'd thought about how he gave her the same looks he'd given me in History class. I didn't make much of it and the night went on.

Winston calmed the room by putting on some slow jams. *My kind of guy*, I thought, as he dimmed the lights. A few couples had gotten up to dance and I knew Winston would soon head my way. I went to the bathroom located in the far corner of the basement, just to make sure my attire was in order. My ponytail was slicked down to perfection, my make-up wasn't overdone, and my dress worked my thick shapely figure. I had to be sure that I was looking good, because Winston didn't seem to be giving me the attention I thought I truly deserved, or for that matter, had earned.

When I left the bathroom, my eyes went straight to Winston. I was in disbelief. He was slow dancing with Carlease—very close. My stomach turned even more and I felt as if I wanted to throw up.

Why was he dancing with her? I thought. Maybe he was looking for me and I was in the bathroom. *Damn, he wouldn't play me like that, would he?*

At least three or four slow jams played and Winston was still dancing with Carlease. By now, he was whispering in her ear and caressing her backside with his hands. I wanted to fuck him up, but instead, I sat in a chair with my legs crossed, pouting.

The floor got crammed with people slow dancing, and as I focused my eyes from a distance, I saw Winston and Carlease kiss, and then go upstairs. He had the nerve to hold her by the hand and I sat looking like the biggest fool ever. *How could he diss me like this? Didn't I mean anything to him?* To top it off, Carlease knew I liked him. She didn't know we were together last night, but she knew I had a major crush on Winston. I wanted to go upstairs and kick his ass for how he dissed me, but I didn't want anyone to see my hurt. More than anything, I was humiliated! Many of the people there knew I was just with Winston last night. I felt so stupid. Bottom line...I got played! Big time!

For the next hour or so, I continued to watch for Winston and Carlease. Eventually, I headed upstairs, and as soon as I reached the top stair, I could see that his bedroom door was closed. This was a gut-wrenching feeling! *Somebody...anybody just get a gun and shoot me—please!* I thought. Paying much more attention to me than I thought, Winston's friend, Joe, took a seat next to me on the couch. He asked if I were okay, but I just rolled my eyes.

"I thought you and Winston were supposed to be kickin' it," he said, adding insult to injury.

I swallowed the huge lump in my burning throat, feeling pretty darn bad about what had happened. "I thought so, too, but I guess I was wrong about the way Winston felt about me."

Joe chuckled, while shaking his head. "If you don't mind, let me give you some words of advice. Don't fall for my boy 'cause he ain't nothin' but a playa. When I say playa, I mean true P-L-A-Y-A. You don't need that kind of boyfriend, do you?"

I didn't even respond, but he should have told me that before I let Winston get the goodies. I doubt that his words would have mattered either way, and even though I had walked away from Joe, it wasn't his fault that I'd let myself get played.

I did my best to keep my cool, but deep down, I was hurting. I had never known what it felt like to be dissed by a boy, and this was not a good feeling. I waited for Winston's door to open, and when it finally did, he came out, closing the door behind him. Shirtless, he walked into the kitchen, and slapped high-five with one of his friends. They chuckled and not once did Winston look my way.

Shortly thereafter, Carlease came out of his room. Her hair was a mess and all of her make-up had vanished. She walked directly over by me, conversing as if nothing had happened. I wanted to inquire about what had transpired, but I didn't want to give her the satisfaction of telling me the details. After all, it was pretty obvious.

We didn't leave Winston's house until 1:00 a.m., and he never said one word to me. Not only was I crushed, but in addition to that, Jesse and I knew we were in deep trouble with Mama. If I had known my night would turn out as it did, I never would have lied to Mama. I would have stayed my ass at home! It was funny that I saw it that way now, and as far as I was concerned, my feelings for Winston were a wrap.

On the drive home, Carlease bragged about what she and Winston had done. A virgin she was not, but as far as I was concerned, he'd made fools out of both of us because we were the ones who considered ourselves friends. What a true lesson I'd learned, but this one was just the beginning of many more to come.

No sooner had we got home, we were made aware that Mama was still awake. Our house was lit up like a Christmas tree. We rang the doorbell and Mama yelled through the door, "Jesse and Brenda, is that y'all?"

"Yeah, Mama, it's us," I yelled back.

"Good! Stay y'all trifling asses out there!" she yelled louder. She turned off the lights and we stood on the dark porch looking like idiots.

Jesse and I slept on the ground in the garage that night, and in the morning, Mama let us back into the house. We continued to lie about Shantell's mother, and even though Mama believed our story, we paid dearly for it. Our backs were killing us from sleeping on the concrete floor and I was left with a true broken heart. I wrote about my experience in my notebook: *So-called friends ain't shit, and neither are yucky boys who say whatever to get some pussy! My feelings are bruised...battered and the next time Winston looks at me and licks his lips, I'm gonna punch him right between the eyes. Hmmm...maybe not because he is still cute, but being cute won't be enough for me to drop my panties again...*

***

The school year was finally over. My sophomore year was a true struggle; it was so bad I even failed gym. Since it was a requirement, I had to take it over next year, along with the freshmen. I'd become so particular about myself that I hated swimming and changing clothes in gym. Eventually, I'd have to deal with it or else fail, again, and face the possibility of not graduating because of gym.

Summer break was well needed. Mama continued to work nights, and the moment she left, the partying was on. All of our friends hung out at our house—boys included. I'd hooked up with a new boy in the neighborhood, Chris, only to stop by his house one day to find my friend, Loretta, working him over. I hadn't had sex with him, and he made it clear that since I wasn't upping the goods, I was out and she was in. I was starting to learn a lot about friends, and as far as I could see, I really didn't have any.

Jesse and I made sure that everybody left our house by ten o'clock at night. We cleaned up any mess we'd made during the day, and when Mama didn't get a ride home from her friend, I left to pick her up from work by eleven forty-five. Being very deceitful, I'd always have my pajamas on as if I hadn't done much all day. I hated to lie to Mama and sneak behind her back, but I felt as if she just didn't understand us. I knew it would be a matter of time that the lies would catch up with us, but that was a risk we were willing to take.

Every day, it was the same routine. Mama would go to work and we would cut loose like wild animals being released from a cage. It had gotten to the point where the whole neighborhood knew our house was the hangout. I'd even caught up with Winston one day, and unable to decline his offer about us finishing up something we never got started, I was down with his suggestion. Unfortunately for me, it was that time of the month. He didn't seem to care, but when we made it back to my house, he regretted his suggestion. From that moment on, I knew that sex during my monthly cycle wasn't going to work. I was embarrassed by my blood flow, and the smell was horrible. I should have left well enough alone, and I was sure...positive that he'd felt the same.

Near the end of the summer, things started to get out of hand. Many of the kids in the neighborhood, known for bullying us, started doing stupid things like toilet papering our yard, throwing eggs at the windows, and even dumped horse manure in the driveway. We were able to hide those incidents from Mama, but when the word "bitches" was spray painted on the side of our house, that immediately got her attention. She confronted us about it and made us take her over the people's houses that were responsible. One by one, Mama cursed them out, and to get back at us, they told her about the daily parties we'd had while she was at work. Mama had a way with words and told the boys, along with their parents, that she was no fool. "I'm well aware of what's been going on in my house while I'm not there, but all of you muthafuckas better stay the hell away from my daughters and stay off my damn property! If not, I promise y'all a shotgun up the asses!"

On that note, we left each house worried about what Mama would do to us. I wasn't sure if she knew what was going on at her house or not, but once we got home, she put Jesse and me on punishment and told us that we were on lockdown until school started. Mama's threats had shaken up everybody, and the rest of the summer remained cool, calm and collected. However, the upcoming school year wasn't and it was the school year from hell!

Chapter Four

The first day of my junior year, trouble was in the air. Jesse and I had many more associates, but lots of enemies. I had gotten fed up with the constant insults from classmates and my actions showed it. I'd become a hard-ass chick...wasn't taking much off anybody anymore. My close associates and I hung tight because, in addition to the rude boys who kept their bullshit up on the school bus, it seemed as if many of our classmates despised us for befriending some of the football players at Riverview Gardens High School.

During school, damaging rumors started to circulate about us and many of the rumors were false. I hated to be talked about or lied upon, and it infuriated me that some classmates could be so cruel. I made my anger known, and if anybody even looked at me the wrong way, I felt a need to confront them. For protection, I kept a baseball bat and mace in my locker, ready to do some damage. Eventually, the bat came in handy one day, when Jesse and a football player named Derrick disputed over Hazelwood East's loss to Riverview in a football game. Jesse was walking up the stairs, talking about the loss and the football player turned around.

"The game is over with, bitch! Why you still talkin' about it?" he charged.

Jesse gave him a look as if hell had swarmed over her and pointed to her chest. "Are you talking to me?" she asked.

All he had to do was say "yes" and he did! By that time, I was already at my locker, which was nearby. I pulled out my bat, swinging it through the crowd as Jesse, some of our other associates, and the football player went at it. They were kicking his ass, and when two more football players joined in to help, everybody was getting it in. I was cracking my bat against the backs of anybody in the way, and if they had on a jersey, nine times out of ten, they were hit. Many teachers rushed to break up the fight and Dana, Tina, Jesse and I were the only ones suspended. Shortly after returning to school, Jesse and I were suspended, again, for fighting two girls in the cafeteria. The fight was wild, and numerous crowds of people were standing around, trying to see where the flying chairs were coming from.

"Fat bitch!" I yelled, throwing the chair at one chick who had just slapped Jesse so hard that her nose was bleeding. Jesse and I hands were tangled in the chick's long hair, yanking the shit out of it. We pounded her face, head and back with our tightened fists. Several other girls were in on it too, trying to get a lick in where they could.

More teachers rushed in, attempting to break up the fight. But when one teacher grabbed my arm, I turned around and shoved her backwards. She stumbled in her high-heeled shoes, trying to catch her balance. My face was twisted from anger and my fists were still tightened.

"Don't put your hands on me, bitch!" I said with a heaving chest. "Are you crazy? I will fuck you up!"

She took a few steps back, but a man teacher intervened and snatched my arm. He escorted me to the principal's office, right along with Jesse. By now, we'd had a bad reputation for causing trouble and the principal at Hazelwood East wanted us out! He advised us that we couldn't come back to school until he had a hearing with our parents.

"We didn't even start nothing," I said, pouting while sitting in his office with my arms folded. "They started it!"

"They'll be suspended too," he said. He stood behind his desk with his hands in his pockets. "As for you and your sister, the two of you can't return to school, until we speak to your parents first."

I stood up, rolling my eyes. There was no need to involve Mama in this, and I knew darn well that Daddy wasn't going to show his face. "Parents my ass," I said to the principal. "I don't need this school and you don't have to suspend or expel me because I quit!"

The principal's face turned beet red. He couldn't believe the tone I'd taken with him, but there was a whole lot of anger inside of me, waiting to come out.

"Let's get the hell out of here," Jesse said, walking next to me. "Fuck Hazelwood East!"

We left the principal's office and he, as well as the staff, stood in disbelief.

"They're nothing but troublemakers," the assistant principal said as Tina and Dana joined in to leave with us. "Good riddance."

I could hear the principal calling security, but I turned at the door, giving the assistant principal a mean mug she'd never forget. "Insult me again," I threatened. "And I will lay your White ass out on that floor."

She didn't dare open her mouth again, and by the time security reached us, we had already gone to our lockers to clear them out. I left the front doors of Hazelwood East with a bat in my hand, and mace in my pocket, knowing that I would never, ever return.

Weeks had passed by and Mama didn't notice a thing. Doing the norm, Jesse and I got dressed every morning, leaving the house as if we were going to school. In reality, we went straight to Tina's house and kicked it with her and Dana, who had left school that day too. We spent our down time doing nothing productive. Gossiping, listening to music and cooking. I had become obsessed with writing, and had filled many more spiral notebooks with my thoughts. Thoughts about my life, my parents, my friends, bullies...everything I thought of was basically spilled on paper. I even started coming up with rap lyrics for our group, The Hazelwood Gangsta Gang. Couldn't believe I had all of this inside of me, and writing made me feel good.

We had discussed returning to school, but not that often. Jesse was in her senior year and only had a few months to complete before graduation. As far as she'd come, dropping out of school didn't seem like the sensible thing to do. I, on the other hand, had almost a year and a half to go. At this point, for me, school was a wrap.

For the next month or so, we all could be classified as one thing—dropouts. We hadn't made any decisions about telling our parents of our unfortunate situation at school, nor had we made plans to return. When Mama received a letter from the Board of Education, no doubt, we had some explaining to do. Finally, we told her everything that had happened and explained how miserable we had been at Hazelwood East. From the day we'd moved to Black Jack, we never did fit in.

"I hate that school, Mama, and there is no way I'm going back," I said, sitting on my bed and watching Mama as she frowned while listening.

"Me either," Jesse said. "We've always been looked down on and people around here treat us like outsiders."

Mama was so mad at us for lying to her, but she was sympathetic to what we had been through. She sighed, and then gave us an ultimatum. "Find a job to help me take care of these damn bills, or get y'all asses back in school! Any school! Preferably Sumner High School. It's where I graduated from."

Jesse and I shouted at the same time. "Sumner High School!"

"Ain't that in the city?" I asked Mama.

"Right around the corner from your grandparents' house."

"But it's in the city," Jesse repeated. "I don't want to go there."

Mama folded her arms. "You don't have a choice. I call the shots around here, so get those sad looks off your faces and get up to do some chores around the house. It's a mess."

Mama left our room, leaving Jesse and me worried as hell about attending a school dead smack in the city. But by the end of the following week, along with Dana, we were enrolled at the historic Charles Sumner High School, on Cottage Avenue. Tina's mom made her enroll at Hazelwood Central because she was afraid of letting her go to a school in the city. It was funny how things worked out. Mama wasn't upset with us anymore, and we were about to view school in an entirely different way.

Chapter Five

Sumner High School was a muthafucka! Appearance wise, it was nothing compared to the luxurious Hazelwood East and the student body was 99.9% African American. The wood floors were buckling; the lockers were loud hot pink, rusty, and banged up. The stairs looked as if they were about to collapse, and the classrooms were overloaded with students who had to share books. Paint was peeling from the walls, no air conditioners, and graffiti was scribbled everywhere. As for a football field—didn't have one, and games were always played at other schools. I couldn't believe what we'd gotten ourselves into and the school mascot was a Bulldog.

Coming from a school that had swimming pools, plush carpet, elevators, a library, and colorful freshly painted lockers—what in the hell was this all about? Not only that, but again, we had a difficult time fitting in. On the first day, we wore fancy dress pants and silk blouses, all by way of a five-finger discount. High-heeled shoes comforted our feet and our pressed hair hung on our shoulders. No doubt, we stuck out like a sore thumb, because many of the other students kept it simple. The norm was rugby's, t-shirts, blue jeans and tennis shoes. No shorts were allowed and neither were mini-skirts! *Huh?* Sumner High made me feel as if I'd dropped down from another planet. And more than anything, some of the students scared the shit out of me. Many of the boys were rough around the edges, but many were also cute. The girls looked as if they didn't play, and eyes were rolling as soon as we hit the door. When you'd ask people for directions, they looked at you like you had shit on your face. The teachers...well, most of them were more like friends. They joked around with students in the classrooms and the students didn't seem to have many rules to follow. To me, this was an eye-opening experience. I couldn't believe the differences I'd witnessed from being in a city school versus a school in the suburbs.

During the first week of school, after scrambling the halls and looking for the girl's bathroom, Jesse, Dana and I rushed in to use it. It was clouded with thick smoke; smelled like burnt dried leaves from a maple tree. A gang of females stood in front of the stalls smoking pot. We didn't want to leave, but since none of the stalls were available, we stood looking like a White person who had just called someone a nigger and regretted it. The females passed a fat twisted joint around the bathroom, eyeballing us as if we had no business being there.

My heart slammed against my chest. I definitely wasn't about to ask any of them to move aside so I could use the bathroom. Since some of the doors were missing from the stalls, I had no intentions of pulling down my pants and allowing everyone to look at me.

Trying to ease the tension, Jesse walked up to the cracked mirror, and started teasing her hair with a comb. Dana worked her jerry curl and I asked Jesse if I could use her comb to straighten my hair as well. The females stared without saying a word. Normally, being stared down sparked a few words from me, but not this time. I hadn't said one word, and had learned my lesson from being such a bad-ass at Hazelwood East.

"What's y'all names?" one of the girls asked while inhaling the joint.

First, I pointed to Jesse. "That's my sister Jesse, Dana, and my name is Brenda."

"What's up," she said, tossing her head back. "Welcome to Sumner."

"Thanks," was all I could say and we walked out smiling.

I wiped the sheen of sweat from my forehead, realizing that I wasn't so tough after all. I was sure to get my ass beat by saying the wrong thing and the looks on many of the girls' faces said so.

After only a few weeks at Sumner High, things started to get better. We dropped the dress pants and blouses and kept it real in blue jeans like many of the other students did. Jesse kept her hair as is, but I swooped mine into a ponytail with feathered bangs. She had first hour with one of the most popular boys in school—Slim they called him, and he started to show us around. He showed us how to cut classes, how to take as many lunch breaks as we wanted, and how to hang out in whatever class we wanted to. A nearby food joint, Billy Burke's, was the place to go for burgers, and some of the teachers often sent us there to get lunch. No doubt, this was my kind of school, and it wasn't long before I classified myself as being a Bulldog for life! The football games were lively as ever and we attended every single one of them. I was always in Jesse's classes or she was in mine. The only time I went to my own classes was if I had to take a test, and nine times out of ten, I cheated on that. After the test was finished, I'd ask the teacher if I could go to the restroom and never returned. The teacher was lucky to see me the next day, or sometimes, not until the next week! We ate lunch together, and at this school, if you had to get free lunch, so damn what! Nobody made fun of you and the struggle seemed understood. Every single morning, the principal got on the intercom and referred to us, the students and faculty, as "family." A family it truly was, and for the most part, everyone seemed to get along. Oh, yes, it was quite a change from Hazelwood East, as many of the things we had done at Sumner would result in immediate detention or suspension from school.

Being at Sumner High for almost a month, I knew we'd made the right choice. And when Mama bought a new Dodge Aries for us to get to and from school, people started to get friendly. Even the boys, too. I'd given my phone number to a boy in my sixth hour class named Omar and we hooked up.

My attraction to Omar was how smart he was. It helped that he was in good shape, and playing on the football team was always a plus. His lips were thick, he had a smooth chocolate brown complexion and I hadn't seen anyone at Sumner High who had flowing neatly-cut waves on their head like him. Since Mama continued to work nights, I was able to communicate with Omar over the phone almost every evening. He had a great personality, a quirky sense of humor, and when he admitted to being a straight A student, I was overjoyed with my choice.

Hours of conversation, and getting to know each other better, ended a relationship that Omar had with a chick named Theresa. I'd gotten myself a boyfriend and hadn't been this excited about a boy since Winston. Either way, the news hit fast...Omar dissed the city girl for the light-skinned county girl from Hazelwood East. It sure was a way to get popular fast because so many people had approached me about Omar and I being an item. My newly found popularity added to Jesse and me gaining more friends, and the more friends we had the more trouble it caused. The lies to Mama continued and we damn near lived in the streets. It wasn't long before drinking alcohol came into the picture, but drugs were left for a specific few. Crown Royal made me never want to drink again, but Colt 45 forty ounces became a favorite.

After school, Jesse and our new crew made it a habit to stop at the liquor store and find someone who would purchase liquor for us. At times, it was difficult making it on time to pick up Mama from work, who sometimes got off early. Using tic-tacs to calm our breaths didn't help and Mama let it be known that she knew what the hell was going on.

"Brenda, you and Jesse need to be ashamed of yourselves. Are y'all drunk?" she asked while riding on the passenger side of the car and lighting a cigarette.

My mouth opened, but not too wide because I'd confirm her suspicions. "Ain't nobody been drinking, Mama. I don't know what that smell is." I eyeballed Jesse in the rearview mirror and she had a smirk on her face.

Mama blew the smoke out of her mouth, continuing to glare at me. "Y'all got a lot to learn about life. When the two of you fall flat on your faces, don't look for me to be there to pick you up. Y'all some lying ass kids. I be glad when y'all grow up and get it together!"

It was times like this when I'd learned to keep my mouth shut. I looked at Jesse, again, and she cut her eyes as Mama ranted all the way home. Before returning to bed that night, she made us scrub the kitchen floor that was already clean. And after lying to her about the alcohol, and having hangovers, we swore that we would never, ever drink again, but the pact didn't last too long.

***

My relationship with Omar started to get interesting. One of my classmates told me that he was expecting a baby. I didn't mention anything to him because rumors were exactly what they were—rumors. There were so many rumors going around at Sumner High that you didn't know who or what to believe. For one, some people often referred to Jesse and me as ho's, and even though

I'd had five-minute sex with Winston and Victor Smith, a senior at Riverview Gardens High School, I suspected Jesse was still a virgin. I didn't quite understand how we'd gained such a reputation, but as out of control as we'd gotten, people were left to assume. Jesse's first boyfriend, Jeff, encouraged us not to let the rumors affect us. He was known for drinking, getting high, fighting and even killing, but he insisted that the rumors about his character weren't exactly true. As cocky as Jeff was, I wasn't sure what to believe. Jesse had him by her side for protection, and being around him made us feel safe. We gravitated to boys who were popular, rough around the edges and who could be classified to some as thugs.

Omar was no thug, but I liked him. I was ready to take our relationship to another level. My popularity brought about much pressure and it wasn't as if I hadn't had sex before. Besides, everybody I knew, with the exception of Jesse, was having sex. Sex was no big deal to me and all it meant at the time was opening my legs to let a boy get his nut. With that in mind, my first experience with Omar took place on Rita's birthday while Mama was away at work. Omar arrived around seven o'clock that evening, wearing a baseball cap, his letterman jacket and a pair of stone-washed jeans. I was happy to see him, but still a bit sad because I hadn't heard from Rita.

Always knowing how to perk me up, Omar's jokes made me smile. We sat on my bed and talked about his plans after graduating from high school.

"I know I'm going to get a scholarship. Not really sure what school I'm going to yet, but college is definitely in my plans. What about you? What are you going to do when you graduate from school next year?"

I shrugged, not having a clue. Mama was already complaining about the money she had been paying back for Rita's student loans, so going to college didn't seem possible. "I really don't know yet. I'm sure I'll find a job or something, but I doubt that I'll be going to college. Besides, my grades aren't all that great."

Omar sat silent for a moment, and then he leaned in for a kiss. Following the kiss, the lights went out. Like with Winston and Victor, I expected Omar to use a condom, but he insisted that he didn't have one. Neither did I, but that didn't seem to deter us.

"Forget a condom. I want to feel it," he said, lying on top of me in the pitch-black room. "I'll pull out when I get ready to come."

"You promise," I asked a bit skeptical, as well as dumbfounded. I figured when he came that he would pull out, but as he lay on top of my stiff body, that barely moved, I wasn't so sure. I lay staring at the ceiling, unable to get into the rhythm he had chosen. Didn't really know what I was doing, but was basically "giving it up" because I thought I was pleasing him. I never left my sexual encounters feeling satisfied and I doubted that the boys I'd been with were satisfied either. Sex was just sex to me, and I honestly did not understand the hype.

Nearly ten minutes in, the phone rang off the hook. Since Jesse was gone, and I knew it was probably Rita, I interrupted Omar.

"I have to answer that. It may be my mama," I said.

Omar moved over in bed next to me, and I felt for the phone on the floor to answer it. To no surprise, it was Rita. I scooted to the edge of the bed, talking to her for about fifteen minutes. I was so glad to hear she'd been doing well and she assured me that she was coming home soon. After we ended our call, I turned to Omar who was already up and putting on his clothes.

"Are you leaving already?" I asked, feeling sticky between my legs.

"Yeah, I gotta get my mom's car back to her. I'll see you tomorrow."

Within the hour, Omar was gone. He didn't even call me when he got home, and the next day at school, he seemed rather distant. During our lunch period, instead of eating lunch with me, he ate with his boys. Towards the end of the day, I saw him talking to his ex-girlfriend by her sewing class. I was boiling with anger. *Not again,* I thought. No way was this happening to me again and what was up with getting dissed all the damn time by boys? I wasted no time confronting him.

"So, what's up with you?" I asked, walking down the hall with him. "Why are you playing me shady?"

He laughed and held my hand as we made our way to class. "You trippin'. I was just asking her about something, that's all."

I could feel something wasn't right with Omar, but I felt that giving up the goodies would bring us closer. That was in no way the case. As the days passed, he became more distant.

***

During the next several weeks, my body started feeling strange. Every morning, I felt sluggish and sick to my stomach. I vomited on the way to school, and if not then, right before first hour. I thought all the drinking I'd been doing had finally caught up with me, but when I missed my period, reality kicked in. At sixteen years old, I was pregnant! Pregnant and confused as hell! I thought one thing, *I ain't telling nobody!* Maybe Omar, but that was it. I also thought about Mama. She was going to kill me or kick my ass out of the house. Until I figured out what to do, I had to avoid her. I'd thought about telling Jesse and Rita, but that was just a thought. What would they think? I was the baby girl and this wasn't supposed to happen to me. Why me and what in the hell was I going to do with a baby? Thoughts of having an abortion crossed my mind, but since I didn't have money for one, an abortion was out of the question.

I had a few conversations with Omar over the phone, but couldn't find the right time to tell him. He was either too busy to talk, or always had something to do. For some reason or another, I kind of thought he knew because he was acting just as strange as I was. During one of our conversations, we made plans to meet up at his house after school on Friday. That would be the perfect opportunity for me to break the news.

Friday came in a flash. Jesse dropped me off at Omar's house and she and Dana went to Tanesha's house. Dressed in my blue jeans, legs warmers and sweater, I climbed the red concrete steps that led to Omar's front door and knocked. My hands were shaking like leaves. They were also sweaty, so I eased them into my front pockets to stop them from trembling. My bottom lip was sucked into my mouth and I took deep breaths to stay calm. Omar opened the door with the phone pressed up to his ear. He invited me to sit on a plaid sofa and continued his conversation in another room. My eyes searched the living room. I looked at pictures of Omar and his mother that hung on a wall. There were a lot of whatnots around the room and an old floor model TV sat in the far corner. The carpet was a fuzzy brown, and even though the house itself was pretty old, everything appeared to be neat and in order.

Minutes later, Omar came back into the living room, where I remained on the couch thinking deeply about our baby. When he mentioned sex, I was in no mood. Had too much on my mind, and I couldn't believe that after a few minutes of him lying on top of me, it had resulted to this.

"I'm going to the kitchen to make me a sandwich," he said. "Want one?"

"No," I said, rubbing my sweaty palms on my jeans. "When you get finished, though, I'd like to talk to you about something."

Always being playful, once Omar finished making his sandwich, he sat on my lap, teasing me with it. He could tell I wasn't in the mood, so he finally slid over to the spot next to me, giving me his attention.

"Are you sure you don't want a sandwich?" He asked. "It's good and you don't know what you're missing."

I opened my mouth to take a tiny bite of his sandwich, but he snatched it away. We both laughed and when I tried to take another bite, he did the same thing again. I knew Omar was trying to ease the tension. He could tell I had something heavy on my mind.

"Can you be serious for one minute," I suggested. "I have something very important I need to get at you about."

Omar chilled and rested his arms on top of the couch. "Shoot, Brenda, what's on your mind?"

I sighed. The thoughts of what I had to say caused water to rush to the brim of my eyes. "I…I wanted to tell you that I missed my period this month—and the month before. I've been really sick," I paused, as the stone-faced look on Omar's face made me fidget. He didn't respond, just rubbed his hands on his wavy hair. "Omar, did you hear me?"

"Yeah, I heard you. Do you think you're pregnant?"

I nodded. "Uh-huh. I really do."

Omar pointed to his chest. "Is it mine?"

My brows went up. "Who else could it be?"

He shrugged. "I don't know. That's why I'm asking you. If you say it's mine, then I'll just have to take care of it."

On that note, our conversation about the baby was over! Omar changed the subject and it wasn't long before I called Jesse to come get me.

I thought hard about my situation that night, and cried until I couldn't cry anymore. I wrote for hours in my notebook, circling every tear that had dropped on my paper: *Why me? I can't be nobody's mama. How am I going to take care of this baby? Omar sure as hell ain't gonna help. I sure hope that I'm wrong because I can't do this all by myself. Not by myself. Maybe he'll ask me to marry him, so me, him and the baby can be a family. Then, I doubt that 'cause he be messing around with those other girls too. What do he get from those other girls that he can't get from me? I don't know, but I do know that Mama ain't going to be happy about this. She is going to disown me when she finds out and where will I live when she put me out? I got myself in a big mess and I gotta be the one to clean it up...*

Writing my thoughts helped me to release my emotions, and when there was no one to talk to about what I was going through, putting the pen to the paper worked just fine. I wasn't sure what I'd do with a baby at seventeen, which I would be that age before the baby came. But I'd known some girls at Sumner High School who'd had more than one baby. Omar said he'd help me take care of the baby, but something inside of me didn't believe him.

The next morning, my eyes were red and swollen from crying so much. Mama couldn't help but notice, and when she asked what was wrong, I told her I wasn't feeling well. I wanted to tell her the truth, but I didn't want to be homeless with a baby on the way.

During the next several weeks at school, I tried to keep my pregnancy a secret, but some of my friends noticed I was gaining weight. They kept asking me, but I denied it to everyone. Still, the news was circulating, and rumors about Omar having another baby on the way were circulating, too. His phone calls diminished, his walking me to my classes came to a complete halt, and he did his best to avoid me. Some days, the only time I would see him would be in sixth hour, and because of his work, he never said much to me in that class to begin with.

Eventually, I started skipping sixth hour because I couldn't stand to be in his presence. I couldn't believe how his whole tune had changed, once I told him I was pregnant. My friend, Tanesha, confirmed everything for me, when she discussed my situation with Omar in her first hour class. Bottom line, he wasn't interested in me, the baby wasn't his, and his only concern was graduating and going to college. I was truly devastated, but there wasn't nothing I could do about it. I couldn't make him be a daddy if he didn't want to be, and as far as I was concerned, this was now my problem, not his.

The last few weeks of school, I avoided Omar and he avoided me. We walked by each other in the hallways, as if our relationship had never existed. The only reason I attended the 1984 graduation ceremony was because Jesse had made it through. I was so proud that at least one of us made it out of high school and we both knew that it was a tough year, especially with me getting pregnant. I still had one year to go, but there was no way I would return to school. Jesse didn't say much about the pregnancy, but considering my situation, she didn't think I'd return to school either.

Chapter Six

Over the summer, and only four months before the baby was expected, I spent many days hanging around the house with Mama. I wore big shirts and baggy jeans, in hopes that she wouldn't notice my sudden weight gain. She questioned me about my weight, but I just couldn't break her heart. Every day she'd complain about me eating too much, but not once did she suspect I was pregnant.

Getting worried about my weight gain, finally, Mama called the doctor and made an appointment for me. She said there had to be a reason why I'd picked up so much weight, and she wanted to know the reason. The night before my appointment, I tossed and turned all night. I promised myself I'd tell her in the morning, and had even written a letter to give to her. But when morning came, I kept the letter in my pocket, where it stayed.

We arrived at the doctor's office around nine o'clock that morning. The words almost came out of my mouth in the waiting area, but once again, I failed to tell her. Soon, the nurse called my name and Mama went into the examination room with me. With an extremely wide belly, I sat jittery on the examination table, biting my nails and fidgeting. I was under enormous pressure and had no idea how Mama would handle the news. She sat in a chair beside me, complaining about her rough days at work.

"I'm getting sick and tired of that old job," she griped. "They working me to death and all I do is work, work, work. I wish I had some money saved for a long vacation, but all I got is ten damn dollars in the bank. All I do is work to pay bills; bills that just keep on piling up. Something has got to give."

I felt horrible, because even though we didn't have much, Mama had worked her ass off to keep a roof over our heads. As much as we'd talked that morning, the real reason why we were at the doctor's office never came out of my mouth. The doctor came in, inquiring about our purpose for the visit.

Mama quickly spoke up. "Dr. Paris, Brenda is picking up a lot of weight. I was wondering if you'd run some test on her to see what's going on. I just want to make sure she's okay."

I shamefully lowered my head, continuing to bite my nails. Dr. Paris lifted my chin and stared into my eyes. He smiled, but my face remained flat. He then scooted a chair in front of me and turned to Mama.

"Just by looking at Brenda, I can tell she's pregnant. Now, I'll run some test to be sure, but I'm almost positive."

"Pregnant?" Mama shouted and jumped to her feet. Her head snapped in my direction and I'll never forget the serious hurt I saw in her eyes that day. "Bre...Brenda, you ain't pregnant, are you?"

I kept my head lowered, slowly nodding. As many tears trickled down my face, Mama dropped back on the chair in disbelief, but more so denial. Dr. Paris excused himself, leaving Mama and me in the room. She awaited a response from me.

"I'm sorry, Mama," was all I could say, as distress was written all over her face.

"Sorry?" she gasped. "Brenda, how could you? What do you know about sex? You know your Mama ain't got enough money to take care of no baby. How do you think you're going to take care of a baby?"

For some stupid reason, Omar's name came out of my mouth. "He said that he'd help me take care of it."

Mama didn't say another word, and after Dr. Paris completed his examination, he confirmed the pregnancy to her again.

Never, ever did I think about the consequences. And to top it off, Omar had left me to handle this all by myself. I didn't even think about how much this would affect Mama, and she was barely making ends meet. Who in the hell was I to go out and get myself pregnant, just to make matters worse. Dropping out of school, and finding a job to help out was not an option anymore. It was inevitable.

On the drive home, Mama couldn't stop crying and neither could I. We didn't say anything to each other, but when we got home, she asked for Omar's telephone number. When I gave it to her, she called to ask him about the baby. I don't know what he told her, but all I heard her say was he would have to help take care of his responsibilities. So much for that.

Adding to my misery, Mama called many of our family members, telling them about my pregnancy. She sniffled as she talked, but for some reason, when she told my Aunt Gerry, Mama was more at ease. Aunt Gerry's daughter had a baby and she told Mama about how delighted she was to be a grandmother.

Things had settled down that day, and finally, Mama came into my bedroom, ready to talk about the baby. I thought she was still upset with me, but I guess she realized that being angry wasn't going to help my situation.

"Brenda," she said with a serious look on her face. Her forehead lined with wrinkles as she spoke. "What are you going to do with a baby? Have you thought about it?"

I was mortified, but I did have *somewhat* of a plan. "Yes, Mama, I have a plan. I'll have to get a job and take care of it. If I don't find one, I'm going to apply for welfare and food-stamps."

Mama walked further into the room and sat on the floor next to Jesse's bed. She handed Jesse a bag of pink foam rollers to roll her hair. Jesse took the bag from Mama and sat behind her. Before Jesse got started, Mama placed her fingertips over her eyes, releasing her emotions again. I looked at Jesse's eyes fill with water, feeling so bad about the hurt I'd caused my family. I hated myself. Mama had already been through so much. This was definitely a low point in my life.

"Jesse," Mama sniffled. "Did you know that Brenda was pregnant?"

"No, I...I thought she was just gaining a lot of weight."

Mama was silent, and then she picked up a cigarette and lit it. "I guess I gotta help you take care of this baby because that fool I spoke to earlier ain't gon' do nothing. You still gotta go back to school, and I don't know how you plan to do that. As for finding a job, do you know how hard it is to get a job without a high school diploma?"

I moved my head from side to side, implying no. I didn't think it would be difficult, but that's because I hadn't faced reality. I wasn't prepared to tell Mama that I wasn't going back to school, so I kept my mouth shut and watched as Jesse rolled her hair.

That night, I was thankful that Mama hadn't made me a homeless child. More so, I was shocked by her acceptance of my situation. If I'd known she'd respond the way she had, I never would have kept my pregnancy a secret. For now, she seemed to have my back and I sure as hell needed all the support I could get.

The following week, my situation took a major turn. During an ultrasound, the doctors insisted that they'd heard two heartbeats and assured me that I was having twins. I was speechless. *Why me?* I cried. *Why was God punishing me?* One baby was already enough, but there was no way I could afford to take care of two. This was just one setback after another and how much more could a girl my age take? I had to go to Mama, again, with the news. I was so sure this would send her over the edge.

Since Jesse went to all of my doctor's appointments with me, I broke the news to her first. She was my rock, and was there for me in every way that she could possibly be.

"You may as well tell Mama and get it over with," Jesse said as we rode home from my appointment. "Don't hide it from her, Brenda. I don't think she's going to be mad about it."

"I do, but I really and truly do not believe that I have two babies inside of me. I'd have to see it first to believe it."

"If the doctors told you you're having twins, then you're having twins. Stop being in denial and face the facts. It is what it is. I just hope they don't come out looking like Omar. Uggh."

We laughed and I playfully pushed Jesse's shoulder. "He ain't all that bad. I could've done better, but you know those muscles and waves get me every time."

"That's about all he's got. The rest, no comment."

We laughed, again, and the conversation helped ease my mind about telling Mama.

Surprisingly, Mama didn't take the news as bad as I thought she would. She said that twins were common in our family, as well as triplets. Lucky me. She was back on the phone telling everybody the news. Rita was expected to come home soon, so Mama asked me to wait before telling her.

During the course of my pregnancy, there were times that Mama seemed onboard with it, and then there were times that she'd stare at me with true regret in her eyes. And if Mama's looks weren't enough to shake me up, when Daddy showed up at the door, I could have died! I was upset with Mama for telling him. Exactly what did she expect to gain from his presence? He couldn't wait to talk to me about my situation, and when Mama called me into her bedroom, I sat in a leather recliner that was directly in front of her bed.

"Give your daddy a chance, Brenda. Go in the kitchen and talk to him about the babies. Don't be so angry at him. If I've forgiven him, you should, too."

I pouted and folded my arms. "Talk to him for what? You've already told him about the babies."

"He might have some questions about the babies. Ju...just go talk to him. Do it for your Mama, okay?"

I frowned, but stood up. I walked slowly down the hallway, making my way to the kitchen. As soon as Daddy saw me, his eyes dropped to my big belly.

"Twins, huh," he said, holding his stare. "I can't believe I'm gon' be a granddaddy."

I didn't say anything, but Mama walked up behind me. "Well, believe it," she said. She went over by the kitchen counter and picked up a plate of food. She put the plate in front of him. "And I hope that your grandbabies don't have to see you drunk all the time. You really need to stop all that drinking."

"Baby, let me do what I want to do, please! I'm a grown-ass man and I don't need no woman telling me what I should or shouldn't do."

"Mama only trying to help," Jesse said, coming into the kitchen. "Besides, drinking ain't good for nobody."

Jesse took a quick glance at me and we both snickered. We certainly couldn't sit there and preach to Daddy, because both of us had been drinking like drunken sailors. Being pregnant caused me to chill, but the beer drinking didn't stop until I was at least four or five months.

Daddy gazed at Mama, while taking sips from his brown paper bag. He cleared his throat and belched. "Baby," he yelled out to Mama. "Let's get married again. Eat'em, Beat'em, and Cheat'em," he said, referring to Rita, Jesse and me, "They need me and I need them."

Mama sat at the table, trying to take the bag away from Daddy. "I wouldn't marry your ass again to save my soul. Now, cut out all that clowning and eat your food."

"Aw, come on baby," he slurred. "After today, I ain't drinkin' no mo. This shit makin' me sick and I want to be around to take care of my grandbabies."

Mama cut her eyes, and then snatched the bag from Daddy's hand. She poured the contents from the bag down the sink, but all he did was smile, knowing that there was more where that came from. She and Daddy had a very strange relationship, and aside from all of the bickering and fighting, I sensed that they had love for each other. Daddy kept his cool and lit a cigarette instead. He looked at Jesse and me sitting across the table from him, while holding the lit cigarette close to his ear. A few seconds later, sparks came from his hair and his dripping wet jerry curl was on fire.

"Your hair is on fire!" Jesse and I screamed. Daddy jumped up from the table, fanning away the flames with his hand. By then, Mama had a huge pot of cold water and tossed it on Daddy's head. The fire went out, and we all couldn't help but laugh at the situation. It had been a long time since we were able to laugh together and thank God that Daddy was in no way seriously injured.

After we ate dinner, Mama rolled the television down the hallway and into the living room. We all took seats around the sectional couch and Daddy looked at me with his red eyes.

"Brenda, I'm gon' take care of you, alright? Anything you need, just let yo Daddy know. To hell with that ole punk-ass muthafuckin' nigga. You don't need his ass, especially when you got me. You understand, baby girl, you got me!"

All I could do was nod. I'd definitely heard that before and I wasn't depending on anybody but Mama to help me with my situation. As the night went on, Daddy talked about his drinking habit and he mentioned us visiting him in the hospital after he'd been shot and stabbed years ago. I vaguely remembered going to see him at City Hospital, but as he spoke about it, thoughts of being in the hospital was in my memory. We were little girls, and Mama never told us who we were at the hospital to see.

Daddy promised to be there for me and said that maybe my getting pregnant would bring us closer together. That same day, he and Mama discussed how things could have turned out differently, and even though I didn't say much, I didn't hold anybody responsible for my own actions.

***

Daddy never broke his promise and I held him to it. Every day, he bought me whatever I desired to eat, which was usually a large sausage & pepperoni pizza or Chinese food. He took me for long drives so I didn't have to stay cooped up in the house, and even took short walks with me so we could "walk the babies down." He was a completely different person—so was Mama. Even though my pregnancy wasn't planned for, it seemed to bring the family together. I was starting to believe that everything happened for a reason, and if the babies were there to help me change my life around, I was all for it.

Even Rita came home for a week to visit. She didn't criticize me for getting pregnant, and seemed to be just as excited about the babies as the rest of the family.

By the time Rita had left to go back to school, later that week, I started getting severe pains. I knew it was getting close to my delivery date, but I couldn't tell if it were labor pains or pains from a fall I'd taken earlier on in the week. During my doctor's appointment, I was hooked up to a monitor to make sure the babies were fine. The monitor showed contractions, and the doctors confirmed that a delivery would be very soon. I was nervous as ever. Didn't quite know what to expect. According to the doctors, in a few days, I, Brenda Hampton, would be somebody's mama. Those words gave me great fear and it all seemed so unrealistic.

Chapter Seven

My frizzy long hair was scattered all over my head and my skin was pale as ever. Tears streamed down my face as I watched the round clock on the wall tick away. After lying in the hospital bed at St. Louis County Hospital for seventeen hours, I knew exactly when the next contraction was coming.

The minute hand hit the twelve, causing me to brace myself. I squeezed the sheets on the bed, balling them up in my hands so tight that they turned red. I squeezed my eyes together and took quick breaths that I was advised to do. My legs flopped around like fishes. I did my best to cease the excruciating pain from the ongoing contractions.

"Somebody...anybody, please help me," I shouted, as the rigorous pain took over my entire body. It lasted for a few minutes, and then it went away. I sighed from relief, recognizing that I would only remain this calm for the next twelve minutes. It was time to beg for help again, but the nurses and doctors were delayed with their response.

As I screamed out again, the nurse came into the room, smiling at me as if there was something to smile about. She reached for my arm to take my blood pressure. I was mad as hell by the way things were progressing, and the twisted look on my face showed it.

"Brenda, you must keep the oxygen over your mouth so the babies can get oxygen and breathe too. If you keep removing it, you'll put their lives at risk and yours."

She placed the oxygen mask over my mouth, again, but it was sure to come off. At this point, I didn't give a damn. How long did this have to go on? As the nurse took my blood pressure, the doctor entered the room. He was grinning from ear-to-ear, too, and I didn't understand what the fuck was so funny. Maybe they were trying to make me suffer; after all, I was a seventeen year old pregnant with twins. Through their eyes, I should have known better than to put myself into a predicament like this one. Basically, I was getting what I deserved and they were doing nothing to help me ease the situation at hand.

The doctor eyeballed the clock, knowing that my outburst was coming soon. He massaged my arms, before wiggling his fingers into a pair of sterile white gloves. Walking to the end of the bed, he stood in front of it. He ordered me to bend my knees and widen my legs. I frowned. Exposing myself to him was very uncomfortable. But at this point, I was willing to do whatever was necessary to get this over and done with.

The nurse held my shaky legs apart, while he inserted his fingers inside of me. *Nasty*, I thought. *Just nasty*. And for making me wait this long, I hoped he got a whiff of my pee since I had already peed on myself.

"I can feel one of the baby's heads, but we're still not quite there yet. Relax," he said, patting my leg. "We're almost there."

That was so easy for him to say, and as soon as those thoughts left my head, it was that time again. The oxygen mask was driving me nuts, so I snatched it off and reached for the nurses red long hair, yanking it.

"Can't you see that I need some damn help?" I said through gritted teeth. "When does this shit stop?! Why can't y'all do nothing for me? Damn!" I pounded my other fist on the bed, displaying my frustrations.

The nurse did her best to remove her hair from my fingers, but the grip was so tight that the doctor had to come over to assist.

"Calm down," he said, pulling my fingers away from the nurse's hair.

"I can't go on like this," I cried out. "Make this stop, please!"

He tried to calm me, but the nurse had given up and walked out. I guess she'd thought I was one crazy bitch, and under these conditions, yes, I was.

"Deep breaths," the doctor repeated. "Take deep breaths and keep the oxygen over your mouth."

He waited until I calmed down, and then he left the room. The deep breaths weren't working and he knew they weren't. I swear, if I could've left, I would have. This was ridiculous and did it take all of this, just to bring a child...children into the world?

As my raging anger ceased, I listened to another lady who was in the same room as I was. A dingy white curtain separated us, and even though her contractions weren't as rapid as mine, she was going through as well.

"I swear to God that I'm never fucking again!" she shouted. "This shit is for the birds! No more pussy for you, man. Do you hear that, Jake? No more pussy for you!"

For a second, I couldn't help but laugh. I felt what the White woman had said, but my thoughts had turned to that deadbeat Negro who had gotten me knocked up. If he only knew what I was going through. *Damn him*, I thought. What a lowlife bastard to make me experience something of this magnitude alone. I didn't realize how much I'd hated him, up until I sat in my bed, watching the clock and waiting as the minute hand struck twelve. I braced myself again, thinking of ways I could kill him.

At 7:53 a.m. the next day, twin A was born and twin B followed at 8:03 a.m. Completely exhausted, I barely had enough strength to look at the babies in the nurses' arms. All I could see was him, and hating him so much gave me something I could look at every single day. I turned my head, wiping a slow tear that had rolled from the corner of my eye. My only thought was... *where in the hell do me and my babies go from here?*

***

Mama and Daddy didn't come to see me until the next day, per my request. Daddy brought me a Teddy bear and he and Mama couldn't stop talking about *their* precious little girls. They wanted to name the twins, but kept coming up with ridiculous names. I appreciated their efforts, but naming the twins would be left up to me.

Once Mama and Daddy left, I was in the room all alone with, for the time being, Twin A and Twin B. With the little strength I'd had, I held both of them in my arms and smiled. They weighed six pounds five ounces each and were quite a load. More than soft, they were precious and I couldn't believe they were actually mine. I rocked my babies in my arms and thought about how Omar didn't know what he was missing.

Being back at home was busy. The babies never got any sleep because they were always in somebody's arms. Mama had supplied almost everything for them, and the rest came from Jesse who had gotten a job at Sears and used her discount to purchase items for the twins. Eventually, I started getting welfare and food-stamps to assist and it helped take some of the burdens off Mama and Jesse.

As time went on, no one ever asked about Omar again. He never called to see if or when the babies were born, and I never called to tell him about them either. I guess I wasn't up for his rejecting us, so I closed that chapter of my life and decided to move on.

By early October, Jesse and I talked about me returning to school. I really didn't want to, but since I had only missed one month of my final school year, I figured it would be in my best interests to at least get a diploma. Besides, something was nagging at me to go back and finish, so we agreed that during the day, she'd watch the twins so I could finish school.

Returning to school, not too many people remembered I was pregnant. And for the ones who did remember, they were surprised I'd had twins. At first, all I was interested in was getting my diploma, but soon, I was up to my old tricks again. I started skipping classes and hanging out with my friends after school. Jesse was at home with the babies, and as long as I let her know my whereabouts, she didn't seem to mind. Sometimes, we would ask Mama to watch the twins and Jesse would come up to Sumner High to hang out with me.

I was so sure that becoming a mother would change my life, but I was making very little effort to change in a positive way. I had even gotten myself a new boyfriend and his name was Dwayne. On a scale from one to ten, he was a twelve. He had coal black natural curly hair, hazel eyes, and a muscular frame of an athlete. His skin was a golden brown and his bad-boy persona attracted me to him.

Through spending so much time with Dwayne, I rarely went straight home from school. Jesse was spending more time with my kids than I was. They were very close to her and I knew they thought she was their mother, instead of me. I continued to tell myself that things would turn around, once I graduated from school, but my actions showed differently.

Mama had picked up more hours at work to make ends meet, but it wasn't long before her and Daddy had gotten into an argument and he was out of the picture again. In order to keep my relationship in good standings with him, I had to take the twins to visit him at my grandparents' house on Vernon Avenue, where Daddy lived too. Mama wasn't happy about it, but I had grown to respect Daddy and missed having him around.

By early January, 1985, I had enough credits to graduate from school, but enjoying my *freedom*, I decided to wait and graduate with the entire class. Besides, I only had a few more months to play around, and then I would definitely have to grow up and handle my responsibilities.

Graduation was only two months away and I had no plans to get a job or go to college. Simply put, I had no direction. I was pleased to get my diploma, but I wasn't sure how far having a diploma would get me.

My past mistakes with boys continued to follow me. I hadn't learned from my mistakes, and when Dwayne brought up the subject of sex, it wasn't as if I hadn't thought about it. He didn't pressure me, but he made it clear that it was something he wanted to happen. Needless to say, my next experience didn't occur with Dwayne, but it happened with another popular football player, Lloyd. I was starting to gain a reputation that I didn't want, but my feelings for Lloyd superseded the ones I'd had for Dwayne.

The opportunity to be with Lloyd presented itself one night at a Toga party I'd gone to with Jesse and some friends. We cut up white sheets, wrapping them around our naked bodies. Old English was the drink for the night, and after guzzling down a 40 ounce of Colt 45, I was hyped.

We arrived at the party a little after ten o'clock that night. The unfinished basement was filled with a cloud of thick smoke. It was dirty and so musty that we started to turn around and go back home. There was a DJ in the corner spinning Salt-N-Pepa, and since he allowed Jesse and me to break out with one of our raps, we opted to stay.

As the night went on, the alcohol took over. Lloyd was looking even better, and his coco-chocolate skin, shoulder length jerry curl and popularity guaranteed him many choices. But when his eyes shifted in my direction, I refused to look away. He excused himself from a conversation with some friends and stepped up to me.

"Brenda, right?" he said.

I blushed. "How'd you know my name?"

"It's easy to find out things I want to know."

I continued to blush and Lloyd's whispers in my ear couldn't be ignored. "That...that sheet you got on is bangin'!" he admitted. "You wanna get out of here and go to the park?"

I nodded and left the party with Lloyd. He drove to Fairground Park, and as planned, one thing led to another. After that night, we continued to hook up, but like always, sex was just sex. Lloyd was one of the first who hadn't gotten what he wanted and jetted, so needless to say, I liked him a lot.

When several people inquired about my intimate relationship with Lloyd, I didn't deny anything. It was so funny how news traveled fast, and it didn't take long for the news to get back to Dwayne. He'd enrolled into another school, Beaumont High, so we didn't see each other anymore during school. He'd gotten into a fight at Sumner, and according to some witnesses, Dwayne almost killed the dude he'd had a fight with. I had a hard time believing that the Dwayne I dated was violent, and when we talked about the fight, Dwayne insisted that people had exaggerated.

Either way, I had some explaining to do. Instead of going home that day, I got to Dwayne's house about 3:30 p.m. He sat on his porch, watching as I walked down the street in my pink t-shirt, black jeans and white tennis shoes. My hair was pulled back into a ponytail, without bangs and showing my full round face. As I walked up the steps, Dwayne was leaning back in a plastic green lawn chair. He glared at me with his hazel-nut eyes, wasting no time to ask what was up with me and Lloyd. It was the first time Dwayne had raised his voice at me, and it surely wouldn't be the last.

"I know what the fuck you did," he said, inquisitively rubbing the trimmed hair above his lip and on his chin. "It's cool, though, Brenda. You won't have sex with me, but you'll have sex with another muthafucka. What sense does that shit make?"

I liked Dwayne, truly I did, but I liked Lloyd more. Still, Dwayne and I had gotten really close and he'd already made a connection with my kids and Jesse. I didn't want to lose him. "Do...don't break up with me," I begged, standing in front of him. "I'm sorry and I was drinking—"

Dwayne cracked his knuckles and bit down on his bottom lip. "Save that bullshit for another time. You had sex with him 'cause you wanted to. This shit between you and me ain't happenin', so get off my porch and take yo ass home, bitch!"

Well damn! I never had anyone speak to me in such a way, and even though I was wrong, Dwayne's rejection and his words really hurt. I swallowed the lump in my achy throat, chalking up this relationship as another loss. My ride home on the bus was long, but I pulled out my notebook and started to write about how I'd disappointed someone I cared about: *I don't deserve nobody like Dwayne and that's what I get for trying to be a player. I'm lucky he didn't knock the hell out of me, but I could tell by looking at his fiery eyes that he sure in the hell wanted to. He's the first boy to show me that he really cares for me and my stupid self than went and fucked things up. I want him back and I'm going to keep on apologizing to him, until he forgives me. I'm sure he didn't mean to call me a bitch, but he had better tone that mess down. I feel so horrible right now, but whatever it takes I'm going to make this right. And when I say whatever, I mean whatever...*

Later that night, I was surprised to get a call from Dwayne. Jesse gave the phone to me and the first thing I asked is if he was still upset with me.

"Nope," he said. "I'm over it."

"Earlier, you told me—"

Dwayne interrupted. "I like you, Brenda, and I don't want to break up with you. You gotta make up yo mind about me and Lloyd, though. I got a lot of friends at Sumner and I got ways of findin' out shit. If you ever hurt me like this again, I promise, I'll make you pay for it." He spoke stern and his tone made me wonder about the reputation he had for being extremely aggressive. Still, I wanted my boyfriend back so I agreed to never hook up with Lloyd again. As a matter of fact, Lloyd made sex partner number four for me, and I was gaining a reputation I didn't want. I was done and decided to take my relationship with Dwayne more seriously. Dwayne told me he loved me that night, and for the first time in my life, somebody had said those words to me. I had no problem telling him I'd felt the same, and at this point, I would do whatever to please him. What I didn't realize at the time was pleasing him wouldn't come easy.

Chapter Eight

Graduation day was finally here. A week ago, I'd had an accident in Mama's car and had to catch the bus to my graduation because the car was totaled. Mama and Jesse said they would try to find a way there, but wasn't making any promises. I also invited Daddy, Dwayne, and Dana, and they all assured me they'd come.

The ceremony had gotten on the way, and I hadn't seen anyone I'd invited. During the announcements, I kept turning my head to see if Mama or Daddy—or anybody else had shown up, but they hadn't. By the time they started calling the graduates' names, tears kept filling my eyes, but I blinked them away. I'm sure everybody thought my emotions stemmed from being enthused about graduating, but having no one there to share this moment with me was agonizing. Especially after having the twins, I expected Mama to be proud of me for completing school. Yet again in my life, I felt so alone.

Finally, when my name was called there was light applause. The claps came from the two students by my sides, but for the most part, the auditorium was pretty quiet. My stomach turned in knots and I walked across the stage with weakened legs to get my diploma. *What was the point?* I thought. A diploma didn't mean anything to anybody else, so why should it have meant something to me? I was delighted when the last graduate was called, just so I could hurry and get the hell out of there.

Making it to the exit doors was the beginning of my torture. Many graduates stood around taking pictures with their families and embracing friends. Other than me, everyone seemed happy, and just so my pain didn't look too obvious, I stood with a fake smile.

I removed my white cap and gown, holding them in my hands. A lady complimented me on the white silk v-neck dress I wore and told me I'd had some of the prettiest hair she'd ever seen. Her compliments brought a quick smile to my face that vanished when she walked away. I busted out of the two heavy doors in the back of the building, making my exit. I walked swiftly down the street, smacking the flowing tears away from my face, but they became too rapid to brush away. When I came to a sewer, I tossed my cap, gown and tassel inside. I'd thought about trashing my diploma, but I held it close to my chest. I made my way to my grandparents' house on Cote Brilliante Ave., which was only a few blocks away.

I knocked on my grandparents' door and my grandfather opened it. His eyes were ice cold and I was surprised that he let me inside. I guess my puffy eyes said something was wrong, but he surely didn't ask what it was. He was a grumpy old man and hated for people to show up without calling.

"Gon' in the living room to see what that nigga wants," he told my grandmother.

My grandmother came into the living room with a smile on her face. Knowing that I had graduated, she secured her arms around me.

"Congratulations," she said, unaware of what her hug was doing for me. "I knew you'd do it."

All I could do was hold her tightly and thank her for having faith in me. I asked if I could use the phone and she put it right in front of me. When I called home, Mama answered.

"Mama," I said, swallowing the baseball-sized lump in my throat. "What happened to y'all?"

"Brenda, we couldn't find a ride. I asked one of our neighbors to take us but she said she had something to do. I didn't want to worry nobody else about a ride."

"Where's Jesse?"

"She's in there looking at TV."

"Where are the twins?"

"They're asleep. Jesse and me just put them down for a nap."

"I'm at grandma's house. I'll be home soon," I said, as my throat ached.

"Alright," she said. "Put your grandmother on the phone."

I gave the phone to my grandmother and left the room. Mama really disappointed me. I knew I'd made some mistakes, and I felt as if I'd have to pay for them for the rest of my life. The way I felt at the time...nobody expected me to graduate, and as a matter of fact, nobody expected nothing but failure from me. I wanted to call Daddy to see what his excuse was for not showing up, but I decided against it. Still, I couldn't hold back my emotions. My grandfather was eyeballing me like I needed to silence my sniffles because he was watching TV and couldn't hear. I got up enough nerve to ask if he would take me home, and he grunted, telling me no. My grandmother was off the phone, so I picked up the phone to call Dwayne. When he answered, I was surprised to hear his voice.

"What are you doing at home? I thought you were coming to my graduation," I said.

"I was but...but I went somewhere with my mother. We just walked through the door. Where are you callin' from?"

"I'm at my grandparents' house," I said dryly.

"What's wrong with you?"

"Nothing."

"I'm sorry for not makin' it to your graduation," he said. "My mother asked me to help her at the last minute."

"That's cool. I'll call you when I get home."

I hung up the phone, told my grandmother goodbye and left. For nearly an hour, I stood on the corner waiting for a bus to come. Finally, it came and as it drove by Sumner High School, there were still graduates outside with their families, taking pictures of their celebration. I closed my eyes, wishing that my experience could have been the same. But no matter how sad that day may have been, my memories at Sumner High School were unforgettable. I loved my school, without one single doubt.

The night of my graduation brought about a few more disappointments. I celebrated with Jesse and my girlfriends, only to come across Dwayne, his brother and some of his friends. Dwayne and I got into a brawl about a passion mark that was on his neck, and his brother confirmed that it came from a girl he had been with earlier that day. The fight ended with me telling him to go to hell and that I never wanted to see him again.

The next day was like a new beginning for me. I had no more school to attend, no job and no life. I was supporting the twins on welfare, food-stamps, and of course, with the help of Mama and Jesse. I wanted so much better for me and my kids, but until I could figure out a way to do better, the welfare system that would eventually handicap me had to do.

A few weeks later, I went to Grandpa Pigeons, a small department store, to fill out an application for employment. Surprisingly, I was hired on the spot. I shared the good news with Mama and Jesse, and right after, she informed me that Dwayne's brother, Myron, had called to discuss what had happened the night of my graduation. Since then, I hadn't talked to Dwayne, so I immediately called his brother back.

"I just wanted to apologize to you for lyin' about the passion mark on Dwayne's neck. I pinched his neck to make you jealous. We were only playin' around and I regret that things got out of hand that night, because of somethin' I did."

Please, I thought. *Do I have damn fool written across my face?* It was obvious that due to what I'd done with Lloyd, Dwayne had cheated on me and that's all there was to it. And even though he had done so, I was willing to forgive him, as he'd forgiven me. He got on the phone to speak, after I told Myron I didn't believe what he had said to me.

"Myron ain't lyin' and what he's tellin' you is the truth. But let's squash this shit and be done with it. Are we good or what?"

"I guess so. I don't know what really happened, but I do have some good news. I got a job today, making three dollars and seventy-five cents an hour. I'm excited and I start on Wednesday."

Dwayne congratulated me, and on Wednesday, I headed to work at Grandpa Pigeons. The bosses were cool and my co-workers were very friendly. I was excited about contributing to the household, where I could now pitch in more.

During my first week at work, trouble was on the horizon again. A plain-clothes security guard who worked in the store to catch shoplifters kept eyeballing me. I didn't know why he was always watching me, and even though I'd talked to Jesse and Mama about coming in to get free merchandise, nothing was confirmed.

It was time for my lunch break, so I headed towards the restroom. Right before I opened the door, a masculine voice called my name. When I turned around, the security guard stood behind me—so close I could feel his breath on my neck.

"Yes?" I replied, wondering how he knew my name.

"I keep looking at you 'cause you are one fine looking woman," he said. "What time do you get off work?"

"I have a man," I rushed to say. My heart raced, and even though I hated to admit it, I was enthused by the attention, especially from a much older man. I hadn't forgotten about my promise to Dwayne, and there was no way in hell I'd ever betray him again.

As time went on, work was becoming a little uncomfortable for me. The security guard, Miles, started making more advances towards me and I was confused. Confused because Dwayne had been busted, again, for cheating on me, and after I talked to his other girlfriend, she confirmed that she and Dwayne had been dating since his freshman year in high school. She even admitted to putting the passion mark on his neck. I felt like such an idiot for forgiving him. When I confronted him, he denied it. He expressed his love for me, and when I spoke of dating someone else, he begged me not to. He promised to end his relationship with his ex and I allowed him time to do so.

During that time, I turned my attention to Miles. He'd given me six free skating passes for Tuesday night skating at Skate King on Kienlen Avenue. I didn't know how to skate, but I knew a lot of people went there to hang out. It had been a while since my friends and I had gotten together, so this was the perfect opportunity to kick it with them again.

On Tuesday, I wasn't scheduled to work so, Jesse, Dana, Shantell, Loretta, and I went to the skating rink. I had described Miles to everyone; smooth brown complexion, a well defined pointed nose, medium build and bowlegged as ever. His Caesar cut was flowing with shiny waves that were sharply trimmed. All of my girlfriends said he sounded scrumptious and definitely couldn't wait to meet him. I never mentioned that he was thirty-two, and when we arrived at the skating rink, everyone was surprised that I was interested in a much older man. Dressed in a dark blue uniform, he stood by the door, collecting tickets from skaters. I introduced him to my friends and they gave me thumbs up. We began to mingle, and throughout the entire night, Miles watched my every move. Actually, I turned a lot of heads, and by the end of the night, I felt like a fool implying that I'd had a boyfriend, especially one who cheated. Miles questioned me about Dwayne that night, but I stuck by my man.

"We're having some problems, but I intend for us to work them out," I said.

"I hope you don't. And if you don't, you know where to find me."

He walked away, leaving me in awe and flattered by the attention he was giving me. I watched him in action that night, unsure about hooking up. He had many chicks flocking to him, and it was obvious that he was just as much trouble as Dwayne was. No doubt, I was attracted to bad boys with confidence.

When we got home that night, Mama was tripping. She was yelling about me not giving her any money and about us staying out late at night. My checks were so skimpy and they were barely enough to buy the twins things they needed. I wasn't up for arguing with Mama again, and lately, she'd been on a rampage. She was yelling so loud that she woke up the twins and they started crying. That always made me angry, and as we spewed harsh words back and forth, she knew exactly how to get me where it hurt.

"That's why that nigga Omar left your ass! You need to get your smart mouth together or you and your babies can get the hell out of here!"

I kept my emotions intact. Bringing up Omar's name infuriated me. "And what did Daddy do to you, Mama? He left you too, didn't he? You have some nerve talking about me, and if you want me to get out of your house, I will!"

I guess I'd touched a nerve with her too. Mama rushed over to my closet, pulling clothes off the hangers and throwing them on the floor. "Get out of here, Brenda! Now! I don't give a damn where you and your babies go! Just get out of my house!"

Jesse tried to calm the situation, but Mama gave her an evil stare, ordering her out of the house too.

"This is uncalled for," Jesse shouted. "It's raining outside and we don't have no place to go with the twins."

Mama kept tossing out the clothes in the closet, making it clear that she wanted us to leave. According to her, she'd had enough of the lies, and coming and going as we pleased was a no-no.

"After all I've done for you, Brenda, this is the thanks I get. I am done trying to help you and I want to see you make it on your own!"

Jesse put one of the twins in her arms and I did the other. I realized just how right Mama was. I had to figure out a way to make it on my own, because the entire situation with Mama was draining. She was wishy-washy, and I could never figure out what she really expected of me.

As Jesse and I walked up the partially lit street with the twins, who were only ten months old at the time, the heavy rain poured on us and gusty wind slapped our faces, blowing us around like ragdolls. We'd had one flimsy umbrella, and when that blew away, I shielded my face with my hand. The twins shivering bodies were held close to our chests, tightly wrapped in pink blankets. I wanted to get as far away from Mama as I could and I had gotten so sick and tired of her threats. They became a reality, leaving us with no place to go.

Like the last time Mama had put us out, we stayed at Dana's house. Her mother felt sorry for us with the twins, but she was adamant that we couldn't stay another night. Since Shantell had an apartment off Lindell Blvd., I called to see if we could stay with her. Luckily, she agreed.

For two weeks, our lives were a living hell. I escaped some of my pain through writing in my notebooks: *Back in the streets again. Damn! This time I got my babies with me and it hurts like hell not to be able to keep a roof over their heads. One of my babies is sick, too, and she's been coughing all day. All I do is keep holding her in my arms and rocking her. But she keeps looking up at me as if I'm so pitiful. Am I really pitiful? I'm trying my best, but it just don't seem good enough. I wanna go back home. Maybe I shouldn't have said those things to Mama, but she made me so mad, talking about that fool Omar. I bet he ain't homeless like I am, but forget him. If I keep harping on him, I'll never get ahead. Never ...*

I was so frustrated with my situation. Shantell had a one bedroom apartment and there were eight of us living there. She had a crazy-ass boyfriend who she often had arguments with, and the foolishness between them lasted many times throughout the night. Her kids were screaming at the top of their lungs and so were mine. Her boyfriend had started to make advances towards Jesse and I the whole time we were there, and when Jesse told Shantell about his actions, she got angry. Not with him, but with us. I was so ready to go back home. Sleeping on her hard living room floor with Jesse, the twins and roaches wasn't cutting it.

I still managed to talk to Dwayne sometimes, but it was hard to keep in touch with him because I didn't have a phone. And as for Miles, he'd been assigned to another store, so I rarely saw him at all. Dwayne had become so close to me and the twins, he suggested that we get an apartment together.

"We need to get our own place," he said. "That way you don't have to deal with no bullshit from yo mama."

"Jesse and I have been looking for one, but the ones we like are too expensive. I put my name on the emergency housing list, so I hope to hear from them soon."

"I hope so too. I love you, girl, so keep yo head up."

Lord knows I was trying, but I didn't see this situation getting better. And after two more days with Shantell, finally, I called Mama.

"How my babies doing?" she asked.

My voice cracked. "O…okay. I can tell they miss their baby beds, but we'll be okay."

"You don't sound okay. And if you, Jesse and the twins want to come back home, y'all can. Just promise me that you'll find you and the twins a nice place to stay, and until then, you'll give me some money to help out. I can't do this all by myself, Brenda. It's a lot on me, and, sometimes, I don't think you understand just how much."

I swallowed hard, thinking about what Mama had said. I knew she'd had a lot on her, I just wished that she wouldn't say some of the mean things that she'd said to me about Omar. And making drastic decisions that affected the twins wasn't right. I already didn't have my head on straight, but I felt as if I was trying. Mama didn't seem to appreciate my efforts, and I wasn't sure if they would ever be good enough for her.

"I promise to do better, Mama, and I'm sorry for saying what I did to you."

There was a pause, and then she spoke up. "Then come on home. Bring my babies and Jesse home with you."

Hearing Mama say that was like music to my ears. We quickly packed our belongings and left! No thanks to Shantell, no I'll call you later, no nothing! We got the fuck out of there!

Mama seemed glad to see us, more so the twins. She didn't apologize for kicking us out, but you could always tell when she felt bad behind her actions. I was just glad to be home, and more than anything, I was delighted the twins were back in their own beds, resting peacefully. At least they were at peace. And as things slowly but surely got back to what was considered normal to me, I wasn't exactly sure what a peaceful life consisted of. Normal in my book included occasional arguments with Dwayne, being yelled at by Mama, working my part-time job that wasn't paying much, and being a half-ass mother to the twins. No doubt, something had to give, because I was starting to feel as if I were losing it.

Chapter Nine

Dwayne was rarely at home when I called, and when I'd spoken to one of his friend's girlfriend, Pat, she mentioned that Dwayne had been involved with a chick named Nikki. With all that had been going on with me, our relationship was strained, but he often found time to stop by and have sex with me. He'd spend time with the twins, too, and we talked about getting an apartment together. To him, the problem was sneaking into Mama's house while she was at work, and simply put, we needed to hurry up and get our own place. With or without him, I was all for getting my own place, but the news about Nikki shocked me. I was sick to my stomach and rushed to the bathroom, hugging the toilet as I vomited. A horrible thought came to mind—What if I was pregnant, again? *Couldn't be*, I thought. *Not again!*

Later that day, I took a pregnancy test. When I lifted the white tube-like instrument, a plus sign was revealed. We had celebrated the twins first birthday several months ago, and I was already pregnant again! I knew Dwayne would want to keep the baby because he seemed so good with the twins. But being an eighteen year old, with three babies just wasn't going to cut it.

Upset about the direction my life was headed, I had to find Dwayne so we could talk. He was the only person I could turn to, and even though Jesse and I were always close, I refused to tell her my secret. I drove around to some of Dwayne's hangouts but had no luck with finding him. My luck changed almost an hour later, when I spotted his car parked in front of a friend of his house on Cora Avenue. As I got closer, I noticed a female sitting on the back seat. I couldn't wait to see who my competition was and I could feel my blood boiling. My eyes turned to numerous of his friends standing on a porch, and when one of them noticed my car, he rushed down the steps to alert Dwayne.

By that time, it was already too late. My car was parked next to his, and in the back seat with Dwayne was the chick I assumed to be Nikki. I moved quick, jumping out of my car to get to Dwayne. Nikki hurried out of the back seat and I rushed inside fist first to slam my fist into Dwayne's jaw.

"You son of a bitch," I yelled while swinging wildly. Dwayne covered his face to protect it, and his friend grabbed my waist, pulling me from the car. He held my arms behind my back, doing his best to restrain me.

Dwayne grinned, displaying his new open-faced gold teeth. "You a bold ass bitch, Brenda. I would fuck you up for hittin' me in front of my boys, but you played yourself."

I maneuvered myself away from his friend's grip. "Fuck you! Go to hell, you liar!"

He threw his hand back at me, and ordered Nikki into the car so they could leave. I grabbed Dwayne's arm as he moved from the back seat to the front.

"What's up with you?" I asked. I held back my tears because I didn't want him to see the hurt he'd caused me. "Why do you keep on doing this shit? Haven't you hurt me enough?"

He snatched his arm away from me, and spoke sternly. "It's a done deal. We're finished, au'ight?"

I was stunned by his words. This couldn't be the same person who had told me he loved me and wanted us to get an apartment together, was it? What kind of game was he playing? I swallowed the enormous lump in my throat. "We can't be over because I'm pregnant. I just found out today and I don't want to do this shit by myself again."

I watched as Nikki folded her arms and cleared her throat. Everybody waited for a response from Dwayne, and his friends giggled, as if they got a kick out of the whole ordeal. Dwayne's words stung.

"If you're pregnant, the baby for damn sure ain't mine. You'd better find somebody else to put the blame—"

What? Not him too! The one who dogged Omar for not taking care of his responsibilities. The only one I'd had sex with on demand, when, where or however he wanted it, even in a car while parked next to a church! The one who claimed to love me so much and would do anything in the world for me and my kids! No, Dwayne was not sitting there rejecting me and this baby, was he?

I'd lost it. Dwayne was so good at bringing out this rage inside of me. I wanted to kill him for how badly he'd treated me, and he was so different when we were together alone. My fist tightened, again, but before I could take action, he slammed his car door shut and started his car. I hurried to mine, retrieving a jack handle from the trunk. As he drove off, I threw the jack handle and it slammed against the trunk of his car. I had hoped to shatter the glass, but a dent in his trunk was fine with me. I swiped my hands together, feeling a tiny bit satisfied, but I knew that satisfaction wouldn't last for long.

By the time I got home, I was a mess. I called the abortion clinic to find out how much it would cost to end my pregnancy and the lady asked me to make an appointment so we could talk. *Talk about what,* I thought. There was no way in hell I was going to have another baby, especially by a no-good fool like Dwayne. As soon as I got my finances together, I planned to take care of my situation. Jesse asked me what was wrong with me that day, but I refused to tell her. She had met this dude at the skating rink named Anthony, and he was very good to her. He was a manager at Kentucky Fried Chicken, he drove a red sports car and treated Jesse with much respect. I wished for someone positive in my life like Anthony, and in my book, Jesse was lucky.

***

"Dwayne is using you, Brenda," Miles said over the phone as I discussed my problems with him. "I'm not just saying that because I'm digging you, but you need to remove yourself from that relationship. Besides, if a man doesn't want to be with you, you can't make him."

I listened to every word Miles had said, but defended my situation. "I thought he truly loved me. He's always been there for me and my kids. I just don't understand why he keeps doing this kind of stuff to me."

"Shit, I know why, but do you need a rocket scientist to figure it out for you? It's because you let him. He likes all that fuck-me, fight-me shit and most niggas do. You'd better be careful messing around with that brotha and I'm gon' need for you to wise up. Don't let no man treat you that way. You're a nice gal, Brenda, and you deserve better."

Miles was an older man telling it like it was, whether I wanted to hear it or not. I agreed with most of what he'd said, but it still didn't stop me from wanting to be with Dwayne. I knew he'd done me wrong, but I still felt that he cared deeply for me. He wouldn't tell me that he loved me without really meaning it, and for whatever reason, I trusted his word.

His next attempt to show me he cared came at three o'clock one morning. There was a knock at my bedroom window and I was sitting in bed with the nightlight on, writing in my notebook. I was scared to look out to see who it was and so was Jesse. Then all of a sudden, a whisper came through the window, "Brenda...Brenda." I jumped up to see who it was and it was Dwayne.

"Come outside," he said.

"For what?" I whispered, attempting not to wake Mama.

"So I can talk to you."

Jesse whispered, "Would you go outside and talk to him before Mama wakes up. You know she'll clown, and so will he if you don't go."

Before going outside, I combed my hair back and slid on my Tweety Bird house shoes that matched my pajamas. I tip-toed past Mama's room and she was snoring loudly. As I opened the door, Dwayne stood on the porch with his hands in his pockets, head hanging low.

"Ay," he said. "I've had time to think about what I've done to you. I came here to let you know that I do care about us. I want to be with you and my baby. Me and Nikki—things didn't work out. I told her I wanted to be with you, but she just wouldn't leave me alone. Honestly, I didn't know what was up with you and Miles, and when you told me about the baby, I wasn't sure—"

"Well, I'm sure. I told you that I hadn't had sex with him and you knew it. You're making excuses, Dwayne, and this time, I can't forgive you."

Sadness covered his face and tears rushed to his eyes. I couldn't believe he was standing there getting ready to cry over me! Wow, the moment was touching. "Baby, you're all I got," he said. "I love you so much...but I don't know why I keep doin' this stupid shit.

Maybe I need to go to church and confess my sins to a priest and ask for forgiveness. I'll do whatever you want me to do and you can go with me."

Honestly, at the time, I was moved. Maybe going to church would help a man to be faithful. I wasn't sure, but there was no doubt in my mind whatsoever that this was some crazy shit! "No, I'm not going to church with you. The only place we're going together is to the abortion clinic so I can terminate this pregnancy. Goodbye, Dwayne, and let me know if you have time to go with me." I went back into the house, closing the door behind me.

The day of my appointment, I was numb. I felt terrible for what I was about to do, but I felt as if I didn't have a choice. Mama had been doing all that she could do for the family, and so had Jesse. My paychecks weren't much, and Daddy had been chipping in to help out as well. I had already felt like a disgrace to the family and no one was about to tolerate another baby in the house. So, whether I liked it or not, this had to be done.

Dwayne told me that if I wanted to end the pregnancy, the choice was mine. He stressed how much he wanted me to have the baby, but agreed to go to the clinic with me. He was supposed to pick me up at eight o'clock that morning, but was a no show. I called his home phone several times but no one answered. My appointment was at 9:30 a.m., and since our car needed a new alternator, I hitched a ride on the bus.

I arrived at the clinic on Euclid an hour late, but they were still able to fit me in. And after hours of consultation and pure deep hell, the pregnancy was ended. I hated that I kept finding myself in these situations and I didn't understand why it was so hard for me to "wise up." Deep down, I wanted to get on the right track, but I didn't know how to go about changing things around. I could always envision the "good life" but getting there was so difficult. My pace was slow, so slow that there were times when I just wanted to give up on life and throw in the towel.

While waiting for the bus, I dabbed my eyes with Kleenex. I wanted to hurt myself for being so stupid. It would serve me right for what I had just done to my baby. I wasn't even smart enough to make Dwayne use a condom, and why hadn't I learned my lesson after having the twins? I was depressed...stressed more like it. Many teenagers weren't dealing with this kind of shit and I felt as if the devil had a tight grip on me.

When the bus arrived, I sat next to a White man who carried a piss smell that burned my nose and gave me a headache. I was already sick to my stomach, so in an effort to avoid him, I turned my head towards the window. I thought hard about my on-and, off-again relationship with Dwayne, and I knew we couldn't go on like this forever. I was fooling myself if I thought things would ever work out for us, and it was so obvious that he didn't give two cents about me. Why I couldn't let go, I couldn't explain it.

As those thoughts swam in my head, the bus came to a stop at the corner of Kingshighway and Natural Bridge, which was only a few blocks away from Dwayne's house. I looked at the cars beside the bus, and his car was two lanes over beside it. Inside was Dwayne, his friend Lester, and two chicks I had never seen before. The loud music coming from the speakers had his entire car vibrating and everyone inside was full of smiles and laughter. I watched as his car made a right turn, pulling into The Carousel Motel. If that wasn't my wake-up call, I didn't know what else would be.

Chapter Ten

For a while, it was all about work for me. I had picked up more hours at Grandpa Pigeons, trying to put as much money in my pockets as I could. I had also been allowing Jesse and Mama to come through my line to get things for free, and they always left with a cartful of merchandise. During those times I was extremely nervous, but not as nervous as I was when I was stealing clothes, shoes...items for the twins at Target and Venture. I would carry my items into the dressing room, stuffing my purse, as well as my body with the things I needed, or should I say, wanted. Sometimes, I'd take the items back to get cash, so it was rare for me not to have any money in my pocket. This was my hustle and I was getting what I wanted anyway I could.

I was still getting food-stamps, and they helped out with buying groceries. For months, this is how I was going about "changing" my life, and I was so bad at running from one relationship to another. I felt as if I needed someone in my life to feel complete. This time, Miles was the one who filled that void, because after my abortion, Dwayne was out again. Since Jesse's boyfriend Anthony, and his friends, spent a lot of time at Skate King, so did we. Seeing Miles at the rink brought us closer together and there became a time when I gave in to his advances.

"I ain't seen you in a while," he said whispering in my ear as I stood by the concession stand. "Why don't you go home with me tonight?"

I cocked my head back, not really shocked by his offer and smiling. "Tonight?"

"Yes, tonight."

"And what's at your house, tonight?"

Like always, he was blunt. "You, me, a bed, sex—"

"Hold that thought," I said, putting up one finger. "I'll let you know before we leave."

"Alright, Brenda. Don't play me. I know you're a bull-shitter and a dick teaser too."

I laughed and couldn't agree with Miles more. I was known for being flirtatious, but many times it would go no further than that. The truth...I was afraid of having sex with Miles. I was still very inexperienced, and often thought that my inexperience was Dwayne's reasoning for being with others. Maybe I was being too hard on myself, but if I couldn't please Dwayne sexually, I knew there was no way in hell I could please Miles.

Skate King was getting ready to close and Miles and a few other security guards were patrolling the parking lot. Cars were crammed everywhere. This was, no doubt, the place to be on Tuesday nights. Getting his attention, I told him I was going to walk Jesse and my friends to our car and would be back so we could go to his house. He was delighted, and on the way to our car, we started looking around for Loretta but couldn't find her. All of a sudden, screams rang out and we saw Loretta's ex-boyfriend's car smash into the back of another car. Loretta was inside, pounding the hell out of him and his new girlfriend with a skate that she'd had in her hand. We rushed over to stop her, but she was so enraged and couldn't be stopped.

Blood was all over the chick's face in the back of the car and her ex-boyfriend was taking punches at Loretta, trying to get her to back off. None of his punches stalled her, not even a hard blow to her face that made me cringe.

"Come on, Loretta," I shouted, trying to pull her away from the car. "He ain't worth all of this!"

I had my nerve. Her situation took me right back to my encounter with Dwayne and his girlfriend in the car. Loretta was getting it in, though, and it took Miles and several other guards to restrain her. But by then, friends of the girl in the car had come over to help. I had never seen a posse of women look so rough, but looks didn't mean shit, especially when you were put into a position where you had to fight for your life. My fists went up, and as two of the chicks started to pound on me, I swung wildly, trying to land punches wherever I could.

One of the chicks had her fingers tightened in my long hair, yanking the mess out of it. "Bitch," she yelled, trying to kick me in my side. "I can't stand yo high-yellow ass!"

Now, what I ever did to her, don't know, but I did my best to stay on my feet. I was pulling hair too, and many of my punches landed where I wanted them to. One of the big Amazon-looking chicks lifted her skate in mid-air and was about to come crashing down on my head with it. I thought it was all over with for me, but Miles came out of nowhere, catching the skate and knocking the chick to the ground.

"If you get up and start fighting again," he yelled. "I will have your ass locked up!"

The chick on the ground didn't move, and me and the other one backed away from each other with heaving chests. She had scratches on her face, and so did I. My head was hurting from my hair being pulled so tight, and I tasted blood in my mouth. I wiped it and looked around for Jesse, who I'd seen fighting as well. I hoped like hell she was winning. I spotted Jesse coming near us with a gun in her hand. It was a toy gun that we kept underneath the seat, just to scare people off. The gun, however, looked very real, causing pandemonium to erupt. People were running all over the place, and Miles rushed up to Jesse, yelling for her to put the gun away.

"Now!" he said through gritted teeth. "Put it away now!"

I ran up from behind, telling him that the gun was fake. I didn't want Jesse being arrested, or shot at, and I knew it was her way of scaring the chicks and getting them off our backs. Miles snatched the toy gun, observed it, and then threw it far across the parking lot.

"Get off my parking lot," he said in a more calm tone. "Are y'all fucking crazy? You can get killed out here tripping like this."

No doubt, it was a messed up situation. We were lucky that night, and as the parking lot cleared, my friends and I sat in the car talking about the incident. We shook our heads at Loretta for kicking the shit off to begin with.

"I couldn't help it," she said, putting her earrings back into her earlobes. "Seeing him with that bitch made me mad. I had to show that nigga what was up!"

"You definitely showed him that," I said. "And I guess you showed her too."

I slid my hand across Loretta's, giving her props for handling her business. As we laughed, we watched Miles striding and strutting as he walked up to the car. He squatted beside my window and looked inside.

"Are you still going home with me, or are you going to stay out here all night, looking for more trouble?"

I wanted to go with Miles, but contemplated because I wanted to go to Anthony's house too. His house was the hang-out crib after the skating rink let out, and we always had a lot of fun.

"Gone and go," Loretta said, playfully shoving my shoulder. "You know you want to go and get some tonight, girl. You can get some for all of us. Besides, that man saved your life. You owe him something, so stop being so stingy."

"Tell her, baby," Miles said, agreeing. "Just a little something and I promise to be good to you."

I hesitated, but put my hand on the doorknob and got out of the car. I walked to Miles' car with him, nervous about what might happen when we got to his place. While in the car, he told me to stay away from the rink for a while and ordered me not to come back until matters cooled down. He knew many of the chicks we disputed with, and assured me that coming back would mean trouble.

"Those chicks will hurt you, Brenda, and you got them babies to see about. I don't want you out here fighting like that, and why do you have so much anger inside of you? Life couldn't be that bad, could it?"

He just didn't know. Yes, I did feel bad that I was the twins' mama and I was out there clowning like I was. But what was I supposed to do…fall to the ground and get my ass beat? Miles made me feel real bad, so bad, that I sat in silence until we reached, not his house, but his apartment on Chambers Road.

When we entered his apartment, he mentioned that he had not too long ago moved in. The apartment had very little furniture inside; a sofa against one wall with a picture of a man playing a saxophone above it. A wooden rectangular table sat in front of the couch and two end tables sat on each side. Beige carpet covered the floors and a sliding door led to a balcony. Miles went to the tiny kitchen to get a beer from the fridge and he offered me one.

"It might help you out later," he said, laughing.

I didn't understand how a beer could help me later, so I declined. Miles guzzled down his beer, and then turned his stereo on to some soft music. I kept thinking about our age difference, and the thought of getting pregnant, again, was on my mind. The abortion clinic had provided birth control pills, but since I'd discontinued sex with Dwayne, I didn't think I'd need them.

I rubbed my sweaty hands on my jeans, and told Miles how much I appreciated him intervening with my fight at the skating rink. "I owe you big time," I said. Miles sat close to me on the couch, making me even more nervous. "You saved my life by stopping that skate from busting me upside my head."

He laughed and snapped his finger. "You do owe me, and I expect for you to one day pay up. But all I was doing was my job. I wasn't about to let nobody mess up that pretty face."

I blushed as he swiped his finger along the side of my face. He always knew how to say the right things to me.

"Actually," he said removing his blue uniform shirt. "Your sister Jesse saved y'all by pulling out that fake-ass gun. It was a stupid thing to do, and promise me you'll never do anything like that again."

"You threw it somewhere, so I guess that's a promise I can keep."

"I hope so." He leaned back on the couch, and put his hands on his head to rub his flowing waves. "Sooo, Brenda, getting back to me saving your life. What are you prepared to offer the man who saved your life?"

I shrugged. "It depends on what the man wants?"

Miles patted his lap, inviting me to straddle it. "I'll tell you what I want in a minute, but for now, I want you on top of me."

He scooted down a bit and I lifted my leg to straddle his lap. I could feel his hardness pressing between my legs, immediately knowing and feeling that I was in deep trouble. Instead of telling me what he wanted, he pulled my face to his, sticking his tongue down my throat. I backed up, certainly not ready for such an intense kiss. Miles paused and stared at me with his narrowed dark brown eyes.

"Stand up, Brenda, and take off your clothes."

"Do what?" I'd heard him, but I was known for stalling.

"I said take off your clothes for me. I want to watch you undress."

I hadn't gotten naked in front of anyone, including Dwayne. I was kind of ashamed of my flabby midriff, which resulted from having twins. More than anything, I knew that standing naked in front of any man would be very uncomfortable for me. There were no sheets around to cover up and the bright lamp in the living room was giving off way too much light.

"Miles, honestly, I don't feel comfortable taking off my clothes in front—"

He interrupted. "Why not? You sexy as hell and you don't have nothing to be ashamed of. I need to see what you're working with, cause I don't stick my dick into nothing, unless I see it first."

"But I..."

He seemed irritated, and reached over to turn off the lamp. There was still a sliver of light coming in from the sliding doors, and the room was in no way pitch black how I preferred it. "There," he said. "Don't be afraid to show your body to me. If it makes you feel better, I'll get naked with you, all right?"

I got up enough courage to stand in front of Miles. I kicked my shoes to the side, and then removed my Nike sweatshirt and white lace bra that secured my healthy breasts. Miles smiled, and as his eyes narrowed more, he focused on me like a laser. I dropped my pants and black silk panties to my ankles, giving Miles exactly what he wanted. "Are you happy now?" I asked while holding my crossed arms against my chest.

At first, Miles didn't say anything. He sat observing my body, with his index finger pressed against the side of his face. "Brenda, you haven't had much experience, have you? I have a feeling that you've been giving the pussy away, but haven't been completely satisfied. Why you out here wasting time with these chumps who don't know how to please you? Or, haven't shown you how to please them?"

I shrugged again, curious as to how Miles could read me so well. "Why do you say that? What makes you think I'm so inexperienced?"

"By how long it took you to take off your clothes. I was about to fall asleep waiting for you. Then, you're crossing your arms in front of you and won't even let me see all of you. There's absolutely no gap between your legs, which means that your boyfriend ain't been hitting that pussy like he's supposed to, and neither has anyone else. Relax, though. I can give you just what the doctor ordered, but I want to make sure you're ready for this."

I wasn't sure if I was ready or not, but when Miles removed every stitch of his clothing, my eyes fell below his waist. I went into a trance, admiring his nicely cut abs, bulging muscles, and…I had never seen a man's dick so big! It was too big, especially for a man who was about six feet tall and weighed less than two-hundred pounds. *Just who in the hell did he think he was going to stick that thing inside of?* I thought. It had to be at least twelve inches long, and I didn't think a dick that size existed. I sat back on the couch, biting my nails one by one.

Miles dropped to his knees and eased his naked body between my legs. "Have you ever had oral sex before?" he asked, lightly squeezing my thighs.

My face scrunched up. "Oral what?"

"Your pussy sucked. Has a man ever sucked your pussy or have you ever sucked him?"

Honestly, I was left scratching my head.

Miles shook his head in disbelief. "I'm about to teach you some things that every woman your age should know about. Don't interrupt me, but if you want me to stop, I will."

Miles stretched a condom over his growing muscle and he directed me to pour my legs over his shoulders. He dove in face first, using his tongue to open my slit and tickle my furrows. As his tongue went deeper, my stomach moved around like waves in an ocean. I tried to back away from the tingly feeling that had me trembling all over. My body felt weak and my hands were balled in tight fists. He was giving me something I'd never had before, and simply put, that was pleasure. I had no idea that being with a man could make me get goose bumps all over, and he was definitely teaching me something new.

"Come for me, baby. I won't be satisfied until this pussy talks to me like I want it to."

My orgasm wouldn't come, so Miles changed positions. He lay back on the floor, inviting me to get on top of him. I did, but when he positioned himself to enter me, I wanted to jump up and run. The size of his muscle was way more than what I could handle and I was only able to ease midway down on it. I remained stiff as a board, fearing that he would bust my insides wide open.

"Relax," he suggested while guiding my hips. "You got to move those hips, baby. Don't just sit there and let me do the work. Put some effort into this. Show me what good sex feels like."

I had flashbacks of every single sexual encounter I'd had. Many times, I'd be looking up at the ceiling, wondering what in the hell I was doing. I'd just lay there with my legs wide open, wanting and hoping that the person I was with was satisfied. That it was enough for that person to like me, and he'd fall in love because I gave him the one thing he wanted...a nut.

Miles wanted more than just a nut, and for what seemed like hours, he worked his over-sized goodness inside of me, teaching me the ropes. He spewed nasty and freaky words to me, all of which made me step up my performance. I was shocked by his aggressiveness, and from one position to the next, he had turned me completely out. "Lay on your stomach...get on your knees...straddle my face...suck me here," he ordered. I had honored his wishes, and as we lay in a 69 position on the floor, I couldn't believe that sex could ever feel this satisfying. He calmed my shaky legs, by taking pecks on them and on my inner thighs.

"Your legs soft as hell. I'm going to enjoy making you mine. In the meantime," he said, lightly smacking my butt. "Turn dat ass over again and let me hit that mutha from behind. I need to punish you for making me wait for as long as you have."

I smiled, getting ready to position myself. "What can I say, other than I was tripping. Never again."

"Let's hope not," he replied, as we continued on throughout the night.

As soon as I got home, I filled my notebook with my experience with Miles: *Wow!! That's what I'm talking about! Never knew a dick could feel that good inside of me. It was the first time that I didn't stare at the ceiling and Miles made me feel like a woman. The only thing I ever rode in was a car, but the way he showed me to ride him, umph, umph, umph! I felt his big thang deep in my stomach and how did I get so wet? His tongue made me wet and that thing was so far up in me I wanted to scream! My nipples tingled when he touched them and I liked the way he massaged my breasts together. I can't believe, though, that I put my mouth on his manhood. Didn't know what the hell I was doing, but I liked how my licks made him smile. Mr.*

Miles is a keeper and I hope he asks me to be his girlfriend because I would do so in a heartbeat. He is mine...all mine...

I hoped and prayed that Mama would never get a hold to any of my notebooks, and once I was done, I hid my notebook far back in the closet. I then tried my best to get some sleep, but unfortunately for me, my thoughts of Miles wouldn't let me. I was so sure of one thing...there was no going back to Dwayne, and finally, yes, he was history! Or, so I thought.

Chapter Eleven

Dwayne was on a rampage, and whenever I'd try to move on without him, he wasn't having it. He was calling about us getting back together, but I was so caught up with Miles that I wouldn't even consider it.

"We are no good for each other, Dwayne. Don't you see that?"

"No, I don't. You couldn't be more wrong. Besides, I've been dealin' with some things and I'm now livin' with my grandmother. I was there for you and I need for you to be there for me too."

I felt bad for Dwayne and I didn't want him to have to fight his battles alone. We talked almost every night after that, but I wouldn't allow him to come over to see me, nor would I go see him. I wanted to see if we could just be friends, because our efforts to keep a relationship had failed.

Also, I truly felt that I had made some progress with Miles. I wasn't cussing and fussing with the man in my life, and he'd always have very encouraging words to say to me. "Keep your head up," he would say. "See about your kids and get a grip on your anger. You're a beautiful woman, Brenda. You just gotta figure out a way to get on the right path and stop griping when shit don't go your way."

Miles' *counseling* helped me build up confidence in myself and some of the things he'd say needed to be said. I enjoyed spending time with him, but there became a time when I suspected Miles had been intimate with numerous women. It didn't make sense for me to kick Dwayne to the curb for his cheating ways, and Miles was getting it in too. But according to him, whoever he was involved with was none of my business, and whenever I inquired, he'd get shitty.

"Did you beep me?" he asked, returning one of my calls.

"Didn't you recognize the code?"

"Yes I did, smart ass, but I told you I had to work both jobs today."

"Is that all you've been doing today? One of my friends told me she saw you in the car with—"

He quickly cut me off. "What I do with my female companions ain't nobody's business but mine. If you want the truth, the truth is I ain't fucking nobody but you. There's a whole bunch of women who would love to get some of this, but right now it's on reserve. Will it always be on reserve for you? I doubt it, but that depends on how you act. Regardless, though, you need to understand that we are just friends, and more than that, damn good lovers. I don't want no girlfriend, I ain't looking for no girlfriend and I damn sure ain't looking for no wife."

Damn! Miles had told it like it was, and gave me my wake-up call. This was a fuck thing, nothing more, nothing less. I sure as hell had been looking for love in all the wrong places, and each time I put myself out there, this is the kind of shit I got in return.

"Whatever, Miles. I'll just see you at the skating rink next week. I hope your attitude is much better by then."

"Don't count on it, especially if you keep talking that mess about who I spend my time with. Eliminate that from your conversations and we good."

Miles said he had to get back to work and ended the call. I wasn't trying to be a pain, but what was so wrong with me wanting to know if he was involved with someone else, and who she was? Was it a crime to know what the man I was sleeping with was doing behind closed doors? I guessed so.

***

Dwayne wasn't giving up. His persistence made me feel special, and since Miles had been catching an attitude with me lately, over some naked pictures I refused to take, I did what I knew best and turned my attention to the other man. Didn't matter that he brought along too much drama, I just had a need to have somebody...anybody in my life that I could say was "my man."

"I've been callin' you like crazy," Dwayne said over the phone. "Yo mama been cursin' me the hell out every time I call. Why haven't you called me?"

"I've been meaning to call, but I misplaced your grandmother's phone number. When I called your parents' house, your sister wouldn't give me the number."

"She should have, but what's up with you and me? Are we gon' get back together or what? I miss you and I wanna see you today?"

"I'm taking the kids to see my father today. He called and told me he wasn't feeling up to himself lately and he wanted to talk to me."

"Can I go with you?" he asked. "You can pick me up at my grandmother's house. Besides, I've never met your father before, and you know it's been a while since I've seen the twins."

It had been a while since I'd last seen Dwayne, so I agreed to pick him up from his grandmother's house. Before I left to go see Daddy, I asked Jesse if she wanted to ride with me. She said that she'd already made plans to go to the mall with Anthony, but I knew she wasn't as forgiving when it came to Daddy as I was. She kind of took Mama's side all the time when they argued. I did, too, but I also knew that, sometimes, Mama was as much to blame for their arguments as he was.

As for Rita, she sided with Daddy most of the time. She was coming home next week to introduce the family to her new boyfriend and we couldn't wait to meet him. Mama said they'd even talked to her about getting married. One day Mama would say it was a good thing, and the next day she would say Rita needed to hurry and finish school, move back home and find a job.

I was happy for Rita because she had done what I should have done, once I graduated. Her and Jesse really seemed to have their acts together. They had decent jobs and positive men in their lives. Good brothers too...men who wanted something out of life and treated them with respect. I, on the other hand, had been a sucker for an older man who was sexually satisfying my needs, and for one who lied so much, I didn't know what to believe.

Dwayne got into the car looking spectacular. He knew that all he had to do was put on some stone-washed jeans, snakeskin boots, a cashmere sweater, with good smelling cologne, and I would be moved. His trimmed goatee was a plus, too, and the way it squared on his mouth and chin, it always made him look sexy. On the way to Daddy's house, Dwayne played with the twins in the back seat of the car and had them cracking up. Everything was going well, until he questioned me about Miles.

"Have you seen him lately?" he asked.

"Yeah, sometimes I see him at work," I said, keeping it brief.

"That's the only time you've seen him?"

"I see him at the skating rink—that's only if I go. Why are you asking me about Miles?"

"Because I had one of my boys check that nigga out for me. He said you've been messin' around with him. Said he had a conversion with Miles and he confirmed it. I even went down to the skatin' rink to peep the nigga myself. He thinks he's a little tough muthafucka, but when I stepped to him and showed him my piece, he was singin' a new tune."

I was boiling inside, but didn't say anything because I didn't want to argue with Dwayne. He was out doing whatever the hell he wanted to do, and with whomever. How dare he try to watch over me and it was just like him to seek control. "Why would you confront him?" I asked. "If you've been trying to start some mess with him over me, you're wasting your time. He's been a good friend to me, and that's it. Besides, he's too old for me. I don't like my men that old."

There was no way in hell I would tell him that Miles had been treating me well. I knew Dwayne was lying about pulling a piece out on him because if he had, he would've been dead. Miles wouldn't have thought twice about killing Dwayne, but then again, neither would Dwayne.

Daddy was delighted to see the twins. He kissed all over them with his scruffy beard and tried to tell them apart. They were screaming at the top of their lungs because they weren't used to being around him. I introduced Dwayne to Daddy, and after they shook hands, Daddy led us upstairs to his bedroom. He lit a cigarette and invited us to have a seat. While on his bed, he dangled the cigarette around in his mouth, while holding one of the twins.

"Dwayne, how long have you been datin' my daughter?" he asked.

"On and off for close to two years. I'm surprised she ain't never mentioned me?"

"Yeah, she mentioned you but I don't keep up with names too well. Her mama mentions yo name all the time because she don't like you. She said you make my baby girl cry all the time." Dwayne's brows went up and his nose flared. "Don't panic," Daddy said. "My ex-wife don't like nobody, so if she don't like you, that must mean you're an okay nigga." We all laughed, as everyone knew how Mama was.

Still, Dwayne defended his actions. "Mr. Hampton, I'm not the one who makes yo daughter cry all the time. She's been messin' around with this old cat, Miles. He's the one who makes her cry. I know that for a fact."

That was a lie, but I didn't say a word. Dwayne was trying to pump information out of me, but the truth be told, I hadn't cried since he'd been out of my life.

"Man, I don't give a shit who she messes with or how old he is," Daddy added. "All I care about is her happiness. If you call yourself her man, then you treat her right and take care of her, ya hear me?" Daddy reached his hand out, slamming it against Dwayne's.

We continued our conversation, until Daddy asked Dwayne to put a tape in the VCR that was lying on his dresser. It was a porn movie; showed a Chinese woman and a Black man getting ready to do the wild thang.

"Excuse me, but don't you have something else to look at?" I asked Daddy.

"Damn, Bree, y'all interrupted me when you came over. Let me finish watchin' my movie," he joked.

I playfully hit Daddy on the leg, called him a pervert and headed for the door.

"Gon' in the kitchen and fix y'all somethin' to eat while Dwayne and me finish checkin' out this movie."

I left the room with the twins, and since Dwayne didn't follow me, I figured he was just as interested in the flick as Daddy. *Men*, I thought while shaking my head.

I went in the kitchen and it was lit up with the smell of a hot baked apple pie. I fixed a plate of my grandmother's make-your-mouth-water cooking: roast, fried chicken, greens, corn on the cob, string beans, cornbread, homemade macaroni and cheese, and of course, apple pie. You name it, it was there! She could cook her butt off, and it wasn't like it was a holiday either. She enjoyed cooking big meals, just in case family stopped by, which was often.

As I sat at the kitchen table, Daddy came strolling in singing as his house shoes slid on the floor. "Damn, girl, you sure you got enough piled on yo plate? How many people are you eatin' for, knucklehead?"

I laughed. "I assure you, Daddy, just me."

He looked at the twins on my lap, reaching for one of them. "My…my babies sure are growin' up fast, ain't they?"

"Yeah, time is moving fast. Before you know it, they'll be going to school. Did Dwayne say he was coming down to get something to eat?"

"Nah, he didn't say. I think his ass enjoyin' those flicks more than me. I had a li'l talk with him and he seems like an okay nigga. Am I gon' have to pull out my tuxedo and walk you down the aisle soon?"

I pursed my lips. "No, I don't think so. Maybe for Rita or Jesse, but not for me. Not yet anyway."

He smiled and gripped my shoulder.

"Brenda, you know yo daddy ain't been feelin' good lately. The doctor been talkin' about puttin' me on dialysis because my kidneys are failin'."

My brows rose; I had no idea Daddy was ill. "When they talking about doing that? Is it serious?"

"Very. But I won't know until sometime next week. I might need you to go to the doctors with me to see how to work the dialysis machine."

I kissed Daddy on his cheek. "Sure. Just let me know and I'll come pick you up to take you."

We finished up dinner in Daddy's room and talked half of the night away. The twins had fallen asleep, and Dwayne carried one of them to the car and I carried the other. I said goodbye to Daddy and we made arrangements to hook up in a few days.

"Your daddy pretty damn cool, baby," Dwayne said on the ride home. "I hope that when I get his age, I be as cool and smooth as he is."

"Yeah, he's something else, ain't he? Mama and him are like night and day. I definitely know why they had to get a divorce."

I parked my car in front of Dwayne's grandmother's house. His car was parked in her driveway with the muffler hanging to the ground.

"Can I come over tomorrow?" he asked with his hand on the doorknob.

"I...I don't know. I'm not sure if I'm ready to patch things up with you. And by the looks of it," I looked at his car. "I don't think you're going to make it anywhere in that car."

"I'm gon' fix my car tonight. So, don't forget to call and let me know if I can come over."

I nodded and told Dwayne I'd call him.

When I got home Mama was upset with me for taking the kids to see Daddy. She said he didn't deserve to see them, because he hadn't done much for them. It was funny how when she was mad at Daddy, she wanted us to be, too. But when they were on good terms, she wanted us to be goody-goody with him.

I'd developed my own opinion about him, and forgiving him came easy. He made mistakes just like all of us did. He wasn't perfect and was always the first to admit it. He was there for me at a time in my life that I needed him to be, and I couldn't ignore that. So, shutting him out of me and the twins' lives, because Mama wanted me to, was not an option.

The truth, Mama was afraid I was going to become too close with Daddy and forget about all that she had done for me. She already felt as if he had stolen Rita's love away and couldn't stand the fact that she would lose another daughter's love to him. She didn't realize that I appreciated all that she'd done for us. I knew she was the one who provided everything for me since the day I was born. As a single parent, I understood her struggles and I knew that raising three children wasn't easy. However, my love for my daddy was something no one could deny me. Not even her.

***

Rita visited with her new boyfriend, Clarence. He was about six-one, thin as a pencil, and talked with a southern accent that had Rita tickled pink. I could see the love they had for each other, and right after dinner, Rita decided to break the news. Clarence and her were engaged and planned to marry right after college. Mama pretended to be moved about the news but I could tell she was totally against it. Why? I didn't know, but she had some funny-ass ways. Who wouldn't be happy about their daughter finding the love of her life in college and getting married? I think Mama was afraid of Rita's marriage ending up like hers; seemed like she wasn't giving poor Clarence a chance.

Rita and Clarence finished up dinner, and then left to share the news with the rest of the family. No sooner had they hit the door, Mama started talking about how she thought it was a bad idea for Rita to get married. She found every reason in the book not to like Clarence, and she didn't even get a chance to know him. He seemed pretty cool to me. He seemed to love my sister very much, so that's all that mattered to me.

That night, I told Dwayne about Rita's engagement and he said that he wished we could get married.

"Really," I said. I was surprised and it confirmed how much Dwayne really loved me. He was willing to marry me and maybe we were destined to be together after all.

He also talked about getting a job so he'd have some money to help me with the twins. I thought that was nice of him, especially since the twins weren't even his. If he was serious, time would surely tell.

***

Monday at work, suited-up big shots were all over the place. There were only two cashiers at their registers, when normally there was at least eight. I put on my red smock, and headed towards the back to get my cash drawer. My boss halted my steps, when he asked me to come to his office so we could talk. I thought he was going to confront me about my relationship with Miles, but I was wrong.

"Sit down, Brenda," Mr. Keys said. I sat down with my heart racing a mile a minute. "We've been watching you and a few other cashiers on tape. It looks as if you've been stealing merchandise from our store. Now, we don't plan to prosecute you, but we are asking that you leave now and leave quietly." I couldn't say anything.

I was shocked—sat there with my mouth wide open. I had stolen more than my share from Grandpa Pigeons and had no defense whatsoever. I stood up, handed him my smock and walked out.

When I got home, Mama asked why I was back so soon. I told her I'd gotten fired and she felt the same way I did; we had definitely gotten our share. I assured her I'd find another job, but it wasn't like that would be so easy to do.

Mama headed off to work and I beeped Miles to see if he'd known about the incident at work. I hadn't spoken to him in several weeks and I wasn't sure if he'd call me back. Almost an hour later, he did.

"Speak" he said.

"Are you busy?"

"Maybe."

"Too busy to call me?"

He snapped at me and sounded irritated. "Maybe, maybe not. Stop with the questions. What do you want?"

"I don't want anything. Just called to see how you were doing because I haven't heard from you."

"Hmm...did you go to work today?"

"Yes, I did go to work, but something happened."

"Something like you got fired?"

"Yes. I got fired for stealing."

"I know what you got fired for, Brenda. They've been watching the cashiers for a long time. I didn't tell you because I didn't think you would be stupid enough to get yourself caught up in that bullshit, especially since you got kids to take care of. But somehow, you never cease to amaze me. You just keep on doing stupid shit and losing your job was the worst thing you could have done."

I was taken aback by Miles' sharp tone and it upset me. He sure as hell knew how to make me feel like shit and his words always stung. Yes, I was immature, but he was the one messing with a nineteen year old who just didn't have it all together. "Losing my job wasn't a big deal. I'll just have to find another one and you don't need to worry about my kids. They're taken care of and they will always be taken care of. Besides, I didn't call to get a lecture from you. I called to see how things were going with you."

"Like always, I'm good, baby. I gotta call you back, though."

"You're not going to call me back and you know it. Are you working at the skating rink on Tuesday?"

"Maybe, but I don't want to see you there. You're too much trouble, Brenda, and I've had enough."

I held the phone in my hand, listening to the dial tone. Miles was tripping. He was in major control of what was going on between us and I didn't like it one bit. On Tuesday, I was going to the skating rink to give that sucker a piece of my mind.

Tuesday came fast, and not only did I give Miles a piece of my mind, but I also gave him a piece of something else—Me. I'd written him a letter about him being such a dog and a loser, but I reminded myself to tear the letter up, as we sat in the front seat of his rocking car, having sex. I was straddled on top of him, delivering all the pleasure that he'd taught me. His head was dropped back on the headrest and his eyes were closed tight. I made sure he regretted every negative word that he'd said to me.

"Brenda, I loooove doing this shit with you," he moaned. "You confuse the hell out of me with yo wanna-be tough ass, and your immature ways. Then you always demanding impossible things from me. Understand that I don't play the boyfriend-girlfriend game. I'm too old for it. You get that, don't you?"

I didn't respond. Now wasn't the time. I was just getting all that I could get, and I had a feeling that our time together was coming to an end. I lowered myself, closing my eyes and thinking as I gave him head. He was the only man I had done it to, and it was not an easy task. Miles gathered a bunch of my hair in his hand and squeezed it.

"Sexy, sexy, sexy," he said. "You are on your way to becoming the woman I always knew you could be."

That night, the woman he always wanted me to be turned into the immature, angry little girl he'd kept complaining about. My friends, Jesse and I got into another fight on the parking lot, resulting from something as simple as being stared at. This time, Anthony and his crew jumped in, and the brawl was nothing pretty. Miles was livid and he tore into me over the telephone the next day.

"I know you're only nineteen, Brenda, but you need to think about where your life is headed. You are going to get yourself killed, and I am telling you that there are plenty of women at that skating rink who wouldn't mind doing it. What's going to happen to those babies if they ain't got no mother? From what you say, their daddy ain't shit, so all they got is you! Get yo shit together and do not bring yo ass back down to that skating rink again! If you do, I can guarantee that you will be arrested!"

"Do what you gotta do, Miles! Unfortunately, I'm living day-by-day with no damn direction! I'm trying to do what's right, but nine times out of ten, I keep getting it wrong! Do not judge me, and until you start contributing more to my life, other than giving me some satisfying dick, then don't complain about how I'm living it!

He hung up. And when all was said and done, I couldn't ignore some of the things he'd said.

Chapter Twelve

Rita's college graduation was in two days, and Mama and Daddy decided to put their differences aside and ride together. Rita had made our entire family proud and during her last year in college she was voted in as Miss Tennessee State University. Her picture was posted in many magazines and newspapers around the country and her GPA spoke for itself. No doubt, she was the perfect role model for her younger sisters, but I could never seem to follow in her footsteps.

Mama and Daddy were back from Tennessee. He came in to see the twins, said hello to us and left. Mama said they'd had a few differences on their trip and she was glad to be home. She showed us pictures of Rita's graduation and had her degree in Communications to show to us. She seemed really proud of Rita's accomplishments and Rita had done well for herself. On top of that, to find the man of her dreams was awesome. Mama told us Rita was coming home next week to look for bridesmaids dresses and we were enthused about being in the wedding.

Planning for the wedding was another joyous time for our family to come together. Rita had everything so organized she could have been the wedding planner herself. She knew exactly what she wanted and how she wanted it. There was no sense trying to tell her different.

A few weeks before the wedding, Dwayne convinced me to let him go with me. He promised me that he wouldn't pressure me about us getting back together, but said he found it odd that we could never, ever stay apart. "That's what true love means," he said. "And nothing or no one will ever come between us." Dwayne's theory made sense; after all, we just couldn't seem to go our separate ways.

And since I'd found out that my long-time girlfriend, Tanesha, from Sumner High School, had been having sex with Miles, what we shared was a wrap. Tanesha described her time with Miles as one of the best experiences of her life.

"That dick was off the chain," she said over the telephone. "I could barely sit down on that sucker and he had my ass hollering!"

I was sure he did, and I wanted him to pay for having sex with my friend that I'd introduced to him at the skating rink one day. My plan was to hook up with one of his friends, particularly a police officer who worked with Miles. His name was Lance and I'd seen the lust in his eyes on many occasions. Only because of Miles did I ignore Lance, but not when I'd caught up with him a few days later, after Tanesha had told me what was up. While hanging out on the White Castle's parking lot, Lance invited me to his apartment on Lucas & Hunt Road. I followed him there, and as soon as we got inside, he was all over me. He was rough, and when he pulled the back of my hair to kiss me, I pulled away.

"Damn, do you have to pull my hair so tight?" I asked.

He let go of my hair, but the wicked smile on his face alarmed me. There was something in his eyes that I wasn't feeling, so I backed away from him by the door. "I...I'm sorry, but I think I made a big mistake coming here. I don't want to do this with you, okay?"

My stomach felt queasy as I hurried closer to the door, but as soon as I touched the knob, Lance grabbed my waist. I held my breath as he tightened his arms around me from behind and put his lips up to my ear. "Don't be sorry, because you're not going anywhere."

He shoved me away from the door and I stumbled to catch my balance. I gave him a hard stare, prompting him to shove me again. This time, I fell to my knees, but rushed back up to charge him. I was met with his gun aimed right at my face.

"You can make this easy, or you can make it hard. Take your clothes off and lay your ass back on the couch."

I never, ever saw this shit coming. A police officer going out like this? There was no doubt in my mind that he would shoot me, but if I had to go out under these conditions, too damn bad. He wasn't going to take something I wasn't willing to give. Sex wasn't just sex anymore and I did care about who I let inside of me. Yes, I was wrong for coming to Lance's apartment with him, but I had a right to change my mind. Tears started pouring from my eyes, as I knew my life was in jeopardy. I swallowed and began to plea for him to let me leave.

"I'm not taking my clothes off. I'm sorry, I can't do it."

Lance smirked and placed his gun on the table. He started to unbutton his uniform shirt, while keeping his eyes locked on me. Planning my escape, I took a few steps forward and was met with a hard blow to my stomach. The pain that I felt caused me to double over and squeeze my teary eyes. At that moment, that's when I realized how much trouble I was really in. He pulled my hair, and lifted my head so I could look at him. His eyes...those frightening eyes, I would never forget. "You think you tough," he shouted. "I'll show you tough!"

He pushed me back on the couch where I fell hard. I defensively held up my hands in a panic. "I...I'm not tough," I cried out. "Not at all. But please don't hurt me."

Lance lowered his pants to his ankles and jumped on top of me. I swung wildly, and used my bent knees to force him off me. He was mad strong and when I took a huge bite at his shoulder, he gripped both of his hands around my neck and squeezed. Almost instantly, I could feel the breath being choked out of me. Tears slipped from the corner of my eyes as his hands trembled on my neck while shaking it. My body was getting weak, and as the lights appeared to dim, there was no fight left in me. My eyes fluttered, and that's when I felt Lance release his hands. I started to cough, but he placed his cold hand over my mouth, squeezing my cheeks. He used his other hand to rip open my shirt and roughly massage my breast. His breathing increased, but I was so scared that I continued to hold my breath. He then lowered his hand from my mouth to my skirt, lifting it so he could feel my crotch.

"Mmmmm," he moaned as he pulled my panties aside and jabbed his fingers inside of me. I flinched, but he pressed his heavy body on top of mine and forced my legs further open with his. I was dry as a desert, and my insides burned as he turned his fingers inside of me, scratching against my walls with his sharp nails. I was defeated and my stare into his eyes said so. He had no idea of the affect this would have on me, and at the time, neither did I. Thing is, he didn't care. He released his fingers from my insides and brought his bloody fingers to his face to look at them.

"I don't want no bloody pussy," he said. "Didn't you know you were on your period when you *agreed* to come here?"

I was well aware that my time of the month was near, but I kept my mouth shut. Lance got up and stepped out of his pants. He pulled his white undershirt over his head, and swung his hard dick from side-to-side near my face. "Touch it," he ordered. "Sit up, touch it, suck it, play with it or something."

I slowly sat up and wrapped my hand around Lance's dick. Miles had shown me how to make him come by jacking him off with Vaseline or lotion. I didn't have either, so I wet my hands with spit and went to work on Lance's muscle. I figured he wouldn't let me leave until he got his nut, so I stroked him with great speed. My wrist felt like it would fall off, but I kept it going, just so he wouldn't encourage me to use my mouth.

"Ahhhh," he said with his head leaning back. "That shit feels guuuuuuuud!"

My eyes were so blurred from the tears in my eyes, and my head was spinning in circles. Lance snatched his dick away from my hand, replacing it with his. His semen sprayed out, some slapping my cheek. I sat motionless, hoping and praying that this would all be over with soon. Lance bent down and tossed his shirt over his shoulder. "Get the fuck out," he said. "And don't be no fool and tell anybody what really happened here, because I will deny it. I will make your ass look real bad for coming here to begin with, and who do you think people will believe? You or me?"

I said not one word. Got up, pulled my ruffled blue-jean skirt down and tried to cover my breasts with my torn shirt. I inched my way to the door, feeling as if I was walking on air like a zombie. After I walked out, Lance slammed the door, causing my whole body to jump. My legs were so weak, and as soon as I got into the car, I collapsed in the driver's seat. Unable to drive off, my head dropped on the steering wheel and I sobbed like a baby.

Several weeks later, Rita came home, and for the sake of not bringing anymore disappointment to my family, or embarrassing myself, I kept quiet about what had happened with Lance. I wrote about the incident in my notebook, blaming myself and having no respect whatsoever for men who claimed they were officers of the law: *I feel useless. Men have made me feel as if all I'm good for is sex.*

Hell, I'm not even good for that to be honest. I shouldn't have ever followed Lance to his apartment and that's what I get for trying to make Miles jealous. My so-called revenge backfired. I guess Lance only did what he thought I wanted him to do, but I didn't want to give myself to him in any way. I thought that he would brag to Miles about me being at his apartment, nothing more, nothing less. The way Lance treated me, I feel like trash. And then to spray that shit in my face was hurtful. So hurtful that I never want to have sex again. It ain't all that anyway, I guess with the exception of Miles. But adios to him because he ain't shit either. I wonder if there are any good men out there? I guess Jesse and Rita seem to have one, but why can't I find one? What am I doing wrong and what would make a man treat me like Lance did today? Never will I trust a police officer again. Never would I trust any man, and at this point, to hell with them all...

Everyone was so upbeat about the wedding, and helping Rita get everything together helped take my mind off what had happened. Considering the fact that Rita had broken her ankle a few days before the wedding, and the pastor was two hours late, the wedding itself was beautiful. Rita looked so stunning in her white laced Cinderella gown with pearls flowing through it. The bridesmaids...we also looked gorgeous. We wore red medium-length silk and lace dresses with v-cuts and bows in the back. Clarence and his groomsmen had on black tuxedos with red silk cummerbunds and white shirts. The most beautiful of all were the twins as flower girls. They wore long white silk dresses with red silk bows around their waists. White sheer stockings covered their legs and black patent leather shoes were on their feet.

As I was escorted down the aisle by a groomsman, I saw Dwayne sitting in a two-piece black suit, looking like a true gentleman. Anthony sat next to him, as he watched Jesse being escorted by another groomsman. Then Rita came down the aisle with a walker guiding her, because of her ankle, and Daddy was on her left arm. This was one special occasion our family would never forget, and as Clarence played "So Amazing" by Luther Vandross on his saxophone, he had the entire wedding party and guests in tears. Several times, I looked at Dwayne and he looked touched by the ceremony as well. That day brought us closer together, and after what had happened with Lance, I clung to Dwayne for security and protection. I hadn't told him what had happened either, but he was the only man I wanted in my presence. After the wedding, Rita made a permanent move to Tennessee and our conversations became limited.

Chapter Thirteen

Mama was out of control. Her house was becoming unbearable to live in. She had even gone to the extreme of unplugging the phones and hiding them so we couldn't use them. Money was an issue, and I didn't know how she expected us to give her money when I was supporting myself and the twins on welfare. I had been returning so much stolen merchandise to Target and Venture, they now had my name on a "watch list" and I couldn't return anything. Jesse was still at Sears making minimum wage and she could only contribute so much as well. During a heated argument, Mama was so upset that she threw a hot curling iron that damn near hit Jesse in the face. Then she made a comment about us being ho's and said we knew how to get "street money."

That just about did it for me, and yet again, Mama and I found ourselves in an argument that was full of disrespect.

"Whatever, Mama," I shouted. "It takes a ho to know one!"

"Yeah, bitch, keep on with that smart mouth of yours. When yo ass living on the streets, I hope that mouth of yours can get you by."

Mama continued to go on and on, but Jesse whispered to me, asking me not to say anything. She was so good at holding her tongue when it came to Mama, but I would lash out in a minute. The back and forth arguing, I felt bad about it. I knew it was time for me to get the hell out of Mama's house, and the truth of the matter was, that if I was grown up enough to have kids, then I was grown up enough to make it on my own.

By morning, Mama hadn't forgotten about my harsh words. She told me to pack my belongings and go. I wasn't going to argue with her anymore, and rightfully so, it was her house, not mine. Since the phones were still hidden, I walked to a payphone and called Dwayne to come pick me up. He said that if I ever wanted to, I could live with him at his grandmother's house.

In less than an hour, he came for me. I went back and forth, loading up his car with my personal belongings. Mama was in her bedroom with the door shut, and Jesse was in our room begging me not to take the twins.

"Don't go, Brenda," she sadly said. "You can't take the twins over to Dwayne's grandmother's house and you know that ain't going to work. Just give Mama time to cool off and stay out of her way. She'll change her mind, like she always does."

I continued to pack my belongings. "No she won't. She's going to keep on putting me out of here, and I'm tired of it. She told me to take the twins with me, and I'm not going to leave my babies behind. We'll be okay. Since I can't call you, I'll call Anthony's house to let him know when we make it to Dwayne's grandmother's house. Don't worry."

Jesse went into the twins' bedroom, while I started to take a few more boxes out to Dwayne's car, putting them in the trunk. When I went back inside, Mama shouted for me to hurry it up so she could lock her door. Dwayne's car was piled high with my things and I had only a few more bags to go.

As soon as I went inside to get the twins, my grandmother came through the front door, inquiring about what was going on.

"Brenda is moving out," Mama answered. "I'm tired of her mouth, and she too damn grown for me." Mama went on and on about what a disgrace I'd been to our family and my grandmother finally stopped her.

"Marie, what in the hell is wrong with you?" Grandma asked Mama. "You can't put her and those babies out like that. You must be out of your mind. Brenda, get that young fella to bring your things back in here," she ordered.

"That nigga ain't coming in my house!" Mama yelled.

"Shut your mouth!" My grandmother fired back. "Brenda, go outside and get your stuff out of that young man's car. We don't know nothing about him, and those babies need a roof over their heads." My grandmother was no bigger than five-two, but I wasn't about to argue with her—neither was Mama. My grandmother's voice carried power and when she asked you to do something, you had better done it.

I took most of my things out of Dwayne's car, but left a few things because I knew it would be a matter of time before Mama got upset with me again. That day, Grandma stayed, just to make sure Mama and me talked through our differences. Grandma sat at the kitchen table, trying to explain some of Mama's funny acting ways.

"Brenda, you, Jesse and Rita have a good mother. She just wants the best for y'all and when things don't go right, it makes her angry. When she acts like this, she's just being like her father. Y'all's grandfather is something else, and the way he raised our children has done more harm than good. All those beatings, cursing at them, throwing them out of the house...that stuff used to make me sick to my stomach. I knew it would affect my children, and watching their daddy and me carry on all the time did them no good. Marie is a good daughter." Grandma touched Mama's hand, as she, too, sat attentively and listened. "I'm proud of her, and I want y'all to get along with each other. Life is too short and God only gives you one mother."

I nodded and so did Mama. I told her I was sorry for cursing at her and promised that I would soon find a place for me and the twins. What grandma had said shed light on the way Mama was. She was a product of the environment that she was brought up in, and nothing could change that. It was up to the next generation to break the cycle, but the question was if we could do it? It was strange that Grandma had only visited us a few times a year. Her showing up at the *right* time really had me puzzled.

For the next few weeks, I searched the newspapers and drove around St. Louis looking for an apartment. I didn't have much money saved, but somebody, somewhere had to work with me. In order to get on the emergency housing list, Shantell had gone to live in a shelter. Within a few weeks, they'd found her a nice apartment, better than the one she had been living in and it had more bedrooms. I promised myself that if I didn't find an apartment by Friday, I would live in a shelter just like some other people I'd known had done.

Friday was approaching fast and still nothing. I had some of the twins and my things packed so we could make our way to a shelter. I couldn't take much with me because I had to show that I was homeless and didn't have anywhere to go with my children. And in a sense, I was. Mama hadn't been saying much to me and I could tell she wanted me out.

On Thursday, I got in the car and drove around for hours looking for an apartment. I came across a deserted-looking complex off Woodson Road that had small apartments attached to one another. The doors were a loud orange and now leasing signs were displayed in some of the windows. I jotted down the number and drove to the nearest payphone to call. The property manager answered and asked me to meet her there in one hour. I was so anxious that I went back to the complex, sitting in the car until she came.

When she arrived, she got out of her Mercedes Benz and introduced herself to me as Katy. She asked if I wanted to see the inside of the apartment and I was delighted to. We stepped into the small, yet cozy living room; it had dark brown carpet and bare white walls. Around the first corner was a medium-sized bedroom with a compact closet and cream colored mini-blinds covered the windows. Straight down the short hallway was a full bathroom, and directly across from it was a larger bedroom with a walk-in closet. The kitchen was at the back of the apartment. It had one small window and a door to exit from. Including a white stove and refrigerator, I was sold on the apartment. It was perfect for me and the twins.

"How much is the rent," I asked.

"The apartment is for low-income people and we base the amount on your income. Depending on what it is, you could wind up paying less than ten dollars, if you're approved."

My eyes widened; I couldn't believe what she was saying. Ten dollars! I could do ten dollars and more, especially for a place like this.

"Most of the apartments are empty right now, but we're looking to fill them soon. I'd say you called me right on time, because the phone calls have been coming in."

"How soon are you looking to fill them? I was thinking about moving to a shelter, hoping they could help me find something quicker."

"Stay put, wherever you are. Complete this application for me and I'm sure we can work something out."

I leaned against the counter, completing the application full of smiles. I couldn't believe this was happening. Katy and I shook hands, and I waited to hear back from her. Hopefully, it would be soon.

On the way home, I had a gut feeling that everything would work out and I sighed with relief. Somebody was looking out for me, but at the time, I had no idea who it was. I mean, we'd spent plenty of Sundays going to New Northside Baptist Church on Goodfellow Blvd., but it took me a while to *receive* the message. I hoped that Katy wasn't giving me the run-around and was a woman of her word. The last thing I wanted to do was live in a shelter with the homeless, but I knew I had to do whatever was necessary to get an apartment.

When I got home, I told Jesse about the apartment and mentioned her living with me. She said it didn't sound like there would be enough room for both of us. I agreed, but could never imagine my life without being close to Jesse. There was already emptiness with Rita being gone, and I wasn't sure how I'd cope without seeing Jesse every day.

It was almost five o'clock in the evening and I hadn't heard anything from Katy yet. It seemed like everybody and their mama was calling but her. By seven, I had given up. The management office was closed and I knew she wasn't going to call after hours.

Finally, she called the next morning. "May I speak to Brenda Hampton?" she asked.

"This is she," I anxiously replied.

"This is Katy from Property Management. I spoke to you yesterday regarding the apartment."

I had my fingers crossed. "Hi, Katy."

"Good morning. I think you will be happy to know that once you come in, sign your lease, pay your deposit, and get a police report, the apartment is yours."

I smiled and was so ready to jump for joy. "Wha...what else do I have to do?"

"There are a few other things we require but I'll discuss those with you when you come in. When would you like to make your appointment?"

"As soon as possible."

"Well, the apartment won't be ready for a couple of weeks, but let's get the paperwork finished today. Your rent will average out to ten dollars a month and I think you can handle that, can't you?"

"Yes," I said and nodded.

"Can you meet me at my office by noon?"

"Yes, I can. And thank you so much for your help."

"You're welcome, Brenda, see you at noon."

I jumped for joy when I got off the phone. Jesse had been listening to my conversation and she knew that I'd gotten the apartment. She was just as excited as I was, but I knew we were going to miss each other. We laughed and talked about all the fun and freedom we would have. She knew that she could come over any time she wanted to.

Mama was in the kitchen making some coffee and asked what all the riff-raff was about.

"I found an apartment, Mama. I go in today to sign the lease and all I'll have to pay is ten dollars!"

Mama smiled, but I could also see that she wasn't as happy as I was. "That's good news, and ten dollars is a blessing. You know I'll help you get anything you need, just let me know."

I reached out to hug Mama, which I hadn't done in a long time. She didn't even put her arms around me, but that didn't matter. I took her word that she would help me anyway that she could.

Later that day, I called everybody I could think of to tell them the good news. Dwayne was the first.

"It's about damn time and I'm glad we don't have to sneak around anymore," he said. "This gon' be sweet and let me know if you need help movin'."

"I will need help and I'll let you know for sure. Thanks and no more sneaking around, because we have a place that we can share."

Dwayne was happy about that, and so was I. Within the same week Jesse, Mama and I went shopping to find things for my apartment. Jesse let me get towels, curtains, dishes, and sheets, using her Sears' discount. I was constantly in Target and Venture, stealing my ass off! Mama picked out a simple brown and beige sofa that matched the brown carpet in the living room. She had also gone through a lot of old things at her house, packing them up for me. The twins had outgrown their baby beds and we picked out two white daybeds for them. My kitchen set was the cheapest: four straw-like wooden chairs and a glass octagon table for ninety-nine bucks. I found a black lacquer bedroom set with mirrors on the headboard and dresser. I put it on layaway, until my next welfare check came.

Moving day was hectic, and needless to say, Dwayne was nowhere to be found. I had more things than I thought I did, and taking charge of my own move, I piled everything up in a U-haul truck and headed to my new apartment. My furniture was set up for delivery the next day, so we had to sleep on the floor for one night. Everyone liked the small two-bedroom apartment. Mama and Jesse stayed over all day, trying to help me make the place look like home. I knew they had a hard time separating themselves from the twins, because when it was time for them to go, they just couldn't seem to do it.

The next day, all of my furniture was delivered. The décor matched well and the apartment had already started to feel like home. I cooked a delicious dinner for us, and when Dwayne called to tell me he had gone out of town with his brother, I invited him to come over. Mama and Jesse couldn't stop calling, asking, "How y'all doing? What y'all doing? Where are the twins?" Question after question. It was all good, though, because I was also missing them.

Dwayne came by around six o'clock that evening. He had a bouquet of flowers, which I put in the middle of the table while we ate. After dinner, the twins went back into their room and Dwayne and I sat in the living room discussing our future. Hours and hours of conversation led to confessions from both of us. We both admitted to wronging each other, and agreed to focus more on our purpose together. After almost three years of a back-and-forth relationship, we hadn't enhanced each other's lives in any way, but it was either now or never.

"I love you, girl," Dwayne said, as he lay naked on top of me that night, looking into my eyes with much seriousness. With my legs straddled wide, I rubbed up and down his back, enjoying the feel of his bulging muscles. "We gon' do this shit and do it right. You have my word that I'ma make yo ass happy and you ain't never gonna have to worry 'bout nothin'."

I felt safe and secure with Dwayne and trusted him, even though I knew I shouldn't have. "I love you, too, but please don't hurt me again. Promise me, okay?"

Dwayne placed my legs on his broad shoulders and navigated his dick inside of me. He closed his eyes, and then let out a deep sigh. "My word, my bond, baby," he said. "All that shit from the past is a done deal."

We stepped up our sexual energy that night, and as Dwayne put me on top to ride him, I put something heavy on his mind. He tightly gripped my hips, as I worked them to a rhythm his wasn't used to.

"Gotdaaaamn," he shouted. "Slow that shit down, before I bust this nut! I can tell yo ass been gettin' schooled by somebody, and you betta not ever let nobody in this pussy again."

I halted my moves and leaned forward to whisper in Dwayne's ear. "When you go out and cheat, you need to bring something worthy back to the relationship. I hope you've been schooled, too, and if so, show me what you learned on your journey."

"My journey wasn't worth it, but I'm sure I can give you what you need and more."

Dwayne returned to his position on top of me, fucking me so hard that I felt like nothing but a piece of meat. Once it was over, he moved next to me in bed and fell asleep. I lay there thinking if he would keep his word and about the journey we both had been on with others. Instantly, my thoughts turned to Miles. I had gotten so accustomed to the way we used to have sex that I had forgotten about what it felt like to be with Dwayne. It was...different, and oral sex or any kinds of foreplay with him wasn't on the agenda. A while back, Dwayne had made it perfectly clear that he would never go down on a woman. And I made it clear to him that if you don't do me, I don't do you. Either with Miles or Dwayne, there was still something lacking. Maybe, a little something known as passion. This couldn't be what sex was all about, and if it was, I didn't see the purpose for it, especially after what had happened with Lance.

I couldn't sleep, so I went into the living room and spent time writing in my notebook. By now, I had a box full and almost every single page was filled with my daily thoughts. There were words of pain, as well as happiness. I just couldn't get enough of spilling my guts, and that night I wrote about my new apartment: *Yes, I'm finally on my own! Freedom rings and I couldn't be more excited. I miss Mama and Jesse already, but I got Dwayne and my kids here with me. We're going to be a happy family. Dwayne has been a decent father to the twins and I'm so thankful to him for stepping in and becoming a father to my babies. Never thought I would see this day come, and it feels like a new beginning. My beginning and I'm going to make the best of it. Dwayne and me both. We say we love each other, but do I really know what love is? Does he? I'm not sure if this is what it feels like, but over time, things will get better between us. They have to and having my own place is a start...*

Chapter Fourteen

After only a few months in my perfect little apartment, things started to quickly change. Even though Dwayne hadn't officially moved in with me, his friends were hanging out all day long and so were mine. The apartment was barely big enough for us, and when other people came over, it was crammed. The only alone time we spent with each other was late at night—usually, after midnight. Many days, I left with the twins to go for walks, upset with him because of his friends. He, of course, was upset with the continuous visits from mine. And if Jesse came over, he had a serious attitude. There was something about her he did not like and vice versa.

Several more months had gone by and things really started to get out of hand. Dwayne had everything in his control. He scared most of my friends away with his bad attitude, and for a while, they stopped coming over. My attitude didn't seem to stop his friends, though. They were knocking on the door at seven in the morning and weren't leaving until way after midnight. Mama helped me purchase a get-out-and-push green Horizon, so the twins and I were rarely at home.

I'd come back from the grocery store one day, and Dwayne and his friends had cleared out. Kentucky Fried Chicken containers and soda cans were all over my living room, smoked blunts were in an ashtray and the whole place was funky. As I started to clean up, I noticed a long slit in my couch and cotton was coming out of it. *Déjà vu*, I thought. *This was similar to what had happened to Mama?* I beeped Dwayne to inquire about it, but hours passed and he hadn't called me back. I paced the living room, fearing that something bad had happened to him. Something had to be wrong, because it wasn't like him not to call me back.

Finally, at a quarter to four in the morning, he put the key in the door and walked in. I was sitting on the couch in my pink cotton pajamas, with foam rollers in my hair, waiting on him with my arms folded.

"Where have you been?" I asked with an attitude.

"What?" he said, pretending as if he didn't hear me.

"You heard me!" I yelled.

"Damn, why you yellin'? I was at Lester's house playin' cards."

"Why haven't you returned my pages?"

"Because my battery was low in my pager."

I got off the couch and turned on the light so I could see his face. I could always tell if he was lying because his nostrils flared as he talked. He was also slurring and his hazel eyes were blazing red. Next thing I knew, he slumped over and fell on the couch. "Dwayne," I said, shaking his shoulder. "What in the hell happened to my couch?"

"Wha...what did you say?" His face was buried in the sofa. I lifted his head so he could face me.

I asked again, "What happened to my couch?" He fell backwards and threw his hands up in the air.

"Shit, I don't know. Why don't you stop yellin' so damn loud? My head hurts."

He quickly jetted off the couch, trying to make it to the bathroom but couldn't. He vomited all over the couch and on the floor. When he was finished, he curled up on the floor and went to sleep. I went to the linen closet and got several towels to clean up his mess. It was disgusting but I didn't want my apartment to smell like a garbage truck.

By morning, Dwayne managed to get off the floor and make his way into the bedroom. He was knocked out until late in the afternoon. I was in the living room combing one of the twins' hair and he sat down on the couch right next to me. He laid his head on my shoulder, but still upset with him, I shrugged him off.

"Baby, I'm sorry," he said. "I got so fucked up last night that I lost track of time. I promise you I won't ever drink again. That shit ain't for me."

"What happened to my couch?" I asked, still pouting.

"I don't know. What are you talkin' 'bout?" He looked down at the couch and saw the slit. "Bree, I'll buy you a new couch, okay? I got a friend who owns a furniture store and I know he'll give me a good deal on some furniture."

"Dwayne, I want my couch fixed or I want a new one. That's all there is to it."

"No problem, I got you covered. Let me use yo car to go see if I can find him. I need a new alternator for my car, and I'll be right back."

"Go ahead, but I need to go see my daddy at the hospital by seven o'clock tonight. He ain't doing so well and I told him I was coming to see him today."

"Aw, baby, it won't take that long. I'm comin' right back." He snatched up the keys and jetted out the door. I could hear my tires screeching as he sped off.

It was getting late and Dwayne still hadn't made it back with my car. I beeped him twice and he didn't call me back. I knew he was lying about the battery in his pager because I'd heard it go off twice while he was in the bathroom. I had gotten to the point of sometimes keeping my mouth shut because I didn't want to argue.

When the phone rang, I quickly answered it. It was Jesse. She called to tell me that she had gotten a new job at the post office making big dollars. They offered her more money than I would see in a lifetime.

"Congrats, girl," I said. "You're moving on up in the world and that's what's up."

"Hey, gotta do what I gotta do. What's been up with you? How are you and Dwayne getting along?"

I never told my family the truth about what was going on, because I was ashamed. Truthfully, things were just okay, and I didn't want to spoil her good news with my concerns. "We're good. He's been out looking for a job so he can help me. This welfare check ain't about nothing, but you know I'm not going to complain."

"I know that's right. But if you don't have nothing up for the weekend, I want to go out and celebrate. Are you down or what?"

"Count me in. I'm always up to partying, so don't leave me out."

By the time Jesse and I had finished talking, it was 7:30 p.m. Visiting hours were over at eight and I felt bad because I promised Daddy I was coming to see him. As I was thinking about Daddy, the phone rang again. This time it was Dwayne. "Bree, it's me," he whispered. "I'm on my way." I just slammed the phone down. And hours later, he came strolling in at almost eleven.

I held out my hand, seething with anger. "Give me my keys and leave!"

He brushed me off and plopped down on the couch. "What the fuck is yo problem? I'm out here bustin' my ass to get you some furniture and this is how you repay me? Yo ass crazy! I ain't goin' no damn where."

"Oh, yes you are. Even if I have to call the police, you're getting out of here tonight!"

"Call'em. Do what you gotta do, but if they come, it's gon' be some shit up in here."

Dwayne and I were yelling back and forth, and the twins stood in the middle, trying to force us away from each other. The yelling and screaming had gotten so bad that I didn't have to call the police, one of my neighbors did. The police banged on the door, demanding that I open it. I cracked the door open, peeking through it.

"Ma'am, we got a call about some screaming and yelling going on in there. Is everything all right?"

"Yes, it's fine." I said, hearing the twins sniffling in the background.

"May we come in?" I opened the door wider and told the twins to go back in their room, while we talked to the officers. One of the officers asked Dwayne for his name.

"Dwayne," he snapped.

"Dwayne what?" the officer fired back.

"Dwayne, none of yo fuckin' business."

The officers smirked at each other. "Dwayne, you need to cooperate or else we'll take you to the police station."

"His name is Dwayne Montgomery," I injected.

"Thanks for your cooperation. I'm going to ask Mr. Montgomery to leave until things cool down a bit."

"I ain't goin' nowhere," Dwayne implied. "Y'all can get the fuck out of here 'cause me and my woman gon' work this out." He opened the door and motioned for the officers to leave.

"Let's go, smart ass," one of the officers said, reaching for his handcuffs. He walked behind Dwayne and tried to push him on the ground. Dwayne resisted, releasing a gob of spit into the officer's face. It must have really pissed him off because he put his foot in front of Dwayne's leg and tried to trip him to the floor. That shit did not work! Dwayne had managed to overpower the officer, and when the other officer stepped in, it only made matters worse. Dwayne had some serious strength and it was a struggle for them to get the cuffs on him.

As the scuffle went on, they'd knocked over my sofa table and broke two of my lamps. My magazines were scattered on the floor and a picture that was hanging was tilted. The living room looked as if a tornado had blown through it.

"Would you please just cooperate," I yelled at Dwayne as they wrestled him to the ground. He was still out of control.

"Fuck you and fuck these muthafuckas too! I can't believe all of this shit over nothin'!"

Dwayne would not calm down, so one of the officers reached in his pocket and sprayed mace directly in Dwayne's face. All of us were gagging and the officer ordered me to open up the doors and windows to clear the air. When I walked back into the living room, Dwayne was laying on his stomach with handcuffs on.

The twins and I stood outside, coughing and trying to breathe in the fresh air. We watched the police haul Dwayne away, and I'll been damned if I didn't have a Déjà vu moment again. Just like my father, I watched Dwayne yell profanities at the officers, but he did it to the extreme. "Y'all White muthafuckas can't hurt me!" he yelled. "Y'all dead as ever! I can promise you that!"

Several of my neighbors had stepped outside to see what the flashing lights were about. I was so embarrassed that I took the twins back inside and shut the door.

I couldn't believe what had happened. How did a little argument get so out of hand? I had no idea Dwayne had that much strength. He had so much power it scared me. Now, I knew why many of his friends feared him and always came to him when they had trouble. And it definitely explained why Mike Tyson was his idol.

Nearly an hour later, the phone rang. It was Dwayne asking me to pick him up from the police station.

"Where is it?" I asked.

"It's right around the corner on St. Charles Rock Road. I'll be outside by the time you get here."

"We need to talk, Dwayne."

"We will. Just come pick me up. I want to get the fuck out of here."

When I arrived, Dwayne was standing outside of the police station. He jumped in the car, gave the twins a kiss and apologized to them. They were all smiles and seemed to really like Dwayne a lot. I truly believed he cared for them, maybe even more than he cared for me. He didn't say anything to me until we got back home. We were in the kitchen and I stood with my back against the counter while he sat in a chair. "Brenda, you really blew this shit out of proportion. All I was tryin' to do was find Stanley to see if he would give me a good deal on some furniture."

"But I told you I wanted to go see my father. If you were going to be late, all you had to do was call."

"I couldn't call because I didn't have a quarter for the payphone. Besides, I wasn't makin' any stops until I found Stanley."

"I beeped you over and over again but you didn't call me back."

"I told you my battery was low. It's probably dead by now." He looked at his pager, pretending to check for numbers.

"I heard your pager go off earlier so I know the battery ain't low."

His voice rose. "I said I didn't get no damn beep! What more do you want me to say?" I gave up because he started to get loud again. I didn't want the police to return, nor did I want the twins to witness more drama.

"So, what happened at the police station?" I asked, changing the subject.

"Them assholes spoke another tune when we got to the station. They told me that they didn't like my Black ass and I told them I didn't like their White asses. We talked about the fight, they told me to watch my temper, gave me high-five, a court date, and then released me."

I was surprised to hear that, but realized that things could have turned out a lot worse. This was the first big argument Dwayne and I had. I hoped like hell that there would be no more.

The next morning, I drove to the hospital to see Daddy. He wasn't looking good but he was able to recognize me when I came into the room. My eyes filled with water and I could barely talk to him. I kissed him on the cheek and held his hand.

"Hi, Daddy. How are you feeling?" I asked.

"Aw...baby girl, I'm doin' okay. They got me hooked up to all these damn machines and I can't do nothin'."

"I'm sorry about yesterday. I had car trouble."

"Damn, that car breakin' down on you already?"

"Yep. But I already got it fixed," I lied. There was no way I was going to tell Daddy the *real* reason I didn't show.

"Where my babies at? I thought you were goin' to bring them."

"They were asleep when I left. I didn't want to wake them."

"Umm...how are things with you and Dwayne?"

"They cool," I said. "But can always be better."

Daddy didn't say much else. For the several years that I'd known him, I had never seen him look so drained. He was a fine man and being in the hospital did him no justice. After a while, I could tell he was getting restless. I propped up some pillows for him so he could rest and I braided his hair. As he fell asleep, many tears fell down my face. I left feeling as if I would lose the father I had only known for such a short time.

He had been very vague about his condition, so I really didn't know nor did I understand what was going on with him. All I knew was his kidneys and liver were failing him and the only thing that could help him was dialysis. I just wasn't sure if it could save him.

When I got home, my cousin Josh had stopped by and he, the twins and Dwayne started playing monopoly. The twins didn't know how to play, but they were having fun with the money. "Bree, you wanna get in on this game with us?" Dwayne asked.

I didn't feel like doing anything because my head was banging. Seeing Daddy had taken a toll on me. "Naw, that's alright. Y'all go ahead and finish playing."

"How yo daddy doin'?"

"He's doing okay."

"You sure you don't wanna get in this game with us? It might help you take yo mind off things?"

"I'm sure. I'm gonna go lay down for a while, to see if I can get rid of this headache." I went into my room, laid on the bed and passed out.

Later that day, Dwayne came into the bedroom, kissing me on my lips to wake me. "Josh and me gonna make a run to my parents' house so I can change clothes. Can I use yo car? You know mine still down and I ain't got no money to fix it right now."

"I don't care," I said in a groggy tone. "Just be careful and don't tear up my car."

As soon as Josh and Dwayne left, I got up and cooked the twins and me something to eat. Shantell stopped by later and we sat up talking about her boyfriend, James, and Dwayne. She was the only friend I had who could relate to my relationship with Dwayne because she was going through some of the same stuff with James. I thought her situation was much worse than mine because James was married, had numerous kids, was on drugs and abused her.

As we chatted for what seemed like hours, Dwayne hadn't called. A ride to the city to change clothes didn't take almost six hours.

By the time they decided to show up, Shantell was still there. They walked in and Dwayne had the nerve to look at Shantell like...what are you doing here?

"What took so long?" I asked.

"You didn't give me no time limit to get back here so don't start bitchin'."

"I just asked you a question. You don't have to get all bent out of shape about it."

His face twisted up. "Why every time I leave you got me on some damn time clock? Don't make no sense that a brotha can't come and go as he pleases." He walked into the bathroom and slammed the door. Slammed it so hard that it knocked one of the pictures in my kitchen off the wall.

I turned to Josh for answers. I knew my cousin would be honest and tell me what was up. "Josh, what took y'all so long?" I asked.

"Nothing cuz. We just went to his house, messed around for a while, and then stopped to get some grub." I thought I could depend on Josh to tell me the truth, but I guess he forgot to tell me why both of them had the apartment lit up with alcohol, and another peculiar smell was coming from their clothes.

For the rest of the night, Dwayne and I didn't say much to each other. He had an attitude and so did I. Shantell whispered for me to follow her outside, so I did.

"What's up girl?" I asked.

"Didn't you say Dwayne don't do drugs?"

"Yeah, but sometimes he smokes weed."

"Well, honey, I'm here to tell you him and Josh look like they on something. They smell just like James do after he's been on one of his crack binges."

"A while back somebody told me they saw Dwayne smoking premos with some dudes in Kinloch, but I never asked him about it."

"You should because I guarantee you, he's on something."

Shantell pretty much hipped me to what was going on, as I had been in denial. It definitely explained why some of these things were happening, and like it or not, he'd have to eventually come clean.

***

Daddy called me to pick him up from the hospital. They were releasing him, provided that he continued his dialysis. When I got there, he looked better. The nurse showed me how to set the dialysis machine so I could operate the one he'd already had at home. While in the car, he joked around about my terrible driving, making me laugh. "When We Get Married" played on the radio and he turned it up, singing it so beautifully.

"One day yo Mama and me gon' get married again. We gon' have a big weddin' and invite everybody from our families to come. The first time we got married, I married her in your grandparents' livin' room on Cote Brilliante. It was nice, but this time we gon' go all out."

I had to laugh, because I figured Mama wasn't down with his plan. She loved my daddy, no doubt, but marrying him again she wouldn't do. Or, at least I suspected she wouldn't, based on our conversations.

When we got to his house, I helped him up the stairs to his bedroom and did my best to set up his machine for him. We talked for several more hours, and once he was tucked in bed, I noticed his voice was getting tired. I told him I was leaving, but before I made it to the door, he stopped me.

"Brenda, next time you come, don't forget to bring my babies."

"I won't Daddy. I promise."

He cleared his throat and let out a rough cough. "I...I don't think I'm gonna make it. If I don't, always remember, Daddy loves you, all right?" I swallowed, and like often, my emotions took over.

"I know you do, Daddy, and I love you too. And you are going to make it, so don't say that. Just get some rest, okay?"

He nodded. "Bye baby."

"Goodbye Daddy."

I left and couldn't stop crying in the car about my daddy. I made a mental note to bring the twins to see him and I wanted him to spend as much time with them as he could.

Josh was at my apartment waiting for me when I got there. "What are you doing here?" I asked.

"My gal put me out and I ain't got no place to go. Would it be okay if I stay with you? It would only be for a short while. I'll give you a little somethin' for lettin' me stay."

I wasn't happy about it, but had sympathy for Josh. His mother was killed when he was a baby and he never knew who his father was. My grandparents raised him, but he'd never gotten along with my grandfather. I couldn't let my cousin be homeless. "I guess so, Josh. If you don't have no place to stay, I guess so."

"Thanks, Cuz. And, uh, Dwayne told me to tell you he'll be back later. He said call him."

I felt as if this was a great opportunity to talk to Josh, so I sat on the couch next to him, turning down the loud TV. "Hey Josh, be honest. Did you and Dwayne get high yesterday?"

"Naw, cuz. We had some weed but it wasn't about nothin'. You be kind of stressin' my nigga, don't you?"

I cocked my head back. "I can't believe you said that. If anything, he be stressing me."

"I know he do. I'm just kiddin'. Do me a favor, though, and don't tell him I told you about the weed."

"I won't."

That day, I could barely focus on anything other than what Daddy had said to me earlier. I'd hoped he wasn't giving up. As long as he stayed on his dialysis, he would be fine. I called to check on him but no one answered the phone. I just wanted to hear his voice to make sure he was okay. Afterward, I called Dwayne to tell him about Daddy because I hadn't talked to Dwayne all day. As usual, he didn't call me back after I beeped him. Josh told me he was probably at his parents' house so I called him there. A voice that I didn't recognize answered.

"May I speak to Dwayne?" I asked politely.

"Who is this?" she asked with a snobby voice. I kept my cool because I didn't know who it was.

"This is Brenda."

"Bitch, don't be calling here for Dwayne! He don't want yo ass anymore!" she said, sounding like a...White girl? Then she hung up.

I dialed the number again, but no one picked up. I called again, but this time, Dwayne answered. I could hear the chick yelling and screaming in the background like she was losing her mind.

"Who is that bitch?" I yelled, too.

"That's my ex-girlfriend down here trippin' and shit." I could still hear her in the background, telling him to hang up the phone.

"Since when did you have a White ex-girlfriend? And what is she doing in your house?"

"Brenda, she just—" The phone went dead again.

Twice I called back, but no one answered. I was so mad that I stuffed all of Dwayne's clothes into a trash bag, asked Josh to watch the kids, and hopped into my Horizon. After I stopped at the gas station for gasoline, I dashed down the street going sixty miles an hour. By the time I reached Interstate 70, I was up to eighty miles. I was going so fast that my car started to shake—felt like it was going to break down at any minute.

I was only about five minutes away from Dwayne's house, when a police car pulled up behind me with flashing lights. Being in the presence of the police made me nervous and I drove on for awhile, seriously thinking about ignoring the sirens. Then, I thought about how much more trouble I would be in if I did.

The officer got out of the car walking like a turtle. I rushed to lower my window.

"Are you aware of how fast you were traveling?" he asked.

Duuuh, hell, yeah, I wanted to say, but I was so anxious to go and my pitiful voice implied just that. "Yes, sir. If I'm late for work one more time, my boss said that he would fire me. I was just trying to get there on time today."

"You won't get there if you crash, will you?" he said, smiling.

I smiled back. "No, sir, I guess I won't."

"Do you have a driver's license?"

"Yes, I do."

"Can I see it?" I reached in my purse and gave it to him. This shit was taking too long. If he was going to write the ticket, I wished he would go ahead and do it. He observed my driver's license, and then gave it back to me.

"Ms. Hampton, slow down before you kill somebody. Have a good day."

"You also have a good day and thank you." Oh, I had plans to kill somebody, but it wasn't going to be by driving.

I signaled and got off at the Kingshighway exit. I couldn't speed because the officer was close behind me. As I made a left on Natural Bridge, he kept straight. I put the pedal to the metal and sped off to Dwayne's crib. When I got there, I felt a sense of bravery. He wouldn't come outside to confront me, so I sat his clothes on the sidewalk and poured the gasoline over them. The smell of petroleum was potent and I soaked his clothes, until the can was empty.

"You cheating-ass coward," I shouted in a rant. "Your word don't mean nothing and how dare you let another bitch disrespect me! Tell that tramp to come outside and talk that mess now. Better yet, bring your happy-dick ass out here!"

Dwayne remained inside, but pulled the curtain aside so I could see him. All he did was shake his head, and that angered me more. I stomped back to my car and looked around for a lighter. I forgot to bring matches, and since I couldn't find anything to set his clothes on fire, I had to turn to Plan B. A bat was in my trunk, so I pulled it out and headed to the other side of the street like a madwoman. Dwayne had attempted to fix up his Monte Carlo, so that was my target. I knew that putting a few dents in his car would get his attention and it surely was a way to let out my frustrations. At the time, I felt like a baseball player, swinging the bat with overbearing power, in hopes that my actions would be a warning for him to cut the crap. With every crack, I smiled. With every dent that appeared, I truly felt as if my mission had been accomplished. I swiped my hands together, telling myself that he would think twice about ever dissing me again.

Out of concern for his car, Dwayne came outside to stop me.

"What the fuck are you doin'?" he yelled, while twisting my arm behind my back. His strength was too much for me, but I had no problem fighting Dwayne. I slapped the shit out of him, and as I tried to get off more punches, his grip tightened on my arm, damn near breaking it. I pleaded for him to let go.

"Please let go of my arm before you break it! I hate you, Dwayne, I swear to God that I hate you!"

"I hate you too!" he said, letting go of my arm, but giving me a shove. I stumbled, but kept my balance.

"Look at my damn car! You gon' pay for this shit, Brenda!"

I sat on the curb shaking and disgusted about this relationship. I listened to Dwayne yell about his car and refer to me as all kinds of crazy bitches and ho's. I damn sure didn't agree with him, especially since he was the one who had made me go there with him. Then again, there were always other options. Options that I didn't want to resort to at the time. Either way, I was exhausted and when Dwayne went back inside, that's when I left. I felt as if I was on the verge of a nervous breakdown while driving home. The pressure of trying to make things work between us had me on edge. The thought of my father's illness stressed me, and the way my life was turning out terrified me. When Dwayne showed up a few hours later at my apartment, I was numb. I moved around like I was in a twilight zone, wanting it all to end.

Chapter Fifteen

For the next couple of days things were awfully quiet around my apartment. I wasn't speaking to Dwayne, but he had no intentions to leave. I felt trapped in my own apartment. He'd called most of his boys and told them not to come over because I was tired of all the company. That didn't move me in no way, and my only concern was Daddy. I called to check on him and I'd taken the twins to see him several times. He looked fine and said he was feeling better. Then, a few weeks later, my aunt Florence called and told me Daddy was rushed to the hospital. I called Jesse and asked her to pick up the twins and me, so we could go to the hospital together.

When we arrived, Daddy looked worn out. I could tell he was in pain, but he was alert and able to talk. He joked around about being back in the hospital.

"This is messed up, ain't it?" he said. "I think the nurses in here like me and can't get enough of my visits."

"Maybe so," I said. "I know you're getting tired of coming back and forth, ain't you? Is the dialysis not working?"

"Not as much as we had hoped, but I'm stickin' to it."

His mouth looked dry, so I asked the nurse for some ice chips for him to suck on. The twins were clinging tightly to my legs, acting as if they were afraid of him. He reached out for one of them and I picked her up to let him kiss her.

"Muaaah," he said. "That's some good ole sugga right there. Give me my other baby."

I lifted the other twin and he kissed her too. Once I put her down, I asked Daddy what had happened to the braids in his hair and I offered to braid it for him again.

"Please do," he said, rubbing his thick hair that had grown several inches long. I started to braid his hair again, while Jesse fed him some ice chips. Daddy closed his eyes and a tear slipped from the corner. "Thanks for takin' care of me. I know I haven't done much as a father, but I've tried to do my best."

Jesse and I looked at each other, knowing that Daddy was trying to give his goodbyes. We were just glad to have gotten to know him, and that's all that really mattered right now. After a while, the nurse came in and told us that she thought Daddy was having too many visitors and he needed his rest. Most of the Hampton family had been up there to see him, but we ignored her request and stayed with Daddy for about another hour.

He slowly opened his eyes to ask Jesse, "How is y'all Mama doin'?"

"She's fine. She said she was coming to see you tomorrow."

Daddy nodded and closed his eyes again. Shortly thereafter he started to snore and we left.

While driving home, I asked Jesse how Mama felt about Daddy's illness. She hadn't said much to me about it.

"You know Mama don't never tell anybody how she's feeling, but I've seen her crying a few times. I know she's worried and she's been smoking a pack of cigarettes a day."

We were all worried, and it felt so strange to know that someone as close to me as Daddy had been was dying and there was nothing any of us could do.

Jesse stayed at the apartment and kept the twins and me company, while Josh and Dwayne went to the liquor store. Dwayne always seemed to be on his best behavior when she was around so she didn't suspect much wrong with our relationship. She told me she'd fallen in love with Anthony and stressed how well things were going for her at the post office. No doubt, Jesse had really changed since I'd left home. She was more mature, more materialistic, and more sophisticated than ever. If money and a man made her change like that, then somebody show me the money and please give me a good man!

Over the next few days, Daddy's condition took a turn for the worse. My aunts Florence and Betty called and told us that the hospital said there was nothing else they could do for him. I rushed out to the hospital as fast as I could. Mama and Jesse were there when I arrived and said that Rita and her husband were on their way. The hospital was packed with so many of my relatives and everyone was in tears. Before I could make it to Daddy's room, everybody embraced me and showed much love. To me, though, Daddy's condition couldn't be that bad; I had just seen him the other day and I prayed for his recovery. He was going to bounce back just like he'd done before.

Jesse and Mama met me at the door of his room. They were both distraught. Mama's hands were trembling and she reached out to squeeze my hand.

"We're going to lose him," she cried. "I'm so sorry, Brenda, so sorry."

I released Mama's hand and walked into the room to see the state Daddy was in for myself. I couldn't understand how his condition had turned for the worse so quickly. He was unconscious and looked like a zombie. Saliva was dripping from his mouth and his skin looked discolored. I grabbed his cold hand, squeezing it tight, just to see if he would respond. He didn't. I even talked to him and joked around with him, but there was no laughter.

"Come on now, Daddy. You've got to bounce back for me and the twins. They've been asking about you and I know you're not giving up on us already. Don't go already, pleeeease." Jesse said that moments before I arrived, she'd squeezed his hand and he squeezed hers back. So maybe, just maybe, he could hear me.

I kneeled beside the bed, touching Daddy's hand with mine. Prayer was going on throughout the room, but I spoke to Daddy through my own words. *Daddy, if you can hear me, I thank you for being there for me. It's unfortunate that our time might have to be cut so short but every moment that I shared with you was precious and dear to me. We definitely made the best of our time together and it meant more to me than you will ever know. What if I had missed out on your love? What if we never got the chance to be father and daughter? I would have been left with an empty heart. I've learned so much about you, and only if you have to, I hope you can go to heaven knowing that your baby girl will be fine. You did the best you could, and deep in my heart, I know that now. I promise to keep your memory flowing through my children and any other grandchildren that you have along the way. Don't worry about your family, as Rita,*

Jesse and me will do whatever it takes to make you proud. I love you…we love you always.

The doctor came in and talked to the family. He told us that Daddy could be like that for days, and it was up to my grandparents if they wanted to end it. He advised all of us to go home because there was nothing we could do for him by sitting in the hospital. My grandparents and aunts said they would call us in the morning and let us know what was decided.

At home, I felt helpless and beat down. I tried to explain what was going on to the twins but they were too young to understand. The only reason they were crying was because they saw me crying. I couldn't sleep, and every thought in my head was being written in my notebook: *Please God, I beg you not to take my daddy. We've gotten so close and I know you want him to be there for me and the twins. Just like before, you allowed him to bounce back. Can you do it again for me? Please. I won't ask you for anything else, but having my daddy in my life is so important to me. I need him, can't you see? Whatever he's done to deserve this, forgive him. I've always been told that you forgive people, so I'm asking you to forgive Daddy and let him live. Let him live and give him another chance…*

As I continued writing, Dwayne sat next to me watching TV, and doing his best to spark a conversation. I still hadn't said much to him, and by three o'clock in the morning, his eyes started to fade. Moments later, the phone rang and he jumped from his sleep. My heart fell to my stomach and I glared at the phone.

"Please answer it," I said in a whisper. Dwayne picked up the phone, and after hearing who it was, he gave it to me.

"It's your aunt Florence." Before I took the phone, I could hear her loud cries. She didn't have to say a word, I could already feel it. Daddy had gone to heaven. Not dead, but had gone to heaven. At that point, I had an out-of-body experience. It seemed as if I was in a dream, but the loss of my father was real. I dropped the phone and buried my face into my hands. Crawled into a fetal position on the couch and tightened my notebook against my chest. Definitely, I felt as if a part of me was gone and could never be replaced.

***

Daddy's funeral was painful. The church was packed with people from the Hampton family, some I had never seen before in my life. Aunt Florence introduced us to everyone as Daddy's little girls. I tried to keep my spirits up but I just couldn't. Dwayne, Clarence and Anthony were there for support and we all definitely needed it. After Clarence played "Amazing Grace" on his saxophone, everybody lost it.

Rita dropped to her knees and had to be carried out of the church. "Daddy!" she shouted. "Not my daddy! God, pleeeease, no, pleeeease!"

Mama kept squeezing her chest and I had never seen her so emotional. She could barely breathe, and many of the ushers fanned her as she, too, shouted out loudly. "Lord, why did you have to do this! Whyyyy?"

Jesse and me couldn't even stand to go look at Daddy. The funeral directors brought his casket to the front pew where we sat, and as I was helped to stand up, my weak legs gave out on me. I fell backwards, grabbing my stomach and pounding my legs. Dwayne hugged me, but his comfort did me no good. I lifted my head and wiped the flowing tears and snot from my face. For the last time I would see Daddy, he looked peaceful and handsome as ever. I sighed, hoping that he was now painless with God.

Chapter Sixteen

Through the sometimes up and many downs, Dwayne and I stayed together. When we weren't disputing with each other, the relationship was doable. He could be considered as a genuinely nice person, until one of his rages sparked. I guessed the same could be said for me, and whenever I was rubbed the wrong way, I could get my clown on, too. A bad girl and a bad boy equaled one explosive combination.

I had gotten pretty lazy, and the next few years of my life was not how I intended it to be. I was still sucking up the welfare system, had no intentions of finding a job and had become addicted to shoplifting. I had stepped up my game to the major department store chains and I frequented the malls on a daily basis. I sold clothes to make money, and it was so easy for me to make about three or four hundred dollars a day. The twins were in kindergarten, and while they were at school, if I wasn't at the mall, I sat around all day long watching soap operas, hanging out with my friends and cooking. I had gained a whopping thirty-five pounds and my self-esteem had plummeted. I was looking awful for a twenty-one year old, and my tinted blonde short hair made me look ghetto.

Dwayne, on the other hand, had a gig of his own. He and his friend, Chris, started stealing cars and selling parts for money. We had become a hustling couple and I was his Bonnie, and he was my Clyde. If anyone said anything negative about him, I would defend him. He was my protector and no one, especially in the neighborhood, dared to step to me the wrong way. If they did, they'd pay, as one dude did who called me a "bitch" for taking his parking spot. Dwayne beat his ass that day, leaving him lying in the street with a busted head.

Keeping money in our pockets was the objective, and I was on cloud nine about being with a brotha who was classified as a thug. I found myself getting a thrill out of watching Dwayne and Chris bust out car windows and start the engine within seconds. Sometimes, I'd drive the getaway car, and other times, Chris' girlfriend, Rosalind, did.

To me, moneywise, we had it going on. I was his Ride or Die Chick and was down with whatever he dished my way. All the money we shared drew us closer and closer together. I had gotten a new car—a baby blue Ford Taurus. Dwayne bought himself a motorcycle and a GMC black truck that came with a sunroof and had a booming radio system. We gave the apartment an entirely new look. Bought a mauve sofa and loveseat, and set it off with black diamond shaped glass tables. Dwayne had purchased a 60 gallon octagon fish tank that he kept Piranhas in and there was a small bar in the corner for drinking pleasures. The twins went from daybeds to canopy beds, dressed in pink and white satin bed accessories. Their closet was filled with the finest brand name clothes, all of which I had gotten by way of a five-finger discount. The kitchen had a new look as well, and was decked out with black appliances.

Everybody in the hood wondered how we were able to afford what we'd had, and it was pretty obvious that something illegal was transpiring. I was the one often being questioned, but nobody questioned Dwayne. He always had a look that said, "Don't fuck with me. If you do, you'll pay." That went for the kids in the neighborhood, too. The twins had experienced some boys outside picking on them, but after Dwayne made his threats, nobody ever messed with the twins again. No doubt about it, having him as a boyfriend definitely had benefits.

Josh had moved out, but only a few doors away with his girlfriend. Him and Dwayne were still making late-night trips to the city, and they'd often come back high as ever. Dwayne assured me that it was only weed, and more than anything, he said their trips were all about making money.

For him, making money had been taken to a new level. Josh and Dwayne rushed in one day, telling me they helped a friend rob a liquor store. According to them, they'd been given a cut of the cash to keep quiet. Shoplifting and car theft were enough, but robbing a liquor store? Dwayne insisted that his other friend did the dirty work and him and Josh were just stand-bys.

"Did anybody get hurt," I asked. "I hope not."

"Nope, nobody got hurt. The clerk was very cooperative." He reached in his pocket, pulling out several hundred dollar bills. "Baby, this is two-thousand dollars. Put this up for us, okay?"

I hesitated to take the money, but opened a safe that I had in my closet and put it with the rest of our money. I didn't feel comfortable doing so, but the money sure did look enticing. I was so afraid for Dwayne, and never in my wildest dream did I think I'd be traveling down this path. Before going to sleep that night, he told me he had a surprise for me. I couldn't wait to see what it was going to be.

Dwayne got up early, telling me he would be back later with my surprise. I dropped the twins off at school and went to Kmart to get some merchandise for a lady who wanted to buy some clothes for her kids. As I was leaving the store, the security guard came after me, flashing a badge.

"Excuse me, Ma'am. I'm going to need you to come back into the store with me."

I wanted to run, but with the clothes I had stacked underneath my own clothes, making me look as if I weighed three hundred pounds, I wouldn't get far. The security guard held my arm, escorting me to a room in the far back. As we walked, all eyes were on me.

"That's a damn shame," one lady said, shaking her head.

Another group of teenagers stood by laughing. The cashiers all stopped waiting on their customers, just to look at me. I was humiliated, and it was the first time I had ever been caught shoplifting.

"Have a seat," the security guard said, being very polite. I sat in the chair, observing the many cameras in which I knew he'd seen me on. He was going through my fat purse, pulling out merchandise. "Why are you out here doing this? Don't you know it makes it hard on customers when we have to raise the prices because of people like you?"

I gave a sob story about being on welfare and having no money. That didn't work for the security guard, especially when he looked through my purse and found five-hundred dollars in cash. I was asked to remove the clothes tucked underneath mine, and having no sympathy for me, he called the police.

The police came and told me that as long as I cooperated, they wouldn't arrest me but would give me a summons to appear in court. They did, and shortly thereafter, I was released.

Dwayne was at home waiting for me. "Where have you been? I've been callin' around lookin' for you," he said.

Uneasy about what had happened, I plopped down on the couch and touched my head to soothe my migraine headache. "I got caught shoplifting today. They let me go, but I gotta go to court in about one month."

Dwayne cocked his head back in shock. "Damn, that's messed up, but don't stress yourself about it. At least you didn't go to jail. I'll go to court with you, if you want me to."

I nodded, feeling a little at ease because he would be with me. "Thanks. I appreciate it."

I still had a bad feeling inside. Things could have been worse, but was this just the beginning of more run-ins with the law to come? To perk me up, Dwayne touched my hands with his and smiled.

"I know that I haven't been right since we've been together and I've been feelin' bad about all the shit I've put you through. None of it was done purposely, but sometimes I get to trippin'. No matter how hard I try, I just can't do right when it comes to you. But girl…I love you. I want to be with you for the rest of my life. I'm not ready to get married yet, but I'm givin' this to you as a promise. I promise to love you, to love yo kids, to take care of you, to stop lyin' to you, to never cheat on you, again, and to treat you like you deserve to be treated." Dwayne reached in his pocket, pulling out a small black velvet box.

I took it from his hand and opened it. The ring was beautiful. It was a huge nugget ring with a cluster of diamonds in the middle. I removed it from the box, sliding it on my finger. It fit perfectly.

"Thank you," I said, reaching over to give him a hug. Yeah, we had been to hell and back, but our relationship felt destined at times. "That was so nice of you. I had no idea you were going to give me a ring."

"Bree, you've put up with my shit for years. At the end of the day, all we got is each other. The ring is the least I can do."

That night, I called my friends and bragged about the diamond/nugget ring I'd gotten. I always felt as if I had something to prove to everyone about my relationship and that was, Dwayne loved me. Truth is, I hadn't even convinced myself of that. Many of them felt that with all the crap I'd been through, a ring was no big deal. I invited them over on Saturday for drinks and some grub. Shantell, Rosalind, and Loretta said they could make it, but Dana declined. I'd met some new chicks in the apartment complex where I lived and also invited them. Jesse said she couldn't make it because she and Anthony had gotten tickets to a play. She insisted that we needed to talk about something she was going through and promised to come see me soon.

On Saturday, I took the twins to Mama's house. She was so happy to see them, even though they visited her every single weekend. Since I'd moved out, Mama and my relationship had gotten a lot better. I talked to her almost every day, and whenever we saw each other, we had nothing but respect for one another. She despised Dwayne, though, and therefore kept her distance.

Before our friends came over, I had put money under my mattress, in my dresser drawer, and in the safe. It totaled every bit of $9,385 dollars. When Dwayne got out of the shower, he double checked me and put nine thousand back into the safe and three eighty-five under the mattress. I headed for the kitchen to cook and waited for our guests to arrive.

My little apartment was packed like sardines with Dwayne's friends and mine. We had a blast watching movies, drinking, playing spades and listening to music. I put together some of my favorite tacos and they were gone before I knew it. Of course, I showed off my ring to everyone, and as usual, there were haters.

"It don't look like it cost that much to me," Loretta said, as I held my finger out for her to look at the ring. "I bet you got that ring at a pawnshop, didn't you?"

"Pawnshop or no pawnshop," Dwayne shot back. "That mutha cost me almost a grand and my baby deserves it."

I blushed, pulling my hand back and thanked *my man* for being so kind.

As the night went on, beer and soda was getting low so I asked Dedra and Charlene, some of my new friends from the apartment complex, to go to the store with me. I asked Dwayne for some money and he told me to get the three eighty-five from underneath the mattress. I looked for it, but it wasn't there. I recounted the money in the safe, but there was only the nine thousand that we had put in there earlier. I yelled for Dwayne, and he came into the room, closing the door behind him.

"Didn't you put some money under the mattress?" I asked.

"Yeah, I did. Why? It ain't there?"

"No, it's not. I counted what was in the safe and it's all there." Dwayne sucked in his bottom lip, which usually meant he was pissed. He opened the bedroom door, storming into the living room.

"Attention everyone," he said, whistling to silence the noise and flickering the light switch. "Listen up. We seem to have a small fuckin' problem. Somebody went into my room and took some money. I know it wasn't none of my boys 'cause y'all niggas know I don't play that shit. So, which one of y'all bitches got my money."

"Dwayne, hold up," I said. "No need to disrespect my friends, and who says none of your friends didn't take the money? They are just as guilty—"

"Brenda, shut up! I got this, and when it comes to my money, don't nobody fuck with that. Fellas," he said, directing his friends. "Go outside for a minute."

Without any hesitation, his friends got up and went outside. That left me, Rosalind, Dedra, Shantell, Loretta, Tanya, Pat, Jerry and Charlene.

"Sit the fuck down," Dwayne ordered. Everybody hesitantly took a seat. We squeezed in on both couches and everybody looked in awe.

Dwayne left the living room and came back within a few seconds. In his hand was a silver pistol, and he pushed the clip inside of it. "What are you doing with a gun in here," I said, frowning and standing to my feet. I had never seen it before and how dare him have a gun in here without me knowing it.

"Sit down and close yo mouth," he said, pointing the gun between Pat and me. "Y'all got three choices here, so listen up. Choice number one, I turn off the lights and y'all move around the table as fast as you can, ring-around-the-rosy style. When I turn the lights back on, the money better be on the table. Choice number two, I take everybody in the bathroom, one by one, and make you strip until I find my fuckin' money. Or, of course, there's always choice number three, and that is, I start blowin' muthafuckas heads off!"

My friends sat in disbelief, but from experience, many knew Dwayne wasn't bullshitting. Shantell pleaded for whoever had the money to return it.

"Whoever got it, just give it up. Don't be getting me involved in no mess like this, especially when y'all already know Dwayne's ass be trippin'."

I added my two cents. "I don't want no mess, so please just hand it over."

"Option one," Dwayne yelled, turning off the lights and putting us in pure darkness. He even turned on the stereo, giving us some music as some of us marched around the table like we were playing musical chairs. After five long minutes of shuffling around in the dark living room, Dwayne turned the lights back on. All eyes dropped to the floor and the money was scattered all over it. Dwayne pulled the trigger on the gun, causing a bullet to go straight through the wall.

"I said put the money on the table, not the floor! Now, get the fuck out!" he yelled, but by then everybody was already at the door, rushing out. "I should kick all y'all stupid asses!" he continued.

I stood in complete, utter shock. I screamed at the top of my lungs. "What in the hell are you doing!"

He cocked his neck from side to side with a smirk on his face. "Ay, you got your money back, didn't you? What's the problem?"

I rolled my eyes and stormed off into the kitchen to clean up. I said nothing else to no one because I was just as mad at whomever the person was who took the money. They were supposed to be my friends and made me look like a fool for accusing his friends.

Dwayne was so mad that he asked his friends to leave too. He cursed at me for putting so much trust in my friends, and when I brought up the fact that he had a gun in my home, he jetted. I lay back on my bed, wondering what was next.

Chapter Seventeen

The judge handed down a $250 fine for shoplifting. Since I was now racking up about six-hundred dollars a day, I easily paid the court on my way out. Dwayne said that stealing would remain on my police report for seven years, but at the time, a police report didn't mean anything to me.

Once he dropped me off at home, he went to the city. His city trips were still somewhat of a mystery, but every time he came home, he added to our bank. There seemed to be no limit for either of us, and I couldn't believe that the bottom-line had come down to making the almighty dollar by any means necessary. I had gotten bold with my game, and strolling out of the store with two or three televisions in a cart was like taking candy from a baby. Dwayne, on the other hand, he was not only bold with his game, but had gotten ruthless. I watched him go after people who crossed him, knocking them out cold. He had become even more protective of me, and when some of my friends and I got robbed at Pantera's Pizza on Kingshighway, Dwayne found out who the dude was and promised me that he regretted it.

Another time, a dude sprayed water from a super-soaker gun on me and Jesse while we hung out with some friends at O'Fallon Park. Dwayne saw what had happened, and all hell broke loose. He removed the blue and white bandana tied around his head and snatched off his muscle shirt. I witnessed him and his friends stomp the dude, knocking out nearly every teeth in his mouth and bashing his head with their fists. I was in tears, listening to the dude beg for them to stop. Dwayne was the aggressor, and even though many of the young women spectators appreciated the look of sweat beads forming on his chiseled abs, I yelled for him to stop. He turned to me with a heaving buffed chest.

"Go get my pistol out of my car," he ordered and wiped the sheen of sweat from his forehead. "This nigga trippin'!"

I shook my head, watching as many people cleared out. "No," I said. "Tell your friends to stop. It's not that serious, Dwayne, and it was just some water."

He sucked his teeth, and after telling his friends to chill, he told me to go punch the dude in his face for spraying water on me. I refused and reached my hand out to help the dude up as he squirmed on the ground. His face was battered and bloody. I felt awful.

"Do you need an ambulance," I asked, as the dude gripped his side.

Dwayne pushed me away, punching the dude in his face again, staggering him. I screamed out loudly to get Dwayne's attention. "Stop it! Let's go or I swear I will find the police and have everyone out here arrested!"

That sure as hell got his attention, and it allowed the dude to limp away.

"I thought yo ass was supposed to be down with me?" Dwayne shouted.

I gazed into his eyes, trying hard to reach his soul. This Ride or Die shit had gone too far, and I started to renege on being that kind of chick. "I am down with you, and I appreciate you protecting me, but I don't want you to go to jail for killing nobody. I want you with me and the twins. Fuck him and let's get out of here."

Jesse threw in her two cents as well. "Yeah, Dwayne, let's go. He ain't even worth it."

We all got in our cars, and on the drive home, everyone in our car rode in silence.

***

Charlene was my card buddy in the complex, so I called her to come over and keep me company. We stayed up until four o'clock in the morning playing spades, and the thought of Dwayne not being there or calling had crossed my mind. I didn't want to alarm Charlene but I think she could tell something was bothering me. Our last game ended at five-fifteen in the morning and still, no Dwayne.

After Charlene left, I didn't want to be disrespectful by calling his parents' house at that time in the morning, so instead, I called my cousin Josh to see if he'd heard from him. Josh answered sounding sleepy.

"I haven't seen him in days," he said. "I thought he was with you."

"I haven't seen him either. I'm really worried about him. I hope nothing bad has happened."

"I doubt it, Brenda. I didn't want to tell you this, but Dwayne be messin' with that PCP. Sometimes, he don't know if he comin' or goin' and he…he also seein' somebody else. I'm sorry I didn't say anything, but I didn't want you to get your feelings hurt. He's probably at her house, so no need to worry. He'll show up soon."

My brows went up, but I really wasn't that surprised about Dwayne seeing someone else. It was pretty obvious by the numerous pages on his beeper, the late nights and our sexual connection had dropped to a two, on a scale from one to ten. I just couldn't give my all, sexually, to a man, who in my gut, I felt had wronged me. What Josh had said hurt, but Dwayne had cheated so much that I started to have little reaction. The PCP did surprise me though. "PCP?" I said. "What in the hell is that?"

"It's like embalming fluid. Makes you feel like you can walk on water and do crazy shit like fly."

"What?" I shouted. "Why haven't you ever told me this and whatever happened to y'all just smoking weed?"

"I didn't want to be caught in the middle. You know how Dwayne is. I didn't want no trouble."

"Well, thanks for telling me, Josh. This explains why so much has been going on with us. I'ma see what I can do about getting him some help."

"No doubt. I'm going back to bed, and you already know what's up. Don't tell him you got yo info from me, all right?"

"I won't. Thanks, Josh, go back to bed."

I hung up and experienced that same painful lump in my burning throat I had felt many, many times before. I had lost so many nights of sleep, worrying about Dwayne and was making myself sick. I couldn't sit still, so I drove around looking for him, and by seven-thirty in the morning, I returned home. Having no luck, I stayed by the phone all day, and every time it rang, my heart skipped a beat. Everybody had called: Mama, Jesse, Rita, Dedra, and many of his friends. Still, no Dwayne.

By the end of the day, I didn't know if he was dead or alive. I must have beeped him a trillion times and called his parents' house more than that. Everyone continued to tell me that they hadn't heard from him.

One whole week had gone by and it was as if Dwayne had fallen off the earth. I was miserable. On Friday, I got up to take the twins to school and went to the welfare office to renew my assistance. My caseworker called my name and I entered the small cubicle area to discuss my case.

"Ms. Hampton, why are you here with such a long face?" my caseworker teased.

I shrugged. "No reason. I'm just not feeling well today."

"Have you been looking for a job?"

"Yes, I have but I haven't found anything yet," I lied.

A look of disgust covered her face and she laid her pen on her desk. She sighed, searching deep into my tired and puffy eyes. "You know, you look like a young lady who has a lot of good potential. Don't let your life go to waste by being on welfare forever. This system was designed to handicap people like me and you, if you know what I mean. There's a program we've being trying to put together to help single mothers like you get off welfare and find good jobs. Would you be interested in participating in such a program?"

"Sure, why not," I said, shrugging with little enthusiasm. She updated the information for me to renew my assistance and continued to talk about the program.

"I'll be sending you some information in the mail, as soon as it becomes available."

"Thanks, Ms. Johnson," I said, standing to leave.

"Uh, Ms. Hampton. Make this your last time coming here to renew your welfare assistance. You can do better."

I nodded. "I know and I will."

I walked out feeling a little better after my conversation with Ms. Johnson. How or why she felt I had potential, I didn't know, but I needed to hear her words. I hadn't thought about finding a job, but maybe it would help me cut back on all the shoplifting I'd been doing.

As I turned the corner on my street, Dwayne's car was parked outside. I rushed inside my apartment, only to find him looking a complete mess with dirty clothes on and hair all out of whack. His lips were chapped and he had the nerve to be taking money from our safe.

"What are you doing?" I asked, pulling him away from the safe.

He shoved me backwards on the bed. "I'm gettin' my money, that's what I'm doin'!"

"Where have you been?" I attempted to snatch the money from his hands.

"Look, I ain't got time for no questions! I gotta go!"

"No...no," I shouted while grabbing his shirt and ripping it. "You owe me an explanation!"

He shoved me on the bed again. I fell back and hit my head on the wall. "Bree, I don't owe you shit!" He pointed his finger at me and spoke stern. "Now, get up again if you want to. Girl, I will break yo fuckin' neck!"

His fiery eyes said I'd better not move, so I didn't. I heard the front door close, and then jumped off the bed to go after him. My big toe slammed right into the door and cracked. By the time I limped to the front door, he was gone. He had taken every dime we'd saved. The only thing I had was forty dollars in the drawer, and that was for the electric bill. It seemed so odd that every time I'd take two steps forward, I'd get pushed two...five steps back. No doubt, illegal money had no benefit and when the devil giveth, the Lord taketh away.

I called Dwayne's mother to tell her what had happened. If anybody could get through to him, it was her.

"Dwayne has been here clowning as well. I know he's doing drugs, but all I can do is pray for him. I'm going to pray for you, too, Brenda, and call me, again, if you need anything."

Her words stunned me because I didn't think his habit was that bad. Drugs had really done him in, and without them, I knew he could have been a better person. I just didn't realize that getting him to stop would be so difficult.

My toe was in so much pain that I drove myself to the emergency room. The doctor gave me some painkillers and told me there was nothing he could do about a broken toe. Having no one to express my disappointments to, I finally called Jesse to tell her about my drama.

"You need to get rid of Dwayne. I know he has some problems, but his issues are much bigger than you. Encourage him to get some help, and that's pretty much all you can do."

"I will, but I haven't heard from him. It's so easy for everybody to tell me to move on, but y'all just don't know all that we've been through. It's been a lot."

"I get that, Brenda, but enough is enough, don't you think?"

I really wasn't trying to hear what Jesse was saying, so I changed the subject. She did too and shared some news with me about her and Anthony. They were still dating, but she had fallen for an older man who she worked with at the post office named Ryan. She explained how her feelings for Anthony just weren't the same.

"I need to tell him how I'm feeling, don't I? Maybe he'll understand," Jesse said.

"I think you should tell him. If the love ain't there anymore, what can you do? I know the feeling of being cheated on is awful, and you can't have your cake and eat it too. Is that what you're trying to do?"

"Not at all. It's just tough because I like Ryan a lot, but he's married. It's not like much is going to come of our relationship, even though him and his wife are supposed to be separated. On the other hand, Anthony is still my heart. We have so much fun when we're together, but my time with Ryan is taking away from that. I'm in a fucked-up situation, and the last thing I want to do is break Anthony's heart."

I felt Jesse's pain, but I wasn't one to give her advice because my relationship was more screwed up than anybody's. However, I did suggest that she try and work things out with Anthony. In my book, he was still the best, and I thought I was the one who made bad choices about men, not Jesse. We ended our call, making plans to get together with Dedra and Charlene for the weekend.

Chapter Eighteen

That weekend, I met a man named Kenneth at The Maxx Nightclub we went to and provided him with my phone number. For whatever reason, I didn't expect him to call, but when he did, we stayed on the phone for hours. He was a meat-cutter at Dierbergs around the corner from my place and was six years older than I was. Other than Dwayne, I hadn't been intimate with anyone since Miles. I wasn't sure if meeting someone new was the right move or not, but there I was, again, not wanting to be by myself and looking for someone to fill that void. It had been almost three weeks since I'd last heard from Dwayne. I made Kenneth aware of my situation and asked him if we could simply be friends. He agreed.

Kenneth and I took things slow. I had lunch with him a few times and I invited him to my apartment for dinner. I bragged so much about my meatloaf, he was dying to taste it.

On Saturday, I went through my normal routine of dropping off the twins at Mama's house. Jesse had moved into her new apartment and Mama was excited to have the twins over because she was lonely. I kept her company for a while, and then headed home to start my dinner. As I was mashing the potatoes, the phone rang. I'd asked Kenneth to call when he was on his way, so I figured it was him.

"Hello," I said in a perky tone.

"We need to talk," he said.

"Who is this?" I asked, knowing perfectly well that it was Dwayne.

"What do you mean, who is this? There betta not be no other niggas callin' there."

I ignored his comment. "Talk about what? What is it you want to talk about now? How you've been out there dirt-ball bad, or how you took all of *our* money? Better yet, let's talk about how you've just disappeared and haven't returned my phone calls in ages."

"Bree, it ain't even like that. You're right, I have been gettin' high and that shit got me trippin'. As hard as I tried to stop doin' drugs *for you*, I couldn't. The urge just keeps hittin' me and ain't nothin' I can do about it. I've been in rehab for the past several weeks, tryin' to get help. They said I shouldn't have any contact with the outside world and that's what I've been doin'. Can I please come over and talk to you?"

I hesitated and thought about canceling my plans with Kenneth. But I knew Dwayne was lying, something he'd gotten pretty darn good at. "Not right now, Dwayne. Maybe later. I have to take care of some business for my mother and won't be back until later. I'll call you when I get back."

"Why are you rushin' me off the phone? I thought you'd be happy to hear from me."

"I'm not rushing you. It's just so hard to stay on this phone with you and pretend that everything is okay and it's not."

"I understand, but why did you get the locks changed? I came by one day and couldn't get in."

"Do you have to ask? You will not come in here, again, and take nothing from me. I mean that."

"It'll never happen again. Call me when you get finished with yo mother. I'm anxious to see you and the twins."

"Sure," was all I could say.

I couldn't believe Dwayne. He thought that one simple phone call would resolve all of our problems. I guessed I'd shown him that coming back to me was easy, but I was determined...not this time, and not again.

Kenneth was right on time. As I finished up dinner, he sat in the kitchen talking to me. He was very intelligent and it was pleasant to talk to someone who had positive things going on.

"I've been working at Dierbergs for the past seven years. I love my job and I make pretty decent money."

"That's good. Everybody can't keep a job for that long. I can't even imagine myself working for the same company for seven years.

I do home healthcare and I have several clients that I see throughout the day."

Yes, I lied. Didn't want to admit to the man I was a professional booster. We continued to talk, and as I started to put our food on the table, there was a light knock at the door. My heart dropped to my stomach; I had a feeling who it was. Dwayne never respected what I said, and as I looked out the peephole, he stood outside with a white and blue sweat suit on. I pretended not to be at home, and slowly backed away from the door. I went back into the kitchen, telling Kenneth it was Dwayne.

"Invite the man in and tell him we're just having dinner. It ain't no big deal and there is plenty of food for him to get his grub on too."

I scratched my head, thinking of what to do. "Uh, I don't think that's going to work."

"Why not?" Kenneth asked. Dwayne was now at the back door knocking and turning the doorknob. He banged harder and harder on the door, as if he knew I was inside. Getting no response, he went to the twins' bedroom window and tried to slide it over, but weeks ago I'd put safety locks on them so no one could get in.

Kenneth was getting irritated with me, and, again, asked me to open the door. I tried to come up with the most sensible thing to do, so I moved the vertical blinds aside and looked out at Dwayne banging on the front door again.

"Dwayne, why are you here? I told you I had something to do."

He wiggled the doorknob. "Open the door, Bree. Quit trippin' and open the door."

"Not now. I...I don't understand why you're here?"

"I'm here because I want to be here." He looked at Kenneth's car parked on the street. "Do you have company?" I didn't say anything. "Open the damn door!"

Once I saw Dwayne's face get tight, I hurried into the kitchen and asked Kenneth to leave out the back door. Before he could get out of the chair, there was a loud boom and the front door came crashing down. I jumped; Kenneth did, too, but he stood with his hands in his pockets. Dwayne walked into the kitchen with tightened fists, while biting down hard on his bottom lip.

"Nigga, get yo ass out of my apartment!"

Kenneth cleared his throat and spoke calmly. "Look, man, I don't want any trouble. Brenda and I are just friends."

"She don't cook dinner for nobody who's just a damn friend, so exit yo ass out of here." Kenneth grabbed his jacket from the chair, and I stood in front of the refrigerator hoping Dwayne wouldn't do anything stupid.

"I'll talk to you later, Brenda." Kenneth said, waiting for my response.

Dwayne swiped his hand across the table, making the dishes and food I'd prepared hit the floor. "Nigga, are you ready to die? You got two seconds to get the fuck out of here!" I softly asked Kenneth to leave and he walked towards the door. My leg was bleeding because a shard of the glass plate had bounced off the floor and cut me. Dwayne gave me a hard stare, and as I bent down to pick up the pieces of glass, he bolted through the living room and out the front door. I rushed after him.

Kenneth was walking down the sidewalk towards his car when Dwayne approached him. I ran up, standing between them.

I touched Dwayne's heaving chest, pleading with him. "He's leaving. Just let him go and leave it alone. Please."

Kenneth smiled and spoke, "Baby, move out of the way. If the man wants to fight then—"

Before Kenneth could finish his sentence, Dwayne slammed him in the mouth with his fist and drew blood. He then pushed me to the ground and they went at it. Kenneth had slid a fork up his sleeve while he was in the kitchen and stabbed Dwayne in the lip with it. Blood gushed down his chin, but it was obvious that he felt no pain. He was all over Kenneth, but he wasn't giving up. His ear started bleeding, and I scurried into my apartment to call the police.

The dispatcher said they'd send someone right over, and by the time I got back outside, Dwayne and Kenneth had fought their way across the street and there were plenty of spectators. Dwayne had got into my old green Horizon and tried to run Kenneth over. He dodged the car and it slammed into a big oak tree. The entire front of the car collapsed to the ground.

Soon, police sirens rang out and they both fled. Kenneth got in his car and took off and Dwayne fled on foot. When the police arrived, they questioned me about the incident. I told them everything had cooled down, but when they asked me for names, I gave fake names so Kenneth or Dwayne wouldn't get warrants.

Since they were already outside, Dedra and Charlene came in to help me clean up. "Girl, that was some wild shit," Charlene said. "Them niggas were throwing some straight-up blows."

"Weren't they," Dedra said. "I ain't never seen two dudes go at it like that and that shit was like watching a heavyweight championship fight."

I was too disgusted to comment.

Charlene and Dedra continued to rant about the fight. I felt bad for putting Kenneth in such a messed-up situation. And from that moment on, I knew that Dwayne would control my life and everyone around me. It was either him, or nobody. I felt trapped, and was so unsure about how much longer this was going to go on. That night, he called to make me feel guilty about my actions.

"You really hurt me today," he said. "I needed you and you lied to me. I'm tryin' to get myself together, but I can't without yo support. You're the only positive thing I got goin' for me, and if I don't have you, I don't know what I'm goin' to do. I may as well just go somewhere and die."

Dwayne sounded pitiful. Was I that wrong for not reconciling with him? Maybe he did need me, and if I was supposed to love him like I said I did, then how could I turn my back on him?

Well, turning my back on Dwayne should have come easy. The next day things took, yet another, turn for the worse. I had just gotten back from Dierbergs, trying to apologize to Kenneth for what had happened. He blew it off, saying that Dwayne wasn't going to stop him from pursuing a relationship with me. Of course, I begged to differ. When I got home and put the key in the door, it was late. I had forgotten to turn on some lights when I left. I could barely see when I got inside. But soon thereafter, my eyes connected with another pair of eyes that stared at me in the dark. My heart raced fast and furious, as I thought I'd walked in on an intruder.

"Where have you been, Brenda?" Dwayne asked with a calm, settle voice.

I fumbled around with my keys, trying to avoid the question. As I reached out for the lights, I felt a powerful fist crack me on the side of my face, and another slammed into my mouth. I lost my balance, falling to the floor. Dizzy, and trying to cease the pain of my brain that felt rattled, I squeezed my eyes to fight back the pain. Seconds later, I blacked out. When I came to, Dwayne stood over me with ice wrapped in a towel. My face was stiff, and when I touched it, it felt numb. I could barely feel my hands on it.

"Have you been out fuckin'?" he asked.

I didn't answer and continued to sit on the floor holding my face. "Alright, since you don't want to tell me, I'll find out myself." He pulled up my skirt and reached for my panties. I struggled to get him to stop, but he was too strong. He felt my crotch, rubbing his hands on my insides to see if I was wet. "Nah, you ain't been fuckin', but who ya been with?"

I was in major shock that he had punched me...no, punched the shit out of me. And having nothing to say, I ignored Dwayne as I walked in a daze to the bathroom. I closed the door and turned the light on so I could see myself in the mirror. My left eye was swollen and red as fire. I looked terrible, and as tears rolled over my high cheekbones, my eyes burned. My head ached so badly, I rubbed my temples, hoping the pain would go away.

A few minutes later, Dwayne knocked on the door. "What you doin' in there? Get out here so I can tell you somethin'."

I ignored him and leaned over the sink, trying to figure out how to handle this messed-up situation. He kept banging on the door, and had threatened to kick it down. It didn't matter to me because wood was still cracked on the front door from when he kicked it. The door barely locked, and if a burglar wanted to get in, he/she would have no problem doing so. In addition to that, my hallway had a big hole in the wall from when he got upset and punched it. The diamond-shaped glass tables in the living room had all been broken. I couldn't forget about the bullet hole that was still in the wall, but according to him, destroying my property made it easy for him not to put his hands on me. Now, things had changed. The security and protection that I had looked to him for was gone. I now feared him, too, and felt sick to my stomach about all that had happened. I was ready to end it, and the only way Dwayne wouldn't have control over me is if I was dead and in my grave. He was able to do whatever the hell he wanted to because my stupid-ass let him.

And then, if I went out and he didn't know where I was, it resulted in this. It didn't make sense to me, and I hated myself for letting things go this far. Allowing my children to witness this ongoing drama was ridiculous. I promised myself that I would never walk in the same shoes as Mama, but those shoes were very similar. Dwayne was beyond anything that my daddy could ever be, but I was always forgiving like Mama was. I didn't understand why she would always go back, but I did understand how difficult it was to let go of someone you genuinely cared for. I cared for Dwayne, more than I did myself. I felt sorry for him, and I knew that his habit had contributed to much of what was going on. Still, this was the last straw for me. I didn't want him anymore, and I hated myself so much that I had no desire to live.

I opened the medicine cabinet and pulled out a razor blade. I looked at myself in the mirror, again, staring at the hopeless young woman in the mirror. Thick snot drizzled from my nose, and flowing salty tears ran over my swollen lip. It was time to die. I wanted out of this life that I had in no way known how to make better. I was a failure and the twins didn't deserve to have a poor excuse of a mother like me. I rubbed the blade against a vein on my wrist and pressed. The way to do it was to slice it and do it fast. I tried, but I just kept pressing the blade against my wrist, hoping that it would be enough to put me out of my misery. *Damn, I couldn't do it!* I opened the medicine cabinet, again, and looked for some pills. When I opened the bottle of Tylenol there were only five pills in there. *This definitely wouldn't be enough to put me away*, I thought. *Shit!*

Dwayne had calmed his voice, asking me to open the door. After I told him our troubles would soon be over, he figured I was contemplating killing myself. He laughed through the door.

"I'ma leave my gun right outside this door, just so you can do it. You're full of shit, Brenda, and you know damn well you ain't gon' kill yourself."

There was silence for a while, and then I heard the front door slam. I waited a while before leaving the bathroom, but when I did, I saw that he'd kept his promise. The gun was right there on the floor, so I could pick it up and use it. I picked it up, putting it in my dresser drawer. I took off my clothes, got in bed and did something I hadn't done in a long time. I pulled out a new spiral notebook from my drawer and started to write. I called Dwayne every name in the book, and before I knew it, I had run out of pages to write on. Front and back, the pages were filled with hateful words I was ashamed to let anyone see: *How in the hell did I ever get myself involved with this sorry-ass motherfucker! That bastard had the audacity to leave a gun so I could shoot my damn self. Is that love? How can he love me and treat me like this? Instead of killing myself, I should go kill his ass for messing up my face like this. It hurts so bad and I can barely see out of my eye. Why do I keep doing this to myself? Why? I'm so stupid and Dwayne is only doing this shit because I keep letting him. How do I stop this? I want out of this relationship, but I don't know how to stop this madness. Why am I with somebody that I hate so much? I hate what he's done to me. My life ain't been about shit with him, but it's what I'm creating. I can't blame him for all of this, but I wish that trifling-ass, low-life nigga would leave me alone before I kill him...*

The next day, Mama called and asked me to pick up some items for her at the grocery store, before I picked up the twins. My face had swelled up even more and my nearly shut eye was bloodshot red. I couldn't tell Mama no, but before I went to her house, I stopped at Dierbergs to get her items and picked up a pair of dark sunglasses. I saw Kenneth stocking meat, and he looked at me with disgust, shaking his head. "Looks pretty painful, Brenda."

"It is painful and looks terrible, doesn't it?"

"Very." He continued to put the meat in the freezer, seeming annoyed.

"Is something wrong?" I asked.

He paused and let out a deep sigh. "Damn, Ms. Lady, something is very wrong. You stand there like it ain't no big fucking deal that this nigga did this to you. Is he locked up? Did you call the police on him or try to get a restraining order? No...I know you didn't. You always trying to protect this fool. You need to be trying to protect yourself and your kids from that...that animal. I swear to you, as I stand here looking at your pretty face, I could just kill him!" Kenneth tightened his fist and shook his head from side to side. "If you want to talk, call me later, Brenda. I don't have time to talk right now." He kissed me on the cheek and went back to stocking the freezers.

While in the car, I'd thought about what Kenneth had said. He couldn't be more right, but I was afraid to go to the police. I disliked them and I didn't trust them to do much. I considered myself a big fool and had paid the price many of times for being so. For whatever reason, I felt as if I had to protect Dwayne, and I didn't want him to hate me for having him locked up. I knew that a restraining order would make him even angrier, and for now, I just had to deal with it in my own way.

When I arrived at Mama's house, the twins were outside playing, while Mama was sitting on the porch watching them. I got out of the car and they ran up to give me a hug.

"Tell your grandma y'all will see her next week, and then go get in the car," I said.

The twins did what they were told, and after giving Mama a squeezing hug, they got in the car. I kept my distance, because I didn't want Mama to question me about the sunglasses. "Thanks, Mama," I said. "I need to get going, because a friend of mine asked me to pick her up from work."

"Your friend can wait," Mama said. "Come in the house for a minute. I need to show you something."

Mama opened the screen door to go inside. I sighed and went inside after her. While near the door, she turned around and squinted as she got a closer look at me.

"What happened to your face?" she asked with her hand on her hip.

I shrugged and dropped my head to look down at the floor. "I fell yesterday, when I got out of the car."

Mama stepped forward and lifted my chin. I snatched my head away from her. "What did you have to show me, because I gotta go, Mama. I'll call you later."

I inched towards the door, but she grabbed my arm and squeezed it. "I don't have to remove those sunglasses to see what's behind them, but you listen to me and listen to me good. What you do with your life is your business, but if you ever bring that no-good-ass nigga near me again, I'm gon' dig a six-foot grave for him in my backyard and bury him myself. And if anything!" she shouted. "Anything ever happens to my grandbabies, I'm gon' have a spot for you right next to him! Leave that nigga alone, Brenda, and I hope like hell that his face looks as bad as yours."

I pulled my arm away from Mama, continuing with my lie, as a tear slipped from my eye. I hurried to smack it away. "He didn't—"

"Yes, he did!" Mama screamed. "I'm not a damn fool, girl! Wake your ass up, before it's too late! You get one life and you sure as hell don't need to be spending it with a fool like that! Now, goodbye, Brenda. Go see about my grandkids and call me later."

I swallowed hard and hurried to leave. I was so embarrassed that Mama had seen my face like this, and I knew she was worried about me and the twins. The look in her eyes implied that she meant every word she'd said. I rarely brought Dwayne around her to begin with, and he was never allowed inside of her house. She despised him that much, and she had never forgotten what had gone down at her mother's wake. It was already a sad day that had gone from bad to worse. As I drove home with the twins, I thought about it.

Mama was devastated by the loss of her mother, and as she hovered over her pearly-white casket in tears, Jesse, Rita and I stood full of emotions beside her. Reliable Funeral Home was filled to capacity with friends and family who came to pay their respects.

"Maaamuuuu," Mama cried out in pain. "What in the world am I going to do without my mamuuu?"

Mama was shaking so badly, and as her legs weakened, we helped her back to her seat. As I sat next to her, that's when I heard a loud voice, yelling my name. Nearly everyone turned their heads, and right at the double doors stood Dwayne in a muscle shirt and jeans. His face was twisted and his eyes were narrowed. I suspected he was high. As he charged down the aisle, my uncle, Tea Biscuit, jumped up to stop him.

"Have some respect for the dead, nigga!" Tea Biscuit said. "Whatever problem you have with her, take that shit outside!"

The look in Dwayne's eyes implied that I needed to move quickly, so I did. I knew he was about to go at it with my uncle and I couldn't let that happen. I rushed out of my seat, already knowing what Mama was probably thinking inside. Embarrassed as ever, I made my way up to Dwayne and asked him to follow me outside. He did, and we stood outside of my grandmother's wake, arguing like doggone fools.

"I checked yo damn messages and I heard some nigga askin' if he could stop by. I went by your apartment to make sure his ass wasn't there, and when I kicked in the door, you lucky nobody was there! But who the fuck was he, Brenda?"

I shook my head with disgust. See, it was perfectly fine for Dwayne to see whoever he wanted to, but not me. Yeah, I had been conversing with a few people, but the conversations were limited because I didn't want to involve anyone in me and Dwayne's mess.

"Can we please talk about this later?" I asked, as Mama and three of her brothers came outside. Her hard stare had broken me down, and, yet again, I felt like her lousy-ass daughter who just couldn't get it together.

"Brenda!" Mama yelled. "You and Dwayne got one minute to clear these premises, and if not, all hell is going to break loose!"

I pleaded with Dwayne, as I knew my uncles were ready to take action and cause some damage. So was Mama. Wrong place, wrong time. "Please go," I said to Dwayne. "We can work this out later. I promise you that I haven't been involved with anyone."

My calm voice helped ease the situation, but as I watched Dwayne walk to his car, I couldn't believe that he was driving a vehicle that belonged to his so-called ex-girlfriend. Yes, this was pretty darn bad, and after I apologized to Mama and her brothers, I left my grandmother's wake. Went home, and sure enough, the door had been kicked open. This was one big mess, and I didn't want to keep on disappointing and worrying Mama. I didn't see Dwayne for almost two weeks after that, but like always, we settled our differences when he called Mama and apologized. To no surprise, she hung up.

I wrapped up my thoughts about that day, ready to face another. As soon as I turned the corner, I could see Dwayne sitting in his car outside my apartment. I wanted to turn around and drive away but he had already spotted me. When I got out of my car, I walked right by him and went inside. The twins rushed up to him, and like always, seemed happy to see him. He played with them for a while, and then came into the kitchen where I was.

"Here you go," he said, dangling long-stem red roses in my face. "These are just a little somethin' to let you know how sorry I am for hittin' you. Baby, I don't know what got into me, but you made me so upset with you. I just knew you had been seein' that nigga, but I can't prove it right now. I was wrong and I hope you can forgive me."

His words went in one ear and out the other. I didn't owe him an explanation at all. I took the bouquet of roses from his hand and removed my sunglasses so he could get a good look at what he'd done to me. He lifted his hand, and fearing that he would hit me, again, I jerked my head back.

"I'm not gon' hurt you. All I want to do is touch it," he said, softly touching my face.

I moved his hand away, and thought about Mama's wish of his face looking like mine. I raised my hand and started to beat the shit out of him with the roses and my tightened fist. He crouched down, covering his face as I pounded his head, back and shoulders. The stems where long enough that they made a whipping sound with each strike. It was nothing like what he'd done to me, and by the time I was finished, not one red petal or leaf was left on the stems.

"Alright Brenda...alright! Damn! I know I deserved that but stop, shit!"

"Get out! Please, get the hell out!" I yelled.

Dwayne stared me in the eyes and started to cry. "Sorry, Bree, I just can't do that. You gotta hear me out, just this last time. Please." I stood with my arms folded, having no sympathy for him whatsoever.

He could barely catch his breath as he spoke. "Please don't end this. All I can say is...I didn't mean to hurt you like that, but somethin' inside of me took over. I'll never do anything like that again."

He broke down on me; sat in the chair crouched over while grabbing his stomach. His performance was pretty damn good—the best one I had seen thus far. I put my hands together, and since I'd taken a seat to listen to him, I stood to give him a standing ovation.

"I...I am not your woman anymore, and the way you've been out here cheating, I haven't been your woman for quite some time. We can't continue on like this, Dwayne. One of us is going to get seriously hurt. I don't care if you beat the living daylights out of me to stay with you, I'm not. It's time that we both go our separate ways and maybe you will feel so much better without me."

Dwayne continued to sob and I couldn't believe when he brought out another diamond ring from his pocket. "I can't just let you go like that, Bree. I got years invested in this relationship and so do you. Ain't nothing we haven't been able to get through and we were destined to be together. Why you wanna give up on us now? If I lose you, some other people will have to lose out too. First, I'm gon' start with Jesse's boyfriend Anthony. If you can't find it in your heart to work things out with me, I'm gon' tell Anthony about Jesse's new man." Months ago, my big mouth had told Dwayne about Jesse messing with Ryan. Not in a million years did I think he would use it against me.

"It would be very stupid on your part to do that. Anthony won't believe you anyway," I said.

"Yes he will. He'll definitely believe me when I play this tape for him. I've taped all of your conversations on the phone, and I have a conversation of Jesse talkin' about her new man."

Dwayne was such a liar, but it would be right up his alley to do something so sneaky. You could easily tape a conversation on my phone, so it was very possible. Whatever he decided to do, I stuck with my decision and told him there would be no reconciliation. He left, feeling good about his blackmail, and I was glad to see him go.

The apartment was a mess, so I spent the entire day cleaning up. I called Jesse to warn her about Dwayne's threat, but she told me she wasn't worried about it. She said that she'd already talked to Anthony about chilling out for a while because her job was stressing her. According to her, they were still boyfriend and girlfriend, but weren't spending as much time together as before. Her sugar-daddy was at her place, so she cut our conversation short.

I was worn out from cleaning up all day. And after the twins and I watched a movie, I fell across one of their beds and dozed off. A few hours later, there was a knock at the door. I peeked out the window and saw it was Anthony. I looked for my sunglasses, putting them on so he wouldn't see my black eye. "Hey stranger," I said, opening the door. "What brings you by?"

Anthony had a frown on his face and could barely look at me. "I don't know what's going on, Brenda. I got a visit from your man today."

"From who?" I played clueless.

"From Dwayne. He told me some disturbing news and played a tape of you and Jesse talking."

I pursed my lips. "He did what?"

"During y'all conversation, she said that she was messing around with somebody else."

"Anthony, I don't know what's going on. Dwayne be lying and playing games so I wouldn't trust anything he says."

Anthony paced the living room. "But...Brenda, it was her voice on the tape. She was the one saying that her and this man was spending all kinds of time together and that she didn't have feelings for me like she used to." Anthony sat on the couch in tears. He put his hands over his face, doing his best to contain his emotions. "Why would she do this to me? I love the shit out of your sister. I made her just for me, not for somebody else. This shit hurts," he said touching his chest, very choked up. "Hurts so bad, I could just hurt somebody." I understood exactly what Anthony was going through. It was a bad-ass feeling when somebody you cared about so much was cheating on you. I couldn't offer him any advice or give him an explanation; after all, Jesse was my sister and I would never betray her.

By the time Anthony left, he had me in tears. I called Jesse to tell her about his visit but she really didn't say much. Anthony was a damn good man, and why Jesse let that one slip through her fingers, I would never, ever understand.

Chapter Nineteen

Several weeks had passed and Dwayne and I hadn't talked. My life was so peaceful and I chose to leave things as they were. Shantell was now living with me. She and her four kids had been kicked out of her Section 8 apartment and had no place to go. When I returned from the twins' school one day, she told me that a friend of her cousin wanted to talk to me. I took the phone and the young woman on the other end confirmed that she had been in an on-again, off-again relationship with Dwayne for almost a year.

"He's been living over here with me for a while. I just want to make sure the two of you aren't still seeing each other anymore, and this thing between y'all is really over."

"I assure you, it's a wrap," I said, handing the phone back to Shantell.

I was so done with arguing with females over Dwayne. It seemed like every time I attempted to put our relationship to rest, some bullshit would come up. I guess the chick thought I was going to stay on the phone and argue with her, but that would have been a waste of time. We both knew Dwayne was no good. What sense did it make to argue over a man who just couldn't seem to settle down with one woman?

That night, I lay in my bed listening to the Quiet Storm on the radio. Sam Cooke's, "A Change Is Gonna Come" was playing, and it was reaching deep into my soul. I could feel a change coming and I wanted it so badly. The taste was so, so sweet and I smiled from the thoughts of my life getting better. Luther Vandross, Whitney Houston and Babyface started throwing down on the Quiet Storm and listeners called the radio station with special dedications. Out of the blue, a dedication to Dwayne Montgomery came across the radio. It was a White girl dedicating "Whip Appeal" to him, and according to her, he definitely had it. I dropped my head with disgust. I snatched the plug out of the wall, shaking my head because the devil was certainly busy. So busy, that the next day Shantell came into my apartment from a party with my grade-school crush, Darrell. Darrell was the one I'd written about as being my future husband, but after he screwed Shantell in my bedroom, so much for that. I started to reevaluate some of the people I called friends, and two days later, Shantell moved out.

I opened the mail and found brochures my caseworker had sent for the Future's Program. She had sent me some literature in the past, but I had thrown it away. I called the number inside one of the booklets, and after making my appointment, I was scheduled for testing in two weeks.

When that day came, the room was filled with a bunch of women who were trying to get their lives in order, just like I was. We sat around a huge square table, listening to the instructor as she prepared us for a test. I was never a good test-taker, so I found myself getting stuck on questions I knew I should have known. The instructor paced the room, making me more nervous; I felt like she was watching my every move. Finally, the time clock went off and the test was over. I turned mine in, feeling like a complete idiot. She told us the test would not affect us, but knowing I did badly didn't make me feel good. According to her, the test was supposed to let them know our strengths and our weaknesses.

She advised the class that she would be in touch within the next couple of weeks to give us our training schedule. The classes were designed to show us how to prepare a resume, how to dress appropriately for an interview, how to type, how to use a computer, and to prepare us for what she called, "Corporate America."

I left feeling somewhat confused about the program. It seemed like something that would take forever to complete and would also take up a lot of my time. Most of the jobs they mentioned paid minimum wage. You had to be really lucky to get one that paid higher than that. *Hell,* I thought, *I could sell some clothes and make hundreds...thousands, rather than bust my ass at a nine-to-five job making minimum wage.* To me, it really didn't make much sense to enroll in such a program, but I was willing to give it a try.

Later, I stopped at the twins' school, Marvin Elementary, because I was scheduled for parent-teacher conference. I sat outside one of the twins' classroom, until the teacher was ready to see me. "Miss Hampton, come right in and have a seat," she said with a big smile.

I sat in the chair waiting to hear how good or bad the first twin was doing. "Thank you for coming," the teacher said. "I just wanted to tell you, personally, that you have a wonderful daughter. She is my best student and I want to thank you for making my job a lot easier. I have no problems out of her and she plays so well with the other students. Now, here is her report card, and I must tell you, there is no room for improvement. It doesn't get any better than this."

I smiled, while looking down at the report card. It was excellent and the teacher had not one complaint. Then she showed me drawings my daughter had done in class, and for a first grader, I was stunned. *Now, why hadn't I noticed this before?* I thought. I had gotten the twins' report cards before, but barely paid much attention to them. I had seen drawings in their bedroom, but could count on one hand how many times I'd picked them up to even look at them. These teachers knew more about my children than I did.

The teacher interrupted my thoughts. "Miss Hampton, from speaking with your other daughter's teacher, you will get the same result. Your children are exceptionally good with art, and if you'd allow them to explore a bit more at home, you never know what their gifts can lead to. Also, I would like to get your permission to challenge her more. She is way above average and I don't want her to get bored."

"Sure, that would be fine with me, Ms. Jeffries. I'd like to see her being challenged as well. You're right," I said, not knowing what else to say.

"Well, I won't keep you any longer. I'm sure you have to get back to work. In the meantime, pat yourself on the back for raising such beautiful, well-mannered children. We don't have these results all the time, and we're always pleased when we do."

"Thank you," I said. I shook her hand and went to the other twins' classroom. Different teacher, but same story. I was happy with the news, but deep inside, I could in no way take credit.

When I got home, I sat at the kitchen table, looking through folders the teachers had given me with all of the twins' work. They had mostly all A's on their assignments and their art work was beautiful. How did they do so well on their assignments? I hadn't taught them anything, except nothing but how to let a man disrespect you and shoplift. They had been in the dressing rooms with me plenty of times, watching as I stuffed clothes into my purse.

"What you doing, Mama," they would ask. "Why you putting that stuff in your purse?"

"I'm going to buy it later. I need to take it home first, just to make sure it fits."

As smart as they were, I'm sure they didn't believe me. And as I dressed them in the finest brand-name clothes there were, materialistic bullshit is not what they needed. They needed me to be there for them. They needed a mother who gave all of her time to them, instead of to her relationships. I felt awful, but it was good to know my stupidity was not affecting them at school. I was so glad they were in a decent school, where the teachers gave a care about the students. Little did the teachers know, though, I wasn't much help at home.

I closed my eyes, knowing right then and there that the Future's Program was just the beginning for me. I didn't care if it took me years to complete it, I would hang in there to get a job. Besides, I was tired of sitting around my apartment all day, being down because somebody had pissed me off. My attitude reflected on my kids. When I cried, they cried. When I laughed, they laughed. When I smiled, they smiled. Being on welfare was not the answer to having a fulfilling life. I was fooling myself if I thought it was. *One day at a time,* I thought. *I could only get through this one day at a time.*

When the twins got home from school, I cooked us a delicious dinner. They loved lasagna with garlic cheese bread, so I whipped it up and set the table. They didn't know what the big fuss was about, but as long as I knew, that's all that mattered. I rented a movie and we stayed up late watching it. As they watched TV, I started writing down steps I needed to take in order to make my world a better place. I started with myself, then my children, and last my relationships. My relationships are what I struggled with; it was important to have a positive person in my life, if I was going to have one at all. He had to be someone who respected me and my children, one who had a job, and one who wasn't afraid of preparing for the future. *Me first, though,* I wrote. In order to find someone with those qualifications, I had to correct myself. I couldn't demand something from someone else, that I didn't have myself. So, definitely, me first.

***

My training schedule had finally come in the mail. All I had to do was sign the registration form, mail it back in, and call the office to confirm. Believe it or not, I hesitated, but deep down I knew it was now or never. I completed the paperwork and called the office to confirm. The lady on the phone told me to bring two black pens, a number two pencil, and a notebook.

"We'll supply the rest and don't forget to mail the form back in. I must have that before you start or else you will not be able to."

I held the form in my hand. It already had a stamp on it. "I'll mail it off today. Thanks and I'm looking forward to starting."

"That's good. Have a nice day and good luck with the program."

After I hung up the phone, I laid the form on the table so I could mail it off later. I was starting to feel really good about signing up for the training class. So good, I wanted to make sure I was nicely dressed for the occasion. I drove to the mall to get some clothes and found some laid out things to wear: multi-colored silk blouses and a couple pairs of linen pants made by Ralph Lauren for a hundred and eighty dollars apiece. On my way out, I swiped up three polo shirts for casual days on Friday.

When I got back to my apartment complex, a chick that lived close by approached me as I got out the car.

"You got any cigarettes for sale?" she asked.

I stole cartons of cigarettes from the Shop-n-Save down the street, but didn't have any on me. "No, I don't have any, but I can get some."

"No matter how many you get, I'll pay you for them. Just knock on my door when you get back."

I told her I would, and since I was low on money, I planned to get about ten cartoons. I drove to the grocery store, stuffing cartons of cigarettes everywhere I could. You could see one of the cartons sticking out of my jacket, and as I tried to secure it, the carton slipped out and fell to the floor. I was right at the door, when the white-haired manager with a thick mustache came up from behind to stop me. His wrinkled face was scrunched even more, and when he grabbed my arm, squeezing it, I snatched away.

"You don't have to pull on me like that," I snapped.

"I'll do what I want to do, now, move it," he said, walking closely behind me as we went into his office. At least I was offered a seat.

He folded his arms, while leaning against the wall. "We've been watching you every time you come in here. The last time you were in here, I almost caught you, but when I went out to the parking lot, you were gone. I don't understand why *you peopl*e just don't get a job and stop expecting society to take care of you. It's ridiculous and you're one of the reasons why we have to drive up our prices to stay in business."

Save the drama for yo mama, I thought. At times, I was still a bit thick headed, especially when people's choices of words didn't sit right with me. "Sir, why don't you go ahead and do what you gotta do so I can get out of here," I said. "And by the way, *we people* aren't the only ones who steal. Maybe you need to visit the courthouse in Clayton. It be full of honkies who steal, so get it right."

"You're a smart nigger with a smart mouth? Let's see how smart you're going to be when the police get here. If I can help it, you won't be going home any time soon." He called the police, smiling when he knew they were on the way.

I was a little scared, thinking about what the police were going to do to me, but I didn't let it show. What if the manager was serious about trying to put me away? The twins had to be picked up from school in an hour and my car outside was full of merchandise from the mall. If they looked in there, I was going down.

I could hear the officer's loud walkie-talkie heading my way. He walked into the room with the manager, asking me to stand up. "Do you have any weapons on you," he asked, patting me down.

"No," I said. The grumpy old-ass manager was still standing there with his arms folded, displaying a mean mug. The officer took my purse and started going through it to make sure I didn't have any weapons in it. It was pretty much empty because I cleared it out, just in case I needed to put some cigarettes inside.

"Is this your ID, Ms. Hampton?" The officer asked.

"Yes."

"Have you ever been arrested before for shoplifting?"

"No." I hadn't been arrested, but had been summons to court three times before for shoplifting. I had even been to shoplifting classes that were supposed to help with my so-called addiction.

The officer and the manager left the room. *Whew*, I thought. *Maybe he wasn't going to arrest me.* If he were, he would have done it by now. I sat in the office for about ten more minutes, before they returned. "I knew she was a damn liar," the manager said, entering the room. "That girl's been in here at least twice a week stealing from our store. You'd better arrest her and I mean now!"

The officer reached for his handcuffs. "Stand up and put your hands behind your back."

"Stand up for what?" I shouted.

"What do you mean for what? I'm arresting you for shoplifting." He pulled my arms behind my back.

"You gotta be so rough," I hissed and frowned. "I can do this on my own." Without resisting, I let the officer put cuffs on me, while the manager stood with a wide grin.

"You...you get a kick out of this, don't you?" I said, turning my head to the side and looking at the officer. "He's been in here disrespecting me and you haven't said one word."

"And you've been disrespecting him by coming into this store stealing. He's exercising his rights to the first amendment of the constitution. If he wants to call you a lying thieving nigger, he can do so."

I shrugged and snatched my cuffed hands away from the officer. "Well, okay, you stupid, dumb red-neck mutha—both of you can kiss this nigger's ass."

The officer got in my face. "Close your freaking mouth or I will charge you with disorderly conduct and resisting arrest. One more word and I will do it."

I guess those first amendment rights didn't apply to me, so I tightened my lip. After all, I already had a resisting arrest charge on my police record from when I'd gotten into a dispute with a police officer who was harassing me while I was parked in front of my apartment. He wondered what I was doing sitting in the car, alone, and I told him none of his damn business. One thing led to another, and when all was said and done, I was handcuffed and thrown into the back of the police car. Called a fat bitch, too—all for just minding my own business. The police in my jurisdiction were known for tripping with Blacks, and they often came into the complex where I lived, causing trouble. In this case, I knew I was wrong, but they didn't have to talk to me like I was a piece of dirt.

As the officer escorted me through the store, all eyes were on me. Again, I felt humiliated. Noticing one of the teachers at the twins' school, I dropped my head, turning it in another direction. I hoped like hell that she didn't recognize me.

While at the police station, the officer rubbed my fingers in black ink, taking my fingerprints. He made me stand up so he could take my mug-shot. As the bright light flashed, my whole future flashed before me. The plan was to get my life together, not to be in a police station getting booked for shoplifting. "Young lady, you're headed down the wrong path," the officer warned. "I probably wouldn't have arrested you, if you didn't already have any prior convictions. Seems like you've made this shoplifting thing a career for yourself."

I cut my eyes at him. "It ain't even like that. I only shoplift to pay the bills. I'm just trying to survive."

"Survival is very important, but you can't survive by shoplifting. The only thing it gets you is a huge fine, a bad police record or possibly imprisonment. Get a job like most of us have to do. I'm not telling you this because I don't like you; I'm telling you this for your own good. If you don't give it up, you might find yourself some place you don't want to be."

The officer handed me a summons to appear in court in six weeks. I thought hard about what he'd said, and even though I didn't like his attitude, he made sense. This had to be the last time I took something that I hadn't paid for. How many warnings would I get, before they decided to keep me behind bars?

Once he released me, I walked back to the grocery stores parking lot and got in my car. It was late, and when I got home there was a note on the door from Charlene, letting me know the kids were at her place. I picked them up and explained to her what had happened.

"I figured it was something, because no matter what, you always be on time picking up your kids. They already ate, and they've been playing in the room with my kids."

The twins were hugging me around my waist. "Did y'all already do your homework?" I asked.

They nodded, and we made our way home. As soon as I got inside, I reached for the registration form and walked to the mailbox to drop it in the mail. After what had happened to me today, putting this off wasn't going to do me any good.

Chapter Twenty

The first day in training class was pretty cool. There were about thirty females in the class, all trying to get some skills. The instructors were some of the most classy, educated Black women I had ever seen. They were very professional and had already made a great influence on me. I wore a dark blue and black paisley printed blouse and my Jones of New York wide-leg black cuffed pants. My hair had grown out again, so it was back to my sleek shiny ponytail with curly tresses of hair dangling down the sides of my face. Earlier, I was paid compliments by the instructors, and compliments always made me feel good.

As the day went on, the class was given a typing test. I'd taken a typing class at Hazelwood East, but all I did was peck at the keys. I wasn't sure how many words I could type a minute, but once the typing test was over, we were shown how to operate a computer. I didn't even know how to turn the thing on, but I didn't feel bad because most of the other students didn't either.

"Anyone in here familiar with WordPerfect?" the instructor asked. Not one person raised their hand. "Well, that's why you're here. You need to know how to use a computer, as well as the programs that go along with it. What about Lotus?"

Everybody shook their heads, implying no. "Then, let's get started," the other instructor said. "This is all about obtaining skills to ready you ladies for the workforce. Find a computer and take a seat in front of it."

Everyone sat in front of a computer that looked so foreign to me. But by the end of the day, I had learned what WordPerfect was and a little bit more about the computer. And after nearly a month in training class, my typing and computer skills had tremendously improved. I stayed after class, many nights, trying to perfect my skills. Sometimes, I would be the only one left in the room, but I was determined to get this stuff down packed. I asked Charlene if she wouldn't mind watching the twins for me on certain nights, and she said she didn't mind as long as I gave her an advance notice.

With the twins having a sitter, I stuck with the class for another month. The instructors insisted that I had what it took to complete the program, and they always used me as an example when talking to the class.

"Brenda Hampton is doing a great job," the instructor Jeanette said. "If you don't understand what you're doing, and you don't feel comfortable talking to us, ask her. She's very helpful and has caught on quite well."

I smiled. Many of the others had already reached out to me for help. I didn't mind not one bit, because I wanted all of us to make it through the program and succeed. I did, however, feel as though the instructors, Jeanette and Melinda, had put me on a pedestal. I didn't want to let them down. I felt like I had a long way to go, and there was no telling what was going to happen before then. I had become content being on welfare, and I couldn't quite get the concept of paying more than ten bucks a month for rent. I knew I had to change my thought process, but there was no denying that it was much easier staying at home collecting a government check. Still, no matter how much I doubted myself, Jeanette and Melinda weren't giving up on me. They told me that as long as I finished the program, they would help me find a decent job to support my family.

With six more months to go in the program, our class was down to fourteen women, and was fading more day by day. I was there to do one thing and one thing only—get a Business Office Technology certificate that was required by many companies who were hiring for secretarial positions. Some of the women had started to cause confusion and I backed away from it. I had gotten to a point where I wasn't trying to make any new friends and didn't care if I was being talked about or not; kind of kept to myself every day. A lot of the women gossiped and shared their personal business with one another. I didn't want anybody to know anything about me. All they knew was I was a sharp dresser with a lot of determination.

My family and the pressure of trying not to let myself or Jeanette and Melinda down is what kept me going. The janitor would come in and tease me about staying so late, basically said that I needed to "get a life." I couldn't have agreed with him more, and I intended to get the life that my girls and I truly deserved. A few months ago, I didn't even know how to start a computer. Now, I was learning how to type professional letters in WordPerfect and use Lotus. I could send and receive e-mails, and was up to typing 45 wpm. My fingers were moving faster and faster on a 10-Key calculator, and my English was getting much better, because we had vocabulary words to learn each week.

After leaving school one night, I sat in my car, listening to some relaxing music. They were playing some of Dwayne's and my favorite slow songs and the thought of him crossed my mind. I hadn't heard from him in a long time. I didn't have any regrets, and being away from him actually made me get off my butt and do something with myself. Going to class sure as hell beat sitting around the apartment all day looking at soap operas, arguing and waiting for him to call.

When I arrived home, I plopped down on the couch, exhausted from my long day in class. I went over the twins' homework with them and could barely keep my eyes open. They were still doing well in school and going over their work with them became my number one priority. After they had gone to bed, I noticed the message light blinking on the answering machine. I checked the messages, and as soon as I heard Dwayne's voice, I deleted it. I shut it down for the night, feeling good about my decision.

***

Jesse came over on the weekend to keep me company. When Charlene and Dedra saw her green Pontiac Firebird outside, they also came over. Jesse was telling us the juicy details about her and Anthony's break-up.

"It's over," she said. "I miss him, though, but everything worked out for the best."

I disagreed. Kept my mouth shut, because I wasn't the one to chime in on other people's relationships. Dedra complained about the phone bill her jailbird boyfriend was running up.

"That sucker up to seven-hundred dollars. I do not have the money to pay for it, but I'll somehow get it."

"If you are lucky enough to get it," Charlene said. "You need to tell that Negro to stop calling so much. It ain't that much talking in the world, and what in the hell can he do for you while locked up in jail?"

Again, I agreed, but kept my mouth shut. Dedra went off on Charlene. "Don't worry about what I be doing, especially with all those dudes you be having running in and out of your apartment. You giving up the goodies for free. At least I get paid by the dudes who visit me."

"That's what yo mouth say. If they paying you, then your phone won't be off next week, right?"

"You can bet it won't be, and as long as I look this good," Dedra said, putting her hands on her hips and sashaying across the room. "I don't ever have to worry about no money."

We were having so much fun talking that we decided to put on some clothes and take our energy to a nightclub. Jesse came up with a bet to see who could get the most phone numbers in one night. Charlene stepped it up a bit and said, "Let's bet on who can have the most sex in one week. One hundred dollars to the winner," she laughed. I wasn't sure about all that, so we booted out Charlene's trifling idea, but the phone number's bet stayed intact.

The outfit I was about to put on—black and see-through like a fishnet from neck to toe—was going to give me all the numbers I needed. I had even shed a few pounds and was feeling better. Of course, everyone disagreed with me getting the most numbers, especially Charlene who had the biggest booty and was confident that she'd win. Then there was Dedra who could easily pass for me and Jesse's sister, but believed her fit body was enough to give her all the numbers she needed. I sent them home to get changed, putting them up for the challenge I'd surely win.

I ran around searching for my eyeliner and black leather pumps. I was already running late when the phone started ringing off the hook. "Hello," I said, barely able to hear who was on the other end.

"Brenda, it's Myron. Can you hear me?" Dwayne's brother asked.

"Yeah, Myron, I can hear you. What's up?"

"If possible, I need to see you. I know it's getting late, but I don't want to waste anymore time." He sounded anxious.

"Is everything okay?"

"Naw, not really. That's why I need to see you."

I was on edge, fearing for the worst. "Did something happen to Dwayne?"

"Naw, he ain't dead or nothing, if that's what you're asking me, but he is in the hospital. I don't want to get into details over the phone, so will you come over?"

"I was on my way out, but I'll stop by on the way to my destination. Will it take long?"

"Nah, it shouldn't take long. Less than thirty minutes."

"Give me a few and I'll be on my way."

"Thanks, Bree. You know I appreciate it."

Damn, I thought. *What is going on now?* I was all dressed up to go kick it and everyone would kill me if I backed out on them now, especially Jesse. I knew she was looking forward to us hanging out and so was I.

I quickly changed clothes and called to tell her I would meet them at the club, after I left Dwayne's house. She wasn't too thrilled, but she knew that for some reason, when it came to him, I just couldn't turn my back.

When I got to his parents' house, his mother answered the door, looking as if she wasn't too happy to see me. "How are you doing, Mrs. Montgomery?" I asked.

"I'm doing fine," she said with a half smile, and then called for Myron to come downstairs.

"Bree...Bree, thanks for coming on such short notice," he said. "Come on back to the den so we can talk." We passed through the kitchen where Mrs. Montgomery was frying some chicken. From the corner of her eye, she looked at me like something deep was on her mind. Myron and I had a seat in the den. "I didn't mean to scare you, but I thought you were the only person who could help when it concerns Dwayne. Last night, he tried to commit suicide. He was in his room all evening with the door closed, and when my mom went to check on him, she found him layin' there unconscious with an empty bottle of pills next to him. When the ambulance came, they pumped his chest and revived him. This morning, the hospital called and said they wanted to have him evaluated. I know my brother ain't crazy. He just needs to stay off that shit and get his life back together."

I was stunned. My mouth hung open and my emotions started to run over. "Myron, I don't know what you think I can do for him. He hates me. From what I heard, he already got several women taking care of him. What makes you think I can stop him from doing drugs?"

"Because, I know my brother. He was happy when he was with you and the twins. That's all he ever talked about. The only thing that messed him up was running here to the city to hang out with his boys. He talked about positive shit when he was with you. He needs to be in that environment again."

I shook my head from side to side. "Maybe you don't understand. Our relationship wasn't all that and we had some very tough times together. Two lost individuals can't make things happen, Myron, and for years, I've been a burden on him and he's been one on me. Our years together have amounted to nothing. We were no good for each other and Dwayne knows that. I think we need to leave things as they are, and me going to see him will not change a thing."

Myron sighed; the look on his face was pitiful. "Before you say no, read this." He handed a letter and picture to me. "I know all about y'all problems because he shared some of it with me. But believe it or not, he truly loves you. When the paramedic opened his shirt to pump his chest, this letter was under his t-shirt, along with this picture." It was a picture of him, the twins, and me. Jesse had taken it two days after I moved into my apartment and we were all smiles. We looked so happy together, and, yes, there were times that we got along just fine. I held the letter in my hand, refusing to read it. Myron touched my hand and told me that the letter expressed his love for me, the twins and for his mother. Tears began to roll down my face. I could barely look at Myron after telling him there was nothing I could do for Dwayne.

"Brenda, would you go see him and talk some sense into him? I'm sure he would love to see you and I know he will feel better once he does."

I nodded, and once Myron told me which hospital Dwayne was at, I left.

My throat ached as I drove; I felt like someone had taken a dagger and driven it straight through my heart. Maybe I did let Dwayne down. He had been there for the twins, and when I was going through with Mama, he was there for me. This was a sickness he had and, many times, he had called out for help. Thing is, I didn't know how to help him. Nothing I did could help him stay off drugs, and I wished that he would just leave that mess alone.

The hospital was cold and I hated the smell of cheap disinfectant. I asked the nurse if she could direct me to Dwayne Montgomery's room and she gave me the room number. I quietly opened the door and entered the room. There was much of nothing in the room, but four white walls and a bed that sat in the middle of the floor. Dwayne was laying on it, and as I moved closer, I could see he had been strapped to it. His eyes were closed and I could see dried blood on his nose and mouth. My heart went out to him, as he laid there helpless. I actually thought he was dead until he moved his leg. "Dwayne," I whispered. "Can you hear me?" No response. I ran my fingers through his natural curled hair and reminisced for a minute about the day we met. Dwayne was so different then. He had been nice to me, and would do anything in the world for the twins. I gravitated to him in a flash, hoping and praying that he would be the one. Then, the drugs came: weed, PCP, crack cocaine...they took over and Dwayne had not been the same since. "I...I'm so sorry that you're going through this. I want to help you, but you gotta help yourself too. Okay?"

There was no response. I couldn't bear to hang around and see him like that any longer. I bent down, kissing his forehead. As I started to walk out the door, I heard his voice.

"Thanks for comin' to see me." I turned around and walked back over to him. His dull yellow eyes were open and a slow tear rolled from the corner of his eye. "You can go. I don't want you to see me like this. I'll call you when I get home. I promise."

"But...but I—"

"Brenda, please," he said, as his tears picked up speed.

I swallowed hard, leaving him at peace. On the way out, the doctor asked me to step in the waiting area for a minute so we could talk. He knew exactly who I was, and said Dwayne talked about me earlier during his evaluation.

"So, the two of you have twin daughters?" the doctor asked. I nodded, knowing that Dwayne had always claimed the twins as his own. "He really loves his daughters, but I understand that the two of you have had a tumultuous relationship."

I didn't know the meaning of the word tumultuous, but would surely look it up later in the dictionary because that was something I had started to do. I assumed he meant we had a relationship from hell, and at times, yes, definitely it was. Therefore, I nodded.

"I just want you to know that after my evaluation, I determined that Dwayne is not suicidal. It appeared to be an attempt to get attention, and that attempt went horribly wrong. He assured me after all the pain and suffering he had been through, he wouldn't attempt it again. I shared my observation with his mother, and I advised her to keep an eye on him."

"Thank you," I said. "I know you didn't have to tell me all of this, but I appreciate it."

I shook the doctor's hand and left. I was in no mood to meet Jesse and my friends at the nightclub, and I figured they would be upset with me for not showing up. Partying was the last thing on my mind, and I was sure Jesse would get enough phone numbers for the both of us.

Chapter Twenty-One

I'd missed the next three days of school. My instructors called me every day, leaving messages on my phone, and trying to find out why I wasn't coming to class. My concerns for Dwayne was one of the reasons why, and after pleading not guilty for the shoplifting incident, and rescheduling my court date for months, finally, the judge hit me with a $750 fine. He also banned me from ever going to Shop-n-Save again and I felt like shit.

Dwayne hadn't reached out to me, but Myron said he was coming home from the hospital that day and I was anxious to talk to him. I left the line clear until seven o'clock, but still didn't hear from him.

I returned to class only to find my instructors livid with me for missing three days. I told them about the situation with Dwayne and they read me my rights.

"You are so vulnerable, Brenda," Melinda said. "If you allow a man to hold you back he will. You act as if you need a man to validate you and that is not the case. Girl, you got it, and I know a woman with potential when I see one. Don't let anyone manipulate you and play on your intelligence. Promise us, right now, that you will not miss anymore days of school and your issues with men will be kicked to the curb."

I didn't know why I was so lucky to have these women in my life, and what they said to me made a whole lot of sense. I promised them that I wouldn't miss anymore days and I intended to keep that promise.

I had to play catch-up at school and asked Charlene to pick up the kids for me. It was almost seven o'clock by the time I left school, and I was about to fall asleep in the car. When I pulled up at home, I noticed lights on in my apartment. I heard voices inside and could smell something cooking. I opened the door, making my way to the kitchen.

"What's up? I picked up the kids from Charlene's and wanted to cook y'all dinner," Dwayne said, smiling. I didn't know how to respond. He was cleaned up with his blue-jean bibs on and Tommy Hilfiger red shirt underneath. His beard had been trimmed and his hair had major shine to it. The good-looking Dwayne I knew was back.

"How did you get in?" I finally asked.

"You know there's at least fifty ways to get in here. Anyway, don't worry about that right now. Can a brotha get a hug?"

I walked over, giving him a hug. "It's good to see you back on your feet," I said.

"It's good bein' back on them. I feel a whole lot better. Anyway, stop talkin' about me. Why don't you take a load off while I finish cookin' y'all dinner? The twins' been tryin' to help, but they keep messin' up my masterpiece."

"Oh really? I doubt that because my babies can cook. They be in here whippin' up all kinds of stuff. And sometimes, I might say, the food taste better than yours."

We all laughed.

Dwayne set the table, as we sat waiting to eat. "So, what's this I hear about you goin' to school?" he asked.

"Yeah, I'm taking a class that's teaching me how to type, prepare for job interviews and use computers. Once I'm finished, the instructors are going to help me find a good job. I can't wait."

"That's what's up, Bree. How much longer you gotta go before they do that?"

"I only got a few more months to go."

"Good for you, baby. I need to work on doin' somethin' for myself, too. Later tonight, I wanna get at you about some ideas that crossed my mind."

I nodded.

The twins and I got down on the meatloaf, mashed potatoes, and string beans Dwayne cooked. I hadn't cooked a good meal like that in awhile, so the twins really appreciated it. They seemed delighted that Dwayne was back and spent most of the evening filling him in on what he'd missed.

Once I finished cleaning the kitchen, I went over the twins' homework with them and sent them to bed so Dwayne and I could talk.

"Bree, before I tell you what ideas I have for us, I wanted to congratulate you on the change I see in you. You seem more in control of yourself and I can't help but notice how much more involved with the twins you are. If goin' to school is what's changin' you then, go on, girl, do yo thang."

I smiled and Dwayne continued.

"I'm tryin' to find that confidence in myself. And the only way I can do it is with you. I admit to doin' you wrong and every time I think about it, it kills me. Give me another chance. I'll find a job and go back to school, too. I'll do whatever you want me to do. After I took those pills, I had a chance to think about what I've done. All I could think about was you and the twins. I don't want to live another day without y'all. Please, baby, just give me one more chance."

Dwayne reached in his pocket, placing another diamond ring on the table. I was up to four rings now, and at this point, rings or flowers meant nothing to me. Giving them to me was truly a waste of money, because love and affection had to come from the heart. Deep down, I knew there was something inside of Dwayne that cared for me, but was it enough for him to get his act together? Was he capable of letting go of the drugs? Everybody I knew would kill me if I got back with him, especially Mama. She would never approve of this, and some of my friends were so sick of the drama that they stopped coming around and calling. Many had witnessed what we'd been through and they'd think I was out of my mind for even considering reconciliation. But I was determined to prove to everybody that this could work, and I rarely listened to the recommendations of others. Besides, we had six long years invested in our relationship, and it seemed like nothing could keep us apart. I'd set him free and he came back, right? So, didn't that mean he'd be mine forever? Maybe I could forgive him for the past...I hadn't been no Saint either. He said he would do whatever *I* wanted him to do, and if he got a job, went to rehab...why not give him another chance? I struggled with my decision, and tried to justify everything that had happened. But it wasn't long before I regretted taking him back.

***

I reconciled not for love, nor because I couldn't depart with Dwayne's dick, as some people had thought. They were on the outside looking in, and had no idea that I felt deeply sorry for Dwayne and had hope that after so many years together, things would eventually turn around. Little did I know, I should have felt sorry for myself. Ever since he'd hit me that day, the high pitch of his voice made me nervous. I was living in fear. Fear that he'd do something to me, or fear that he'd do something to himself. Fear that he'd leave forever, and the twins would never again see the man they had grown to know as their father. I did my best to keep the peace, but I didn't realize that this thing with Dwayne was so much bigger than me. His issues required more than love from a girlfriend who truly didn't know what love meant. No matter what I did to help him, I would learn that it would never be enough to get him on the right track.

He had found a job at a factory making ten dollars an hour and I was in my last few weeks of training class. I'd been sent on two interviews and neither one went my way. I failed the typing test on one of them because the supervisor made me take the test on an ancient typewriter that looked liked it hadn't been used in years. And the other one said they were looking for someone with a little more experience. I was feeling a bit down, but my instructors convinced me when the right opportunity came along, I would get it.

On my last day, the school held a ceremony for me and the twelve other women who stuck in there and did what they had to do to get their certificate. I was so proud of myself, and was tearful when they presented me with it, thinking this day would never come. Like my graduation, no one was there to share this moment with me, but it didn't bother me one bit. I wasn't going to let anyone steal my joy, and I was starting to feel better about my future. I didn't have a job yet, but just by having some skills, I knew a decent job was well within my reach.

As I packed up my belongings, Jeanette and Melinda asked me to come into their office so we could talk about where I needed to go from there.

"You did remarkably well in this program, Brenda," Jeanette said. "We would like for you to share your experience with other young ladies, so that they'll be excited about joining the program."

"I would love to," I said. "Just let me know when and where, and I'll be there."

"There's a catch. You'll have to do it on TV. A talk-show host is going to interview you about the program, allowing you to answer questions. We'll help you prepare for it and I'm positive that you'll do well."

Geesh, these ladies had a lot of faith in me, and yet again, I could not let them down. I agreed to do it and we all were pretty ecstatic about it.

When I got home, I couldn't wait to tell everybody the news. Not only did I have my certificate, I was going to be on TV! My family was happy for me and my aunt Florence said she would tape it. My girlfriends were trying to figure out what they had to do to join the program, but when I told Dwayne, he was negative about it.

"I hope you don't embarrass yourself on national TV, telling people you're on welfare. Not only that, but what if the kids' teachers or classmates see it? I bet they'll make fun of the twins."

My joy quickly turned to doubt. I knew how cruel some kids could be. Did I really want to put my business out there like that? Realizing I didn't, I called Melinda that night to renege on the offer.

"Brenda, no you aren't going to do this to me," she said, sounding very disappointed. "I already called the talk-show host at the station and told her you would do it. If you don't wish to talk about being on welfare, then don't mention it. Our purpose is not to degrade you; it's to give you the opportunity to share your experience with other single young mothers in your situation and give them hope. Brenda, you're an inspiration. All we want you to do is talk about what you learned and what efforts you put forth to make it to this point. Please don't back out on me," she pleaded.

An inspiration, I thought. Could I really, indeed, inspire others? "Alright, I won't back out. I'll meet you downtown next week at nine o'clock sharp."

"Thanks, sweetie. And by the way, I know it wasn't you calling me. It was your boyfriend. This is a prime example of what I meant when I said he manipulates you. Just a little advice from a sista who has been there before. He doesn't want you to succeed. He is intimidated by you and will bring you down as long as you keep him. You're in a pursuit for happiness and let no one weigh you down."

She'd hit it right on the money and that's exactly what I was doing. The weight was heavy, and I just needed to stop it from keeping me down. "Yeah, you're right," I said, trying to talk as Dwayne was sitting right next to me, listening to my every word. "Thanks for the advice. I'll see you next week."

When I hung up the phone, Dwayne couldn't wait to ask, "So, what did you tell her?"

"I told her I would see her next week to do the program. She said I didn't have to mention being on welfare if I didn't want to. Said my only purpose would be to inspire other women to join the program."

"Well, it sounds like a stupid idea to me. Why can't *they* talk to people about the program? Why *they* gotta use you and they ain't payin' you jack."

"Dwayne, I'm not afraid to share this experience with anyone. If I can convince other women to do the same, then I will. So be it."

He threw his hands up and went into the kitchen. I followed, continuing to talk. "You know, I wish you would support me just a little bit. You supported me when I was out there shoplifting, so why can't you support me now?" He didn't say a word; continued making his sandwich as if he didn't hear me.

Over the next few days, I wrote down what I was going to say in my notebook: *The JPC Futures Program is the best thing that ever happened to me. With the help of my instructors, I learned how to type, use a computer and how to prepare myself for Corporate America. If I can do it, you can do it too!...*

I practiced day in and out, and each time I rehearsed, I thought I sounded like a fool. I called Melinda, telling her I was getting cold feet.

"Just speak from your heart," she said. "You'll have no problem doing so."

I thanked her and hung up. Now, how in the heck was my heart going to speak for me? I wasn't sure.

I stood in front of my closet, trying to find something to wear. I must have tried on twenty different outfits, until I came across a brown pin-striped suit I swooped up from the mall a while back. It still had tags on it and when I tried it on, it was perfect. I put on a cream blouse underneath it and accessorized the outfit with gold costume jewelry. I looked like a million bucks and was ready—ready to show the world the new and improved Brenda Hampton.

The day before the TV program aired, I called everyone to remind them to watch it. Mama said she had told all of her friends to watch, and the twins had even gone to school and bragged to their teachers and classmates about their mother being on TV. I got letters from their teachers congratulating me and wishing me well.

Dwayne came in from work that evening, looking tired and with a serious attitude. He didn't even speak, just walked right into the bathroom and took a shower. The twins and I were in the kitchen putting icing on a chocolate cake I'd baked earlier. We had chocolate everywhere and when one of them splattered icing on my face, it was on. We started tossing icing all over the place. Of course, I won the fight, but when I realized I had to be the one to clean up the mess, they laughed.

Dwayne came out of the bathroom with a white towel wrapped around his waist. "Hey, have you seen my razor?" he said, interrupting our chocolate fight.

I licked chocolate off the spatula. "No, I haven't, but can a sista get a hello or something?" He just glared at me, cut his eyes, and then went into the bedroom.

After I cleaned up the mess in the kitchen, I went into the bedroom to see what was troubling Dwayne. I was having a pretty good day, but of course, that wouldn't last for long.

"Are you alright?" I asked. "Seems like you got something on your mind."

"Every time I look for somethin' around this damn apartment, I can't find it. You need to put shit back where it belongs and clean this junky muthafucka up!"

I ignored the part about the apartment being junky—it was. "I haven't seen your razor, and if anybody misplaced it, it was you. Besides, you had an attitude before you couldn't find your razor, so what's up?"

He threw his hand back and started to get dressed. "Nothin' Bree. Ain't nothin' wrong. Gon' in the kitchen and finish cleanin'."

"I will, but I'd really like to find out what's bugging you first. You know, this is why our relationship was messed up before. We didn't communicate with one another. Whenever something is on your mind, I want to know about it. Maybe I can help, maybe I can't. I'd still like to know."

Dwayne sat on the bed, sliding on his black steel-toe boots. "You know damn well what's on my mind. Don't stand there and pretend you don't know I'm upset with you about goin' on TV tomorrow. Every time I try to tell you somethin', you don't listen. You call up all your girlfriends and listen to their advice, but you won't listen to me, and I'm supposed to be yo man. I told you I didn't want you doin' that interview, but you doin' what you wanna do."

I frowned, confused by him being upset. "Hold up a minute. I'm doing this because I want to do this. As for listening to what other people say, yeah, I listen but I don't always take their advice. If I did, we wouldn't be together. I know this is something God—"

"There you go always throwin' God up in yo mess. You be killin' me with that. And goin' forward, I'm not gon' listen to you and you don't have to listen to me. As a matter of fact, I'm quittin' my job and movin' out tomorrow. The reason I got one anyway was to make yo ass happy. The reason I stayed here with you was to please you. I asked you to do one damn thing for me and you can't even do it."

I threw my hands in the air. "Hey, that's fine with me. It's your life, not mine. We both seem to be on the right path, and the reason things are slightly changing is because we finally got off our asses and tried to do something with our lives. If you don't want this anymore, good luck to you and God bless." I left the bedroom and went back into the kitchen. Dwayne followed.

"So, now all of a sudden you got this attitude like you don't need me, huh? You think just because you got a li'l business certificate that makes you better than me? Well, I got news for you, baby. You ain't got what it takes to be a success. You should have stuck with shopliftin' because that's the only damn thing you're good at. And as for this TV interview tomorrow, what a joke. The only reason I tried to stop you is because I didn't want you makin' a fool out of yourself on national TV."

His words stung. I swallowed hard and let out a deep sigh. "If I'm not worth anything, then why are you with me? Just leave, Dwayne, and go live your life without me. Please," I begged.

His voice rose and he held his finger close to my face. "I'll leave this fuckin' apartment when I get ready to leave."

"You just said you were leaving tomorrow. Go ahead and leave now."

He lowered his finger and stood face-to-face with me, gritting his teeth. "What you gon' do if I don't leave?"

"If you touch me, I'm calling the police to have you arrested."

He yelled, and as he spoke, his spit sprinkles dotted my face. "Bitch, I don't give a fuck about the police! You of all people should know that by now. Them muthafuckas excite me! Go ahead, call 'em!" He paused for a minute. "No, I tell you what. You don't have to call them. I'm gonna leave because I can't stand bein' around you. You make me sick, always tryin' to be better than everybody else. If I didn't have another cold-ass bitch waitin' for me, I'd fuck you up." He pushed my head, slamming it into the wall beside me. I held the side of my face, and reached out my other hand to punch his back. I may have been scared of Dwayne, but that didn't stop me from fighting back. When he turned, he landed a hard punch directly at my mouth. I covered it with my hand and looked at the twins, who stood in the kitchen with frowns on their faces. I knew that going after Dwayne would lead to a straight-up brawl between us, and as he turned away from me, I quickly picked up the phone, dialing 911. Like always, Dwayne jetted before the cops got there, but not before kicking the bedroom door off the hinges.

When the police arrived, they already knew the story. I didn't have to provide a name, address...anything, as they already knew the routine. Brenda Hampton and Dwayne Montgomery had been at it again. Through the eyes of everyone standing outside watching me talk to the police, the saga continued.

Once the police left, I went into the bathroom and had to face myself again. My lip was bleeding and it had swelled. I got a towel to make myself an ice pack. I knew I had no one to blame but myself. *Making* him get a job and trying to keep him here with me, so he'd stay on the right track was not the answer. He needed serious help. Help that I, in no way, could give him.

By morning, my lips were numb. Most of the swelling was on the inside of my lips, where it was black and blue. The outside still looked puffy and I covered a tiny cut with foundation and lipstick. I figured I wouldn't have to open my mouth that wide to talk, so maybe no one would notice. The thought of backing out of the interview did cross my mind, but something inside wouldn't let me do it. It dawned on me that Dwayne had planned to spark an argument with me all along. He was determined to keep me needing him, but the truth of the matter was, I didn't need him at all. I'd felt a sudden heap of strength. That same strength wouldn't let me break down and cry last night, and it was my motivation that got me out of bed and made me eager to do the interview than ever before.

I dropped the twins off at school and headed for the TV station. When I got there, Jeanette and Melinda were waiting for me. Both of them encouraged me to go out there and do my best.

"We know you can do it," Jeanette said, holding my hand. "Relax and keep displaying that pretty smile."

"I got this," I teased and we all laughed.

The host who was going to interview me directed me to sit side-by-side with her in a big leather beige chair. It relaxed me, but the butterflies in my stomach wouldn't go away. When I looked at Jeanette and Melinda standing behind the glass window with their fingers crossed, I smiled. My nervousness had subsided a bit, but I wasn't sure how my interview would turn out.

The Director yelled, "Lights, Camera and...you're on." The lights came on and lit up the entire studio.

"Good morning, everyone. My name is Leslie Bridges and I have a graduate from the Jobs Partnership Center here with me today, Miss Brenda Hampton. After a short break, we're going to talk about the program and Brenda is going to explain why she thinks many of you out there should be a part of it. Right Brenda?"

The Director turned the camera to me. "Yes," I smiled. "You're absolutely correct."

The camera turned on Miss Bridges again. "So, don't go anywhere. We'll be right back and you all are in for a treat."

I took a deep breath, and was very impressed by the host. Her words were crisp and clear; she'd obviously been doing this for a long time. She would definitely be a hard act to follow, but I was determined to do my best.

During the break she held my hand and said a prayer. She told me if I got nervous to speak from the heart. Again, speaking from the heart didn't make much sense to me. I had written pages and pages of things to say and that's what I was going to speak from.

The lights came back on and the host introduced me again. It was my turn to talk about the program and I was advised to focus on the big camera in front of me. I immediately froze up and tried to quickly think about what I had written down on paper. I drew a blank and couldn't remember one word. Then all of a sudden, I started talking about my experience with the program. How it helped me? How long it took me to complete the course? What I learned from the program? Hell, I even talked about being on welfare and that definitely wasn't in the plan. I rattled on so much, the host had to cut me off and take another break.

When all was said and done, my instructors were overjoyed. The host thanked me for coming and the lights went out. They all hugged me, congratulating me on a job well done. The host thought I'd done so well, she asked me to fill in for her in her absence. I knew she was just kidding, but it sure as hell would have been nice.

Afterward, Jeanette and Melinda took me to a fancy Chinese restaurant in Clayton, a richy-rich neighborhood. I thanked them for selecting me to do the interview, and was so glad that I'd gone through with it.

Before the waiter served our food, I sat thinking about my interview. I'd spoken from my heart and what a waste of time I spent writing my comments on paper. My heart was trying to reach out to women who were in the same situation as I was. I was trying to convince them that welfare wasn't the answer to having a rewarding and fulfilling life. My only hope was that I'd gotten through to somebody...anybody.

When I arrived home, Charlene and Dedra met me at the door and followed me into my apartment. The message light was blinking, displaying that I'd had twelve messages. Then, the phone rang and it was Mama.

"Well done, Brenda, your Mama is so proud of you." Tears quickly filled my eyes. I rightfully felt that Mama had not been able to tell me that up until now. It was a good feeling. Her baby girl had finally made her proud. And even though I wanted to hear her say it years ago, I really hadn't given her a reason to until now. I asked her to rate me on a scale from one to ten, and she blurted out, "Twenty." I guessed that was just a mother's perspective on things. We laughed and I told her I would call her back, once I got settled.

Most of my messages were from my friends and family, congratulating me on a job well done. But one of the messages was from Dwayne. He spoke in a nasty tone, telling me to gather his belongings and bring them to him—soon! I deleted his message and went back to entertaining my company.

At one o'clock in the morning, Jesse stopped by after work. She worked late nights at the post office, but she didn't want to go the day without personally congratulating me. A card was in one hand, and a bottle of expensive champagne was in the other. I laughed and invited her in.

"Whatever happened to my bottles of Colt 45?" I asked Jesse. "You done stepped it up to champagne now and have forgotten about our Colt 45 days, haven't you?"

"I haven't forgotten. As a matter of fact, I'll never forget. We're just moving on up and I have this feeling that there won't be no stopping us now!"

I couldn't agree with Jesse more. We conversed about my future plans that I was really getting hyped about. Like always, we made arrangements to get together for the weekend and celebrate.

Chapter Twenty-Two

There was a hard knock on my door, waking me from my sleep. When I opened it, it was the sheriff handing me a letter. It was an eviction notice. I had to clear the premises within thirty days or they would get a court order to kick me out. The reason for the eviction: too many disturbance calls reported at my address. According to the letter, the police had been called to my residence a total of nineteen times within a one-year period. The management office stated this was unacceptable. *Damn, damn, damn,* I thought. *What in the hell was I going to do now?* At the time, I didn't realize how much of a blessing this news was.

I called the management office to speak with Katy. I wanted to know if there was anything I could do to keep my apartment.

"The situation is out of my control," Katy said. "The inspectors were in your apartment and noticed holes in the walls, the bedroom door off the hinges, several of the windows cracked, and your front door is unable to lock. Not to mention the numerous calls to the police and you also have a serious roach problem."

I tried to defend what the inspectors had witnessed, as best as I could. "I...I called for the exterminators, but they never showed up. I can also get some new locks for the door and my ex-boyfriend is not allowed to come here anymore, so the police won't be called to come back again. I have nowhere else to go with my children and all I'm asking for is another chance."

"Sorry, Brenda. Within thirty days, you must be out. Good luck."

Katy hung up, but before I could even think about what I needed to do, the phone rang. It was Jeanette. "Brenda, I have good news for you. Our phones have been ringing off the hook since your interview on TV. There have been all kinds of companies calling here asking for you to come in for an interview. And not only that, we're getting so many calls from people who want to sign up for the program just because of you. Thank you so much!" she shouted. "Now, when are you going to come in and call some of these people back for an interview?"

"How about now? I can be there within the hour." I hung up the phone and tore up the eviction letter. They didn't have to give me thirty days. All I needed was a couple of weeks and I was out!

The first place I called wanted to interview me that day, and the other three sounded interesting, so I set up interviews with them later in the week. My self-esteem was working its way back up. I was amazed about being given so many different opportunities at once. Less than a year ago, I had nothing; and now, all kinds of doors were opening for me.

Before I'd left home, I called Jesse to break the news to her about being evicted and asked if she would co-sign for an apartment for me. Since I was going to be working now, there was no reason I couldn't afford to pay regular rent. Jesse agreed to co-sign for me, and said we would spend the weekend in search for an apartment. I thanked her and left to go on my interview.

During my interview for Physician's Health Plan, I wasn't nervous at all. Two White women asked the questions and a Black woman took notes. They laughed and joked with me about how crazy the health insurance industry could be, and said it definitely had its ups and downs. According to them, they were looking for an experienced, friendly person to run the front desk where visitors and some of their most important clients came. They took me to the place where I could possibly work, and needless to say, it was the perfect environment. The floors were hunter-green swirling marble and a mahogany desk sat in the middle of the floor. Old-fashioned cushioned chairs surrounded the room and a matching sofa set sat near the entrance. You had to have a swipe-card or enter a pin number to enter, and when you did, the tall tinted glass doors opened to the receptionist area.

"So, Ms. Hampton. Do you think you can do this?" One of the ladies asked.

I was still mesmerized, looking around. "Absolutely. I would love to work here."

"Let's finish taking the tour, and then we'll go back to my office to talk about a start date and salary." I was all smiles. I couldn't believe I was about to work for one of the largest healthcare companies in the country.

When we got back to the interviewee's office, everyone shook my hand and congratulated me on my new position. They turned me over to the Black lady, who was the Assistant Director of Human Resources.

"Girl, you did a great job," she said with her legs crossed. "It's good to see a sista coming up in here ready to handle her business."

I laughed. "Actually, it's good to see a sista with a position like yours."

"Yes, but I had to work hard for it. It didn't come easy. After being with this company for six years, they had to do something for me."

"I hope to have the same success with this company. It seems like a wonderful place to work."

"Oh, you will. I can tell by your personality and attitude, you'll do just fine. You're exactly what we need out there at that front desk. It won't be easy—we get an enormous amount of phone calls and visitors, so be prepared to stay busy."

"That's fine with me."

The HR Director turned to her computer, and after checking her schedule, she turned to me.

"Okay, Brenda, so when can you start? We want you to train for two weeks, and after that, you'll be on your own."

"Can I start Monday?"

"Sure, Monday sounds fine. That way you can start when the new pay period begins. As for your salary, the position starts out at $28,000 a year. You get a small raise after six months, and then you're evaluated once a year."

My eyes widened and mouth hung open. "How much did you say?"

"Yes, sweetie, I said $28,000 a year. But remember, there's a lot of work involved."

"I know, but that seems like a lot of money for a receptionist, doesn't it?"

"I can always offer you less if you want me to," she said, smiling.

"No, that's okay. I'll take the twenty-eight instead."

We both laughed.

"I'll see you at eight o'clock Monday morning and don't be late. Meet me in the lobby."

"Thanks, Ms. Watson. Thanks for all your help."

"Don't call me Ms. Watson, call me Ruth."

"Okay, Ruth, I'll see you Monday."

I hurried home to make my phone calls. Twenty-eight thousand was a dream come true for a sista on welfare getting $292/month from the government. Not in a million years did I think I would see that kind of money. Why or how something this good happened to me, I didn't understand. I could find the twins and me a nice place, buy a new car, and start saving for the future. Most of all, this kind of money would keep me out the stores. I'd been backsliding a lot when it came to that, but now, I could pay for what I wanted.

Jesse, Dedra, Charlene, and I drove around on the weekend looking for me an apartment. Shantell and I had made up, as we often did. But when I asked if she wanted to go with us, she turned me down. Her boyfriend, James, had her so wrapped around his finger, she couldn't do anything. The last time I'd seen her, he'd blackened her eye. Looking at her situation was a mirror reflection of mine, and as we spoke often on the phone, she cried about getting out of her relationship too. I didn't judge, and I knew, more than anyone, how difficult it was to break that grip. I would judge no woman in her situation and I looked at it as God strengthening a person and preparing them for something better to come. Whatever that would be, He'd be the one to decide, not me.

Jesse had driven to about ten different apartment buildings listed in an apartment guide she picked up for me at the grocery store. Not one appealed to me. They were over-priced and the bedrooms were like matchboxes. Dedra and Charlene complained about me being too picky.

"Any place beats where we live at right now. I don't know why you're being so picky and I liked the last place we were at," Charlene said.

"Well, I didn't. And since I'm going to be paying my hard earned money, the place I move into has to be right."

Jesse agreed, but by day's end, we had almost given up. We sat at QuikTrip on West Florissant Ave., drinking sodas and sharing chips. There was a sign on the corner pointing to some townhouses down the street, so Jesse drove to the rental office. The manager gave us a key to look at the display unit. The outside wasn't bad at all and the premises were well manicured. When we stepped into the townhouse, I immediately knew this place was for me. It had two large bedrooms with walk-in closets that connected to bathrooms. The kitchen had white appliances and a small island sat in the middle of the floor. The living room was bigger than my whole apartment and had built-in bookshelves on one side of the wall. The entire place, except for the kitchen, was covered with shiny hardwood floors. We opened the door to the lower level, and were completely sold. It had a laundry room, another half bathroom and the rest was an open carpeted space.

I rushed Jesse over to the rental office to complete the application. The manager said rent was seven hundred and fifty dollars a month. Even though it was more than I anticipated, the luxury was well worth it. The manager shook our hands and said she would call Jesse on Monday to let her know if her application had been approved.

The twins and I spent the rest of the day cleaning out our apartment. We had accumulated so much over the years, it was ridiculous. I came across the full box of spiral notebooks that I'd been writing in for years. While flipping through the pages, I began to read many of my entries. The bad times I'd written about, outweighed the good. Many of the pages still had dried-up tears on them. Some pages were curled and had me thinking about the past. Other pages had stories where I'd used my imagination to create them. Some were interesting, many not. My fairytale stories where life was good made me smile, and I remembered it as being one of the ongoing stories that I used to read to Jesse. But most of the contents were about a past that I wanted to put behind me. It was time to let go, so I carried the cardboard heavy box out to the dumpster and dumped all of my spiral notebooks inside. Right away, I felt something awkward inside, because I knew I was giving up on something that was close to my heart and often gave me peace—writing.

Since Dwayne had been calling and bugging me about bringing the rest of his things to him, I put all of his belongings in a box to take to him later. I knew packing was a bit premature but my destiny was already confirmed. I was so ready to leave my apartment, and if I could have moved out that day, I would have.

Later that evening, I called Dwayne's parents' house to see if he was home so I could take him his things. Myron answered and asked me to call back because he was on the phone. I told him to relay a message to Dwayne that I was on my way with his things.

Before going to his place, I stopped at a pawnshop, removing the four diamond rings from my fingers. I laid them on the counter and the man behind the counter asked how much I wanted for them.

"Fifty dollars," I said.

He scratched his head. "Fifty dollars? Are you pawning them or do you want cash for them? If you want cash, I can give you a little more than fifty dollars."

"I know how much the rings are worth. All I need is fifty dollars to pay my gas bill. You can sell them for whatever you want to."

The man rushed to give me fifty dollars and he made me sign an agreement that confirmed I didn't want the rings back. Without any delay, I did so.

Dwayne stood on the porch, watching as I pulled up and got out of my car. I grabbed one of the boxes from the back seat and walked up the steps to give it to him. The box was pretty darn heavy and he just stood there with his hands in his pockets. I dropped the box on the porch, turning to go get another one.

"Brenda, don't come down here trippin'," he said in a whisper.

I quickly turned with confusion on my face. "What are you talking about? Trip for what? All I came here to do was bring you the stuff you've been bugging me about."

"Aw. Myron said you had an attitude when you called because he told you I had company."

"Well, Myron was incorrect. He didn't tell me you had company. I told him to tell you I was on my way and he said that he would. If I'd known you had company, I would have waited." Just then, his front door opened. The White young woman stared at me, and I looked at her.

"Dwayne, who is this?" she asked. I made my way to the porch, extending my hand to hers.

"Hi," I said with a huge smile planted on my face. "My name is Brenda. I'm Dwayne's ex-girlfriend and I just wanted to bring him his belongings that were left at my place when he moved out. I'm moving and I didn't want any of his things getting left behind."

"I appreciate you bringing his things to him. He's probably going to need them when we get our place. We've been looking for months and we're so anxious to find one."

I nodded. "What did you say your name was?"

"Stephanie, my name is Stephanie."

"Stephanie, it's been a pleasure meeting you. Take care and good luck to you and Dwayne."

"Thanks, Brenda, it's also been a pleasure finally meeting you. I've heard so much about you and it's good to be able to put a face with the image." *Lord only knows what Dwayne told her about me*, I thought. It didn't really matter, because at that moment, I knew my seven-year relationship with Dwayne was over! I had not one jealous bone in my body; I actually felt sorry for the chick that seemed like a nice person. I almost cracked up at the shocked look covering Dwayne's face when I talked to her. He seriously thought I was going to act a fool over him again, but little did he know, those days had long passed.

I smiled as I pulled the last box out of the trunk and set it on the ground. Dwayne jogged down the steps, and put the box on the trunk of my car.

"So, where you movin' to?" he asked.

"I found a townhouse in North County. I'm moving in a couple of weeks." I didn't even know if it was a done deal or not, but I was claiming it.

"If I can help, let me know."

"No, that's okay. I already got that part taken care of." I moved around him to get into my car.

"Brenda, hold up. What's the rush? I...I miss you. Why don't you call me so we can holla about some things? If you want me to, I'll make her go home and we can talk now."

"That won't be necessary. I don't want to be with anyone right now. I need time to myself. Time to focus on just my kids and me. So, you go ahead and do you. I wish you well, Dwayne, truly, I do. And whether you realize it or not, if she's who you want, I'm happy for you."

Dwayne's girlfriend got agitated on the porch waiting for him. She called his name three times, but he ignored her. She started down the steps.

"I'm getting ready to go," I said, rushing. "I don't want to disrespect her in any way."

"Alright, Brenda," he said, holding the car door open so I wouldn't shut it. "Give me a kiss. Can I have just one last kiss?" I cut my eyes at him and sighed from frustration. Stephanie walked up from behind him.

"Did you just ask her for a kiss?" she snapped, raising her voice.

"Back up! Take yo ass back on the porch until I get finished talkin'! Don't be out here confrontin' me over no bullshit," he yelled.

"What the fuck is your problem?" She blinked the tears from her round blue eyes, and while they stood arguing, I shut the door and drove off. I could hear Dwayne yelling for me to wait, but there was no turning back.

Chapter Twenty-Three

Work was exciting but hectic. Everything was a rush-rush situation. The phones rang off the hook and visitors came in from left to right. The temp who was training me was an older White woman who didn't seem to have it together. Ruth came out a few times to check on me. She pulled me aside and asked me to be patient, because after two weeks with the trainee, I would be on my own.

That day, Ruth invited me to lunch with her. I hadn't eaten anything so lunch sounded good. She took me to a restaurant in Westport Plaza that was owned by baseball legend, Ozzie Smith. Ruth talked about her job and the things she had to do to get where she was.

"If you work hard, you can get here too. PHP is known for giving promotions to those who perform well and African Americans are given a fair chance. The company also pays for schooling, so if you want to go back to further your education, come see me."

I felt as if I had so many angels around me, and it wasn't until I was willing to walk through that opened door, when good things started to happen.

Making our way back from lunch, Ruth and I could see the receptionist from a distance, filing her long nails. Ruth wished me luck and we laughed.

On the reception's desk was what looked to be two dozen long-stem red roses. Ruth walked up to smell them.

"Ah…these smell so good. Who are they for?" she asked.

"They're for her—the new girl."

"For me?" I asked, surprised.

"Yes, for you," she said, getting back to her nails. I sniffed the roses and pulled the card from the envelope.

"You are one lucky woman," Ruth said, leaving for her office. "Must be nice to have such a good man. Also, don't forget to stop by my office so you can get information about returning to school."

I nodded, but I knew the flowers couldn't be from a man because I didn't have one. I quickly opened the card and it read: *Hope you have a wonderful day at work. We're all so proud of you. Love always, Your Instructors at JPC.* I put the card back into the envelope and smiled. Since the receptionist was now on the phone, I used another phone in the lobby to call and thank them for being so supportive. I left a message because they were at lunch. As I walked back to the receptionist area, she told me I had a caller on hold. It was Jesse.

"What's up, dirty?" she said, chewing on some gum. "How's work coming along?"

"It's cool. I just got back from lunch and my instructors sent me some roses."

"Aww, that's so nice," she said sarcastically. "Who was that old woman answering the phone? She couldn't get it together, could she?"

"Girl, that's a whole other story in itself." We laughed.

"Well, I called to tell you my application was accepted. The lady said the townhouse would be available as soon as the deposit was paid. I asked her to give me until the end of the week and I'd come in to sign the lease."

I wanted to jump for joy. "Thanks, Jesse, I really appreciate it. Don't know what I would do without you sometimes. I'll call you when I get off work so we can go over the details."

For the rest of the day, the receptionist let me handle all calls and visitors. I felt like I had worked there for years. When Ruth came up and saw how well things flowed, she asked me if one week of training would be good enough. I told her I thought it would be, and she decided to send the woman back to the temp agency at the end of the week. I was glad; she was spending more time on her nails, than she was showing me the ropes.

***

Everything was packed and ready to go. Rita and Clarence had come to town to visit, so the twins had gone back to Tennessee with them for the summer. That allowed me plenty of time to get things situated in my new place and I didn't have to worry about finding a sitter while I went to Florissant Valley Community College in the evenings. Things were going perfectly for me and returning to school was the best decision I'd made. Surprisingly, I'd done extremely well and my Writing/English courses were my favorites. I was back to writing again, and whenever the teacher would have us write essays, I had no problem doing so. He could tell me to write a hundred page essay, and I'd have it finished within a day, maybe two. I had a new career, a new place and a new attitude. Most of all, I had a new phone number and didn't have to worry about being bothered by no one from my past. I looked at my new beginning as a blessing and this was a moment in time when I realized that God would help me, as long as I was willing to also help myself.

My new place had an echo. I had given almost everything away because I didn't want to drag any of the old furniture into my new place. I had some money set aside for new furniture, but it wasn't enough to furnish my place like I wanted to. With that in mind, it took more time to save money. I still had the whole summer before the twins came home and wanted everything to be perfect when they did.

Like often, Jesse called to check on me. She complained about my life being boring, ever since I'd moved. I did occasionally go out with her and some of her friends, but the club scene just didn't seem to excite me that much anymore. I had given my new number to a few young men here and there, had sex with a couple of them, but went on my way thereafter. Dwayne had left a scar on me; I didn't believe I could ever trust another man for as long as I lived.

I did, however, reflect on the men from my past. The only man who gave me some kind of satisfaction in the bedroom was Miles, but I hadn't spoken to him in years. I lay in bed, thinking about how different sex was between us. Just for the hell of it, I beeped him that day, hoping that his number was the same, and left my number for him to call me back.

Charlene and Dedra showed up within the hour to play spades with me, and during our card game, the phone rang. I had been cheating my butt off in the game, and since I didn't want to get up to answer the phone, Charlene reached for it.

"Yo," she said, flipping through the cards in her hand. She paused. "Didn't nobody beep you, who dis?"

Her mouth widened and she whispered that it was Miles. My brows went up, I had no idea he would call me back. I reached for the phone, placing it on my ear with the biggest grin on my face.

"Hello, Miles," I said.

"Who is this?"

"Who does it sound like?"

"Don't know. That's why I'm asking."

"It's Brenda."

There was a pause, and then he replied. "Damn, baby, what's up?" I could hear the excitement in his voice. "Where have you been? It's been a long ass time."

"I know. I'm surprised your pager number is still the same."

"Yeah, I've had this number for a long time. I'm glad you called."

"I'm surprised to hear that, especially since we kind of ended things on a sour note."

"That was then, this is now. Now, I wouldn't mind seeing you. Can you make it happen?"

I wanted to see Miles, too, but I wasn't sure about moving backwards. Still, I couldn't deny that if there was ever any man that I met who could get it at the snap of his finger, it would be Miles. "See me for what?" I said, and then blushed.

"Don't start playing no games with me, woman. You know damn well why I'd want to see you. I still got a healthy sexual appetite and my dick ain't been right since you left it. Why don't you let me bring it home?"

Charlene and Dedra were looking down my throat, taking in every word. They knew how I'd felt about Miles, and even though they'd never met him, I often talked about his *skills*.

"Where are you?" was all I could say.

"I'm at work, but I get off at ten o'clock tonight."

I looked at the clock on the wall. It was a little after 6:00 p.m. "I wouldn't mind seeing you either. Call me when you get off and I'll give you directions to my place."

"Do you live alone? If not, and if you still mess with that crazy-ass nigga, I need to bring my piece."

"Naw, I'm good. Just call me when you get off work."

Miles said that he would and hung up. Charlene and Dedra had dropped their cards on the table.

"Well, I guess we may as well go home," Dedra said. "It's a wrap."

Charlene pursed her lips and spoke up. "Shiiit, not me. I'm staying right here. Brenda claimed Miles was working with twelve inches and I want to see this shit for myself."

I laughed. "What? Do you think he gon' come through the door with his dick hanging out so you can see it?"

"Nope, but let me hide in the closet or something. He won't even know I'm in there."

I really wanted Dedra and Charlene to see just how much Miles was packing, but letting them watch us have sex was crazy. They continued to bug me about hiding in the closet and when I said no, they accused me of lying. I then made a $100 bet that his goods were not fake, and they agreed to pay me if I were correct. After going back and forth about how I could prove my point, I couldn't believe that I agreed to let them hide in the closet.

"Just give me some popcorn and a strong soda," Charlene said. "I will stay put."

"Oh, you gon' need more than a strong soda. Just wait until you see it, and please, please don't make any noises."

By nine o'clock, I was tipsy from drinking a few shots of Vodka and so was Dedra. Charlene had guzzled down two Heinekens and we were acting rather silly. Miles hadn't called yet, but when he did, it was on. I changed into a black bell-sleeve short mini-dress, revealing my thick thighs. I'd lost several pounds by walking everyday at Flo Valley, but was still a bit thicker since the last time Miles had seen me. My hair was still long and my feathered look was back. Charlene and Dedra tossed out compliments, and when the doorbell rang, it was time to put up or shut up. I knew Miles would come through for me, and after we connected our pinky fingers for the bet, I rushed Charlene and Dedra into the closet. We all giggled and I placed my finger on my lips.

"Shhh, y'all gotta be very quiet. Don't say nothing, and if y'all do, he gon' kill me."

They put their hands over their mouths, silencing the laughs. I swiped the sheen of sweat from my forehead, clearing my throat before opening the door.

I was in a trance. Miles stepped in the foyer, looking down right workable with his security uniform on. He was so, so sexy and my eyes couldn't help but drop to take a glance at the huge lump in his pants.

He smiled, while looking into my glossy eyes. "You fucked up, ain't you?" he asked.

I flirted with my eyes—drinking alcohol always made me the aggressor. "A li'l bit," I said, eyeballing his lips and biting down on mine. Miles blushed and eased his arm around my waist.

"You look damn good, Bree. I can't wait to taste you and I'm gon' put in some overtime tonight."

Sounded like a plan to me, and wasting no time, I took Miles' hand, leading him to my bedroom. I eased back on the bed, resting comfortably on my elbows. Miles stood directly in front of the bed, and as he started to remove his clothes, I turned my head to the right. The sliding closet door had a wide enough crack where I could see peeping eyes. I blinked away, and focused my attention back on Miles. My legs fell apart, and that sure as hell brightened his day. He dropped to his knees, and already knowing the routine, my legs poured over his shoulders. Miles got down to business, tearing my insides up with his fierce tongue. He kept saying, "Mmm, mmm, mmm," and when I inquired about the taste, he pecked my thighs and licked his shiny wet lips.

"This mutha taste like a seasoned fat juicy steak. This some pretty good shit, baby, you just don't know."

We laughed and I heard a clunk in the closet. I turned my head, pretending as if I didn't know what it was.

"Something must have fallen," I said with a shrug. Miles paid the noise no mind and lay back on the bed. I stroked his muscle, holding it straight up so Charlene and Dedra could get a good look.

"I see that some things just never change," I said. "Is it just me or has this *thing* gotten even bigger?"

Miles was proud of what he was working with. "Naw, it's still about the same," he boasted. "That's roughly twelve inches right there and I'm sure you won't have no complaints."

I agreed and couldn't help but take another glance at the closet. There was no way for me to let my friends see how I really got down, and after I got up to turn off the lights, the heat was on. For the next thirty minutes or so, Miles and I connected well. I wasn't sure how Dedra and Charlene would feel about me, especially after witnessing and hearing something so intense. No questions asked, Miles' freakiness was well above average, yet the passion was not there. This was strictly a fuck thing and I still felt like nothing but a piece of meat to him. I couldn't believe Charlene and Dedra had held their peace, and as soon as Miles left, they slid over the closet door and fell out on the floor.

"Girl," Charlene shouted. "Where in the hell did you find his ass at? I ain't never had a man get down like that, and I couldn't believe the size of that thing!"

Dedra was shaking her head. "Me either! I seriously thought you were lying, but when you held that sucker up, I had to cover my damn mouth. I couldn't even imagine nothing like that going inside of me. How in the hell did you ride him?"

"Trust me, it ain't never been easy, but it damn sure has been a lot of fun."

"Yeah, we know, Miss Steakum," Charlene laughed. "He messed me up with that and Dedra's ass poked me in my back. I jumped and your damn shoe fell off the shoe rack."

"I knew something had happened. I thought I was busted. Either way, Miles wouldn't have given a care. If he'd had his way, all three of us would have been in that bed working him over."

We laughed, again, and couldn't stop talking about what had happened. Charlene called Jesse to tell her about it, and when all was said and done, Dedra and Charlene had to pay up!

Chapter Twenty-Four

Life was starting to feel good. I listened to Mama, over the phone the other day, when she reminded me life was too short for a bunch of foolishness, and taking a bunch of shit off men, definitely wasn't where it was at. Miles had already been cut again, but this time, I didn't even trip. Being with Dwayne had toughened me up with relationships, and I wouldn't trade the experiences from my relationship with him for nothing in the world.

I was starting to demand more from my relationships, but I quickly found out that my standards left me at home alone. That was cool, because I threw myself into work, school and exercise. By walking nearly every day at Flo Valley and doing aerobics, I'd dropped about forty pounds. My body was fierce, but the only thing I didn't like was my long feathery hair. It was too thick and made my face look fat—me look older. Trying to change it up, I entered the bathroom, staring at myself in the mirror. I no longer hated who I saw, but I knew the hair had to go. I searched for some scissors and started clipping away. I trimmed my hairline with clippers, and teased my short curled hair with styling gel. I loved my new look and couldn't wait for others to see it.

While at work, I kept busy, organizing my desk and presenting myself as a true professional. The compliments about my hair were overwhelming. Many people liked it, so it didn't take long to grow on me. Whenever customers would come in, I was polite and did my best to service them as much as I could. Some of the people came in angry about their insurance, wanting to talk to one of the Member Service Managers, and many customers demanded it. Even those people left upbeat. I carried on conversations with them, like I understood their problems. It took less than a month for me to be offered a new position, and I couldn't believe that I was already due for a promotion.

"We have a vacancy in Member Services," the manager, Elaine, said. "If you're interested in it, let me know."

"Of course," I said, standing near my desk speaking to her. "I would love to work in Member Services."

Elaine told me to set up an appointment with Ruth, and when I called, she was so happy for me.

"I told you to hang in there, didn't I? And I don't have to tell you that three more grand will be added to your salary."

I was speechless. Why all of this was happening to me, I didn't know, but I was grateful. Ruth told me to come see her later so we could work out the final details. I agreed to do so.

Just as I hung up the phone, a group of White men in business suits entered the receptionist area. One asked if he could use the phone, and I directed him to one that was made available to people in the nearby lobby. Another man asked if I would buzz Jeff from Marketing, just to let him know that Schmidt's Brokerage Firm was there to see him. I smiled, buzzing Jeff and letting him know that he had guests awaiting him. I hung up the phone, appreciating the presence of a Black man who walked into the receptionist area, dressed in a tailored black suit. One hand was in his pocket and the other hand swung by his side. He was cleaner than Mr. Clean, had a head full of natural curly black hair, heart-melting grey eyes, and a physique that showed he was cut in all the right places. Men didn't come this clean-cut and fine, did they? I couldn't keep my eyes off him, and neither could another lady who had turned her head to see who had captured my attention. When the phone rang, it knocked me out of my trance.

"Physician's Health Plan. How may I direct your call?" I asked, keeping my eyes on Mr. Sexy. His goatee suited his chin so well, and as he talked to the other men in the lobby, I noticed his dynamite smile. His teeth were perfect, and when I say this man was flawless, he was every bit of it. He had to be a movie star, and I was seconds away from asking for his autograph.

Jeff came through the double glass doors, greeting each of the men who waited and shook hands with them. He gripped the fine Black man's shoulder, and quite frankly, I noticed all of the men giving him their attention. He stroked his chin a few times, laughed with the men, then they all moved in my direction. Jeff had always been nice to me, and he stopped for a quick introduction.

"Gentlemen, this is Brenda Hampton, our receptionist. Our meeting shouldn't be that long, but if you need anything, please let her know."

I said hello to the men and all of them spoke back. The Black man, however, reached out his hand for me to shake it. "Jay Rogers, Brenda. Nice to meet you."

I wanted to jump up and do some cartwheels. His hand was so soft and strong, I didn't want to let go. The addictive cologne he wore infused the space between us, and not only did I smell his cologne, but I could also smell money. From the top of his head, to the bottom of his sharp leather shiny shoes, he was loaded with cash. I must have looked like a fool with my mouth hanging open, and my words were unable to come out. He pulled his hand back, and after slipping it into his pocket, he joined the other men as they made their way through the doors, and into their Marketing meeting. I couldn't get a grip of myself that day, and I wondered if I would have the pleasure of ever seeing Jay Rogers again.

***

It was a Saturday night, and I stayed home reading a book, *Disappearing Acts* by Terry McMillan. I was so indulged; it was the first time I was on my way to reading a full novel. The characters had me hooked, and as I laid the book on my bed, I wondered if I could write a story like hers.

Over the years, I'd been doing an enormous amount of writing, but to me, none of it made sense. I doubted that anyone would want to read about all the drama I'd been through, but then my mind traveled elsewhere. I picked up some typing paper I'd had lying on my dresser and used a ballpoint pen to write the first thing that came to my head. For whatever reason, I started writing about Jay, the one I had never known and who had only crossed my path for a few short minutes. He seemed like an interesting man to write about, and God only knows if I had a man that intriguing in my life, what I would do with him: *There he stood, tall and finger-licking good as ever. His hair was full of natural curls; curls that I saw myself running my fingers through. His lips were full and thick, I surely wanted to kiss them. And there was something in his addictive grey eyes that were luring. Something about him that made me squirm in my seat and melt shortly thereafter. An intriguing creature he was and as he moved closer to me...*

My imagination went wild, had me laughing a bit to myself and amazed by what I had come up with. I'd finally taken a break, only to pick up Terry McMillan's book, again, and finish it.

Once I was done, I couldn't stop thinking about how well she'd crafted her story. I was right there with her characters, moving along as if I was in the book myself. I re-read what I had written, only to rip up the pages and throw them in the trash. I later retrieved them, planning to let Jesse read them, before I gave up on what I'd written. I had a long way to go, but I truly felt as if, one day, I would somehow piece a story together.

Before going to bed, I called Rita's place in Tennessee to speak to the twins. Rita told me they were coming back at the end of next month, but I couldn't wait for the twins to see their new place. I had already decorated most their bedroom with pink, green and white, some of their favorite colors. They still needed new beds, though, but I waited a while before getting those. I really missed my children, but I was sure they were enjoying their time in Tennessee.

The next day, I stopped by the grocery store to get something to eat for the night. The refrigerator had been near empty all summer, since the twins weren't there, and I only ate when I was extremely hungry. I'd dropped another ten pounds and wasn't trying to do so.

I strolled my cart to the Deli section, picked up a sandwich, and then went down the condiments aisle to get a jar of Mayo. I spotted this dude stuffing a pack of frozen ribs down his pants, and as I got closer, I saw it was my cousin Josh. He was looking terrible. His hair was nappy, pants were dirty and half-way hanging off his butt. His shirt looked like a two year old tried to button it and lips were crusty as ever.

"Josh, what are you doing in here stealing?" I whispered. "I could have been anybody and reported you. Take those ribs out of your pants and throw them in the cart. I'll buy them."

Once upon a time, Josh could be considered a really handsome man. But ever since he'd started messing around with drugs, he'd gone completely downhill.

"Thanks, Cuz. You always seem to come through when I need you to," he said putting the ribs in the cart. I went through the line, paying for the few items I had in my cart. Josh had thrown in some chips and a beer, but I didn't mind. He was family.

On the parking lot, I bagged up his things and handed them to him. He thanked me and started jogging away. My heart went out to him, but the last thing I wanted was him knowing where I lived.

By the time I made a left at the corner, I could see him walking down West Florissant Ave., munching on the bag of potato chips I had just bought. I pulled over because something wouldn't let me leave him.

"Josh, where are you headed to?" I asked.

He shrugged. "I don't know. Anywhere, I guess. I ain't got no place to live. Been out on the streets for a while now, Bren."

"Get in the car. At least go to my place and clean yourself up. Then we'll talk about some living arrangements."

Josh hurried inside and I drove back to my place. He took a shower, and when he got out, I gave him a pair of red jogging pants and an old beat-up t-shirt that had St. Louis printed on the front. The shower did him justice, but the clothes were a little too tight. We sat at the kitchen table, talking. "You got a nice place," he said, sipping from the beer I had just bought.

"It is nice, Josh, and I want to keep it that way. That means I don't want you telling Dwayne where I live."

"I won't. I promise you I won't. Besides, we got into an argument a couple weeks ago. I stopped fuckin' with him. That fool wanted to—"

"I don't even want to know," I said. "All I know is he better not find out where I live."

Josh took another sip from his beer bottle. "So, do you have any room here for me? I see you got a basement. I can sleep down there. I'll stay out of your way and you won't even know I'm here."

I was very skeptical about letting Josh live with me, but what choice did I have? How could I tell my own cousin no? It was another Déjà vu moment for me again. I remembered Mama allowing a relative who'd been on drugs to stay with us while we lived in Wellston. He stole our television and pawned it. Mama was pissed, and I hoped that my situation with Josh wouldn't wind up like hers.

Josh thanked me for letting him stay and went downstairs to watch TV.

Even though Josh cleaned out the tub when he got out, I scrubbed it again. If he'd been living on the streets, I wasn't taking any chances. So, instead of bathing, I took a shower and washed my hair. As the water was on full blast, Josh knocked on the bathroom door and told me he was heading out for a while. I told him to be sure to lock the door.

After my shower was over, I got comfortable in bed, thinking about writing again. All kinds of stuff was in my head, but I was too tired to write. I closed my eyes, and before I knew it, I was out.

On Monday, I sat at my desk, hoping and praying that Jay Rogers showed up again. It's not that I was going to say anything to him; I just wanted to look at him. Many other insurance brokers had shown up that day, but I was shit out of luck. I was a little disappointed, but was happy about starting my new position in Member Services on next Monday.

When I got home from work, Josh was downstairs looking at TV. "Did anybody call?" I asked, looking through the mail.

"Jesse called, Dedra called, your mama called, the kids called, and you had one hang up call too. I got bored so I cleaned up the basement and washed the dishes. Do you think you can loan a brotha twenty dollars? I'm hungry and you ain't got shit to eat in the fridge."

I placed my hand on my hip. "Please. You're living here rent-free and complaining?"

"Damn, I washed the dishes and cleaned up the basement."

"That's what you're supposed to do, especially if you messed up my basement."

Josh sighed and pleaded with me. "Come on, Brenda, give me a break."

I hesitated, but reached into my purse. "Here, Josh. Don't make this no habit either."

He smiled, thanked me and left.

It took me about two hours to return everybody's phone call. Rita and the kids told me about their weekend adventures; Dedra talked about her drama with her boyfriend; Jesse and I caught up on the scoop with her and a Que-dog that she'd met, and Mama was on the phone complaining about her neighbors and about me letting Josh live with me.

"I couldn't believe when I called he answered the phone," Mama said. "I told him to find his grown ass a place to stay and stop running to you for handouts. You need to put him out of there, Brenda. I don't understand why you're always trying to be nice to people. You can't save the world."

"Josh had no place to go, Mama. I didn't feel right leaving him like that, and you know he's had a tough upbringing. I'm going to keep my eyes on him, and if anything gets out of hand, I will ask him to leave."

"When you get done talking, that apartment is supposed to be for you and the twins. Josh is grown! How many times are you going to let him move in with you and tear up your damn place?"

I sighed, really not in the mood to be having this conversation with Mama. I knew how she'd felt about Josh, even though he was her nephew. Mama had been burned by family, so I did my best to understand her position.

"He will only be here for a little while. I'm going to see if I can help him find a job and get his own place."

Mama wasn't trying to hear me, so she hung up. I started to call her back and go off, but the last thing I wanted was to argue with her about Josh. She and I had been getting along well, and I wasn't about to ruin it.

It was one o'clock in the morning, and as soon as I shifted in bed to another position, I heard hard knocks on the door. I staggered to open it and it was Josh. "Damn, Josh, it's almost one o'clock in the morning. Where have you been all night?" I asked, yawning.

"None of yo business. Remember, that's what you told me when I asked you."

I threw my hand back. "Really, I could care less. I'm too tired to fuss with somebody who claims to be homeless."

Josh laughed and sat at the kitchen table, watching me pour a glass of water. "I saw Dwayne tonight," he said. "He told me to tell you to call him. He said all he wants to talk about is seeing the kids."

I pursed my lips. "Yeah right, whatever. He'll wait on it. Besides, why you keep bringing up his name?"

"Because y'all were made for each other. He loves you and you love him. Y'all need to work on gettin' shit together."

Josh straight-up touched a nerve and I snapped. "We don't need to work on nothing. I wish everybody would stop saying how much love we had for each other, as I hadn't felt it. We've moved on and there's nothing to work on. Got it?"

Josh looked taken aback by my tone. "Your blood is boilin', ain't it? If you really want to know, I was just playin'."

I rolled my eyes. "Well, don't play like that. I get so tired of hearing it."

Josh didn't say much else to me about Dwayne. I didn't mean any disrespect, but I didn't trust him when it came to Dwayne. They were too close and I suspected he really wasn't kidding. Something was up.

Chapter Twenty-Five

Work was busy. Phones were going crazy with complaints. Apparently, Physician's Health Plan changed pharmaceutical companies and some members were furious. I had to listen to upset customers all day long. The ones who couldn't get through on the line came in to visit and the lobby was packed with irate customers, wanting to talk to someone from Member Services.

I was so glad the weekend had finally arrived. I went to the bank to cash my check, and then stopped at the car-wash to wash my car. As I was getting a towel from the trunk, someone approached me from behind, tapping my shoulder. I turned and it was Dwayne. He wore a red, white and blue Fila jacket and stone-washed jeans. A one-inch herring bone gold chain hung from his neckline and a diamond earring sparkled on his earlobe. He was hooked up, but like the last time I'd seen him, I wasn't moved.

"What's up, Brenda?"

"Hi," I said dryly.

"Did Josh tell you to call me?"

"Yes, but I forgot."

"That's bullshit and you know it. I ain't tryin' to argue with you, but I would like to see the twins when they get home."

It was interesting that he even knew they weren't at home. "I don't know if that's a good idea. I think it's only going to complicate things for them."

He put his hands in his pockets and his face twisted up. "What do you mean complicate things for them? You mean complicate things for you. This ain't even about you no more. I've been in their lives since they were babies. I'm the only father they've ever known. You would be wrong for tryin' to keep them from me."

I was silent for a moment, and then spoke up. "Let me think about it. I'll call and let you know."

"When they comin' back home?"

"They'll be back the last week in August."

"Alright. Don't forget to call me," he said, making his way back to his truck. He honked the horn, turned up his loud music and drove off.

As usual, Josh wasn't home when I got there. I marked my calendar to count down how many days before the twins came home, and there was only a month left. I missed them tremendously, and even though they were with Rita, I had a difficult time letting them go. I'd become very overprotective, but that was a fear I had of something happening to them or someone doing them wrong.

I changed my clothes and decided to go look for some furniture for their bedroom. They mentioned twin waterbeds, so I knew the waterbed store would be my first stop. I opened my drawer to get my money out of the jewelry box and couldn't believe it was gone. I plopped back on my bed, trying to figure out where else I could have put it. I knew I had dug into my stash a couple of times, but I always put the money back. Then, all of a sudden, it hit me. Josh.

I picked up the phone and started calling around for him. I had gotten so desperate that I beeped Dwayne to see if he'd known where Josh was. Ten minutes later, Dwayne called back.

"Did somebody page me?" he asked.

"Have you seen Josh?"

"Who is this? Brenda?"

"Yes. I'm looking for Josh. Have you seen him?"

"Yeah, I've seen him. He was down here early this mornin'. I'm sure he'll be back, and when he comes, I'll tell him to get at you."

"Dwayne, don't forget. It's important."

"Why you lookin' for him?"

I hesitated to answer and wiped my tears. "Be...because, he took some money from me."

"How much did he take?"

"Seventeen hundred dollars," I said choked up. "I...I was saving it for the twins furniture and he took every bit of it."

"Calm down, Brenda. What are you doin' with that kind of money around Josh anyway? You know what he about, don't you?"

"Yeah, but I didn't think he'd do me like that, especially after as much as I've helped him."

"Well, lately, he's been down here flauntin' a lot of money. If I see him, though, I'll tell him to call you."

I hung up and closed my eyes for a moment, thinking about how stupid I was for letting Josh stay with me. I thought I'd had a good hiding place in my drawer, but he must've seen me go in there to get some money before. I was so mad that I called Mama to tell her about what happened. What did I do that for, as she went ballistic.

"His ass better hope I don't ever see him. What kind of man is he, taking money from you and those kids! I warned you, Brenda, but you do not listen to anything that I tell you. Stop trusting so many damn people and kick Josh's ass the hell out of there!"

Again, she said what she had to say and hung up. I continued looking around for the money, just in case I placed it somewhere else and forgot. I even went downstairs to check through his clothes, only to find a straight shooter he used to smoke crack. As I made my way upstairs, I heard the front door close. It was Josh, and when he saw me coming from the basement, his eyes widened. I could tell he was high; he was fidgety. I held out my hand. "Where's my money at?" I asked.

He avoided eye contact and tried to walk around me. I grabbed his arm to stop him. "Brenda, I ain't got twenty dollars on me. I told you I would give it back when I got some money."

"Don't mess with me Josh. Give me my damn money!" I was getting pretty emotional, but Josh continued to deny it.

"Girl, look, I don't know what you're talkin' about."

"You know damn well what I'm talking about. I called Dwayne and he told me you've been in the hood with some money. If it ain't mine, then where in the hell did you get it?"

Josh turned, increasing his tone. "I said I ain't got yo fuckin' money! You better go call them thieving-ass girlfriends of yours who took your shit the last time because I ain't got it!"

As we argued, thunder roared outside and heavy rain started to pour. The lights blinked on and off and finally stayed on. Lord knows I didn't want to put him out; after all, I had also been put out in the rain and it wasn't a good feeling. But I wasn't getting anywhere with him. All I wanted was my money back, but he wasn't bulging.

"I refuse to stand here and argue with you over my money. It's either you give me my money or you get the fuck out! I can't believe you did this to me, Josh. No matter what, I stuck by you and gave you a place to lay your head. Not once, but twice. And this is how you repay me? You need to leave or I'll call the police."

Josh fell back on the couch. He rubbed his temples and lightly mumbled underneath his breath. "Damn, I'll give yo money back to you. I only took a hundred dollars, but the rest, I don't know what happened to it."

I tried to pull him off the couch, but he snatched away from me. My thoughts of calling the police made me think about what had happened at my last place, but I still threatened to do it. "You took more than a hundred dollars and you know it. I'm calling the police, right now, if you don't give me my keys and go."

Josh quickly stood up, threw my keys on the floor and ran downstairs to get his belongings. I heard him talking to himself, calling me every foul name in the book that he could think of. The lights were flashing again, and rain was beating so hard on the roof, it sounded like it was about to collapse. Josh came upstairs with a trash bag full of clothes. He opened the front door and the smell of stormy weather invaded my townhouse. I could hear the wind and the rain splashing on the porch. The door slammed, and all kinds of hurt went through me. I had no choice, and the feeling of putting him out wasn't a good one. I sat on my bed upset because every time I tried to be there for somebody, they screwed me around. My money was history and there wasn't a chance in hell Josh would ever give it back.

I tried to figure out what I could avoid paying to get the twins beds for them. I had another paycheck coming, but it was already spent on bills. I decided to skip some bills and play catch-up later. As for the rest of the place, I'd just have to start saving again.

A few hours later, I was coming home from the grocery store, and when I got out of the car, I could see Dwayne standing on my porch. I walked up to it with bags of groceries in my hands, ignoring him.

Dwayne held out his hands. "Damn, that's how you greet a brotha who stopped by to make sure you're okay?"

I unlocked the door, walking away from it. "Come in, but there's no need to check on me because I'm fine. I guess I don't have to ask who told you where I lived."

"Please," he said, closing the door. "I've known where you lived since the day you moved here. I know you wanted your space so I didn't bother you. And the only reason I'm here today is to help you."

"Help me how? I don't mean to sound cold or anything, but I don't need your help." I put the bags on the kitchen table, then went into my bedroom and sat on the edge of my bed. My eyes were puffy from crying and I looked a mess. I hated for Dwayne to see me like this; the last thing I wanted him to think was things had been going downhill since we'd broken up. That was in no way the case.

"Look, I'm just being honest. Josh took yo money. As a matter of fact, he gave some of it to me. He was buyin' his product from a dude I got doin' some hustlin' for me. So, I came here to repay you." Dwayne reached into his pocket, pulling out a thick wad of money that he was barely able to grip with one hand. He tossed the money on the bed, grinning as if he'd done me a favor. "There's a little somethin' extra in there for you. Buy yourself somethin' nice."

I picked up most of the money, flipping through it. Had to be at least three grand. "So, I see the drug game is treating you well, huh?"

He reached into his pocket and pulled out some little white rocks wrapped in a plastic bag.

"You see this shit here? This made me a rich man. I got all kinds of shit. Jewelry, more cars, you name it. I'm about to invest in some rental property and I got some corner boys workin' the streets for me. All I need is you and the twins back in my life and things will be even better."

I was downright disgusted. Dwayne knew better than to come over here, boasting about his so-called good fortune. Drugs had fucked him up and my cousin as well. How he ever thought selling and using was profitable, I didn't understand. I held out my hand. "Can I see those rocks," I asked. "Maybe I need to hook myself up." Dwayne chuckled, giving the bag to me. I lifted the bag up high, pretending as if I were studying the rocks. "You know, it's a shame how much you can make off some mess like this. I can't believe people crave for this. How many pieces are in here?"

"About twenty. That's enough to buy that big-screen television you've been talking about for years and then some."

I nodded and wasn't the least bit interested in his new career, or how it could benefit me. I made my way into the bathroom and Dwayne followed, still bragging about how much money he had. As I ripped the plastic bag, dropping the contents into the toilet, Dwayne tried to push me out of the way. I flushed the toilet and he stuck his hand inside.

"Fuckin' bitch!" he shouted, unable to save not one rock. He fell to his knees, trying to see how far down the toilet the rocks had gone, but it was too late. He rushed up and tightly grabbed my neck. My body was thrown against the wall and he tightened his grip with every word he gritted through his teeth. "Do you know muthafuckas die over shit like this every day? You just flushed a whole lot of money down the toilet, and if I didn't care about the twins havin' a mother, I'd kill yo ass right now!"

I scratched at his hands, straining as I spoke. "Do...do whatever you got to do. And you'd better go get your money before I flush that down the toilet too or burn it."

Dwayne quickly released his grip and rushed into my bedroom. He snatched the money off the bed and was in total disbelief about what I'd done. Needless to say, I was too. It was a risky move, but I wanted to make it clear to Dwayne that I wanted nothing to do with him, or his money. When he left the room, I remained against the wall, soothing my scratchy and sore throat with my hand and coughing. He squeezed his fist and stood face-to-face with me. My eyes did not blink, nor did they water. I was definitely afraid of what would happen next, but refused to let my fear show. He lifted his hand to squeeze my cheeks. "That's the last time I try to help yo ass. You're gonna need me one day, and when you do, I'm gon' tell you to kiss my ass."

He stared me down for a few more seconds, waiting for me to say something. I kept my mouth shut, and my eyes fluttered with relief as he let go of my cheeks and walked out the door.

I wasn't sure if he'd come back, but I predicted he would. I rushed to call my other cousin, T-Bone, to see if he'd bring me a gun.

Chapter Twenty-Six

The twins were coming home tomorrow. I took my entire paycheck to purchase their waterbeds, along with pink and white bedding ensembles. Imaging exactly how I wanted their room to be, I sat in the middle of their bedroom floor painting ceramic letters that spelled their names. I carefully hung the pink painted letters on the wall and couldn't believe how beautiful their room had panned out. I'd promised them that we'd go to Show Biz Pizza, but due to the lack of money, that had to be put off for another day.

As I was cleaning up my mess, there was a rapid knock on the door. I asked who was there, but got no answer. Not knowing if someone had just walked away, I opened the door. Two thuggish looking brothas, one with thick braids and the other with a wild afro, stood on the porch. Before I could say a word, they rushed inside. I backed up to the coat closet behind me, staring at the gun in the one with the braids hand. My breathing increased, I had never been so afraid in my life!

"Take whatever you want," I rushed to say with a heaving chest. "I…I don't have much money, but what little I do have is in my purse."

The one with the gun aimed it directly between my eyes. I stared down his barrel, waiting for a bullet to shoot through. Tears had already soaked my face and I was frozen in time. I couldn't even breathe any longer and my whole body felt like cement had been poured over it. "Where dat muthafucka Dwayne at?" he shouted while sucking his teeth. "Have you seen that nigga?"

I slowly moved my head from side to side. "No," I said softly. "I…I haven't. He doesn't live here."

"That bitch lyin'," the other one shouted out. "She knows where that fool at!"

My hands trembled and I tightened my fists to calm myself a bit. "I swear to God that I don't know where he is. I swear it."

The brotha with the gun grabbed my collar, shoving me towards the living room. I was very cooperative, and he ordered me on my knees. He squeezed my neck, and pressed the cold tip of the gun against my cheek. By now, I was shaking all over and my cries were uncontrollable. My stomach was queasy; I felt as if I had to throw up.

"If or when you see that nigga, you tell him Big Rick stopped by. That nigga stole ten g's from me, and I want every damn dime of my money back!"

He was squeezing my sweaty neck so tight, pinching it. I swore up and down that I didn't know where Dwayne was, nor did I have anything to do with him.

"I can't tell him anything because I...I don't know how to get in touch with him. Please believe me," I begged tearfully. "I wouldn't lie to you at a time like this."

The dude pushed my head to the ground, forcing me to lay execution style. This was it for me. I couldn't believe my life was about to end like this. I squeezed my eyes together, thinking about my babies...my family and hoping and praying for a way out.

"Knock this bitch off," the one showing the gun advised the other. "She don't know shit, but I don't want her snitchin'."

He walked out the door, leaving the other dude behind to do his dirty work. Since I was about to die, I felt a certain urge to face my killer. I wanted to see the person who was responsible for taking my life away from me, leaving my kids without a mother, and my family suffering through years and years of hurt. I slowly rolled on my back, eyeballing the gun that he'd pulled from his pants. My body was stiff, and since I hadn't taken any breaths, I already felt dead. I shifted my eyes to my possible killer, staring at him without a blink. My mouth was dry, and when I opened my mouth, my lips felt as if they were stuck together. A sudden calm came over me, and I softly spoke out with trembling lips that were laced with my tears and snot.

"Please don't do this to me. I have two babies that need me and please don't destroy their lives. I'm begging you not to, and if you let me live, I will pray for you, every single day, for the rest of my life. God help you and me, please, I'm begging you not to kill me."

The brotha stood stone-faced, twitching his beady eyes and hesitating. He took a few bites from his lip, staring at me and contemplating his next move. After a few seconds, he ran towards the door. Two gunshots rang out, causing my whole body to jump. I sat still for a few minutes, without moving from my spot. I then heard screeching tires, and that's when I crawled over to the door to close it. I lay flat on my back in the foyer, tightly gripping my stomach and sobbing uncontrollably. It wasn't long before I gagged and threw up right there on the floor. Over and over again, I thanked God for sparing my life.

***

The twins were so happy to see me, and from the loneliness I felt, I knew I would never let them go away for that long again.

Rita and Clarence were tired from the long drive, so we ordered pizza and went to the basement. Jesse came over, too, and as we all sat around talking, Rita hit us with breaking news.

"I wasn't going to tell anyone yet, but I'm pregnant."

Jesse and I were surprised and we congratulated Rita and Clarence. It was about time one of my sisters had a kid.

"Does Mama know about this yet?" I asked. "I suspect that she doesn't because I know my phone would be ringing off the hook."

"Well," Rita said. "I haven't gotten around to telling her just yet. You know how Mama is. I'm not up for a bunch of negative talk right now. Clarence and I are on our way to tell her, but I don't know what to expect."

"Yes, I do know how Mama is," I said. "So don't expect her to jump for joy right away. Whenever me and her talk, we rarely talk about my personal business and she never asks."

Rita and Jesse agreed. Mama hadn't said much about any of the men we'd dated. It wasn't that she didn't care, but in her eyes, nobody was good enough for her daughters. And if you weren't good enough, then you weren't worth discussing.

Clarence laughed. "Y'all need to stop talking 'bout y'all's Mama. She gon' be happy to have another grandbaby. When she finds out we're having a boy, she really gon' be excited."

We all pursed our lips at Clarence. "You don't know how Mama is," we said in unison and I gave Clarence a "welcome to the family" pat on the back.

"So, do you like your new place, Brenda?" Rita asked.

"Girl, I love it. Much better than the other one, ain't it?"

"Yes, it is and way more room."

"I know. I definitely needed more room. Now, we got a place where we can chill, instead of cluttering up the living room."

"Ay, whatever happened to Dwayne," Clarence asked clearing his throat. I was sure everyone had thought back to the time Dwayne had gone to Tennessee with me and we got into an argument at Rita's house. He called me a bitch, and called Rita one, too, when she intervened. Clarence spoke up for us both and Dwayne cursed him out. He left in a rage, and we drove around for hours trying to find him. I was so embarrassed. Rita and Clarence had witnessed for themselves the ongoing drama in our relationship. "Y'all still together?" Clarence continued.

"Uh, no. That didn't work out too well."

"I'm glad to hear that, but I know the twins really like him. They talked a lot about him while in Tennessee."

"Yeah, the twins' love for him is unconditional. They care a lot for him. He's all they've ever known as a father."

"It takes a lot of courage for a man to step up when another man didn't. I'm sure you appreciate that, but you can always do much better."

"Trust me, I know that now. Things are getting better for me."

I changed the subject and everyone spent the next few hours telling me about the twins' visit to Tennessee. It had gotten late so Rita and Clarence were on their way to go see Mama. I wanted to go, too, but the twins were already asleep. I thanked Rita and Clarence for keeping them over the summer, and they left. Jesse stayed to talk to me a while longer.

"I wanted to tell you that I read those pages you gave me. I loved it, Brenda, and you straight up took me there. I was feeling your characters and you got that character, Jay, hooked up, don't you?"

I was grinning from ear-to-ear, because Jesse enjoyed my story. "He does have it going on, don't he? Do you think the story is going overboard?"

"Not at all. Keep writing. I'd love to see what else you come up with."

I got up and Jesse followed me upstairs to my bedroom. "I've written about thirty more pages," I said, handing them over to her. "Read those and let me know what you think. Don't lie, Jesse. If you ain't feeling it, let me know. More than anything, be honest."

"You know I'm your biggest critic, and you can count on me to tell you the truth!"

I walked Jesse to the door, thanking her, again, for reading over several pages of my story. She left, but I tossed and turned all night, thinking about the story I had been piecing together. I remembered where I left off, and since I was so hyped, I sat up in bed and started writing again.

Nearly an hour later, my writing was interrupted by a bang on the door. I jumped, as I had done so at the sound of every little noise that I'd heard, since the incident with those intruders. I cautiously got out of bed, peeking through my window, first, just to see who was out there. From my window, I couldn't see much. I thought it could be Rita and Clarence coming back to tell me they'd got into it with Mama, but I also thought it was those two thugs coming back to finish me off. This time my children were home, and I regretted that my cousin, T-Bone, wouldn't bring me a gun.

I was so nervous that I reached for the phone. I carried it to the front door with me, where I had a chair against the door to secure it. I had been that scared about the intruders coming back, and was prepared to call 911 if need be. I turned on the porch light and looked through the peephole. It was Dwayne. I sighed, and then spoke through the door, trying to keep my voice down so I wouldn't wake the twins.

"I came to see the kids," he said. "I know they're back by now."

"They're asleep. Come back tomorrow."

"Nope. Can't do that. I'm here now so open the door." He continued to bang, so I moved the chair away from the door and cracked it open.

"What is up with you?" I asked irritated as ever. "You can't be coming over here without calling. It's too late and—"

"I can do whatever I want to do. Now, let me in before I force my way inside to see them."

I hesitated, thinking maybe if I let him see the twins, he would do so and then leave. I widened the door for him to come in. "You got five minutes to see them—and I mean just see them. Please don't wake them up."

When Dwayne walked in, I could immediately tell something was wrong. His eyes were a dull yellow and his words slurred. He stumbled into the twins' room and hit his leg on the edge of one of their beds. "Ouch," he yelled loudly. They lifted their heads, and I stood in the doorway counting the minutes down. By then, I'd realized it was a bad idea letting him come inside. He'd dropped down to one knee, and they both had their arms around him, giving him hugs. Of course, they didn't know any better, but I did. He mumbled his words as he spoke, looking spacey as ever.

"You...you can come back tomorrow to see them," I said, trying to rush him. He ignored me. "Dwayne, did you hear me?"

"Yeah, I heard what you said." He stood up, barely able to keep his balance. "I don't take orders from you." I kept my mouth shut, anticipating my silence would encourage him to leave. Instead, he got louder and continued his disrespect in front of the twins.

"You...you get on my damn nerves. Here I am tryin' to spend just a little time with the kids and you over here tellin' me what to do. You broke-ass slut, I'll leave when I get ready to leave."

I shook my head, disgusted that this was happening again. The twins first day back and they had to deal with this. I had seen this play out many, many times before. He was high on PCP, crack...whatever, and would claim not to remember a thing. No matter what, though, he was getting out—now! I walked to the front door and opened it.

"Goodbye, Dwayne. We'll talk to you tomorrow." He came out of the twins' room and slammed the front door shut. He sucked in his bottom lip and bit down on it. I knew what was coming next and had to think fast.

"Didn't I tell you I wasn't goin' anywhere?" He pushed me away from the door. "Get somewhere and go sit down."

The twins stood in the hallway right by the door with sad looks on their faces. I could tell they were about to burst out in tears and I lost it. Something inside of me snapped and I ran to the dark kitchen to search for any object I could find to protect myself from what was about to happen. I wished like hell my cousin had brought me a gun, but he told me that he didn't want me getting into any trouble. Dwayne charged into the kitchen, grabbing me by my shirt and slinging me against the wall. His fist punched the wall beside my face, causing a gaping hole. I put my hands over my face, screaming so loud that my whole face shook. He backed up and I fell to the ground screaming even louder for him to get out of our lives.

"Get ooooout!" I yelled. "And stay out!"

Feeling as if I couldn't do anything else to defend myself, I got on my knees, praying out loudly. "Lord, please help me," I begged. "Remove this man from my life, because I have no need for him."

As I continued in a tearful prayer, I could hear the twins' cries echo through my ears. Dwayne's voice rang out the loudest, but I did my best to tune him out and kept on praying.

"You're a silly bitch! Don't go callin' for Him now," he said standing over me. "He ain't gonna help yo ass."

I kept at it. "Lord please, right now Lord. You've shown me time and time again that this relationship wasn't for me, but I ignored your signs. I've paid the price, and from now own, I promise to be obedient. Look upon me and my children right now and save us! I need peace and I need him removed from my life." I lifted my head, wiping the tears from my face.

Dwayne squatted face-to-face with me. "Yo ass is stupid. God don't hear people like you. You're a thief, a liar, a cheat and a poor excuse for a mother. " He gathered saliva in his mouth and spat in my face. I took a hard swallow and didn't say a word. I got off the floor and walked over to a drawer that carried the butcher knife that I'd seen right before he'd entered the kitchen. I knew this wasn't God answering my prayer, but it was only me, trying to seek satisfaction for all that had been done to me. I charged at Dwayne with the knife in my hand and for several seconds, my mind went blank. Silence fell over the room. My vision was blurred and when I snapped back into the moment, I saw dripping blood on the razor-sharp knife. The twins arms were tightly gripped around my waist and Dwayne had run towards the door while holding his bloody shoulder. I dropped the knife to the floor, and grabbed my terrified children in my arms.

Moments later, I locked the front door, put the chair back in front of it and hurried into my bedroom. I thought about calling the police, but I didn't want them taking me to jail, leaving my kids behind. And I definitely didn't want to contact anyone in my family. They were frustrated about what had been going on between Dwayne and me too. I checked the windows in every room to make sure they were locked. Surely, I feared for our lives and I didn't know what Dwayne would do after this incident. He had been shot before, and the dude who was responsible didn't live much longer after that. I knew what Dwayne was capable of and I had no idea how bad his injury was. I put the twins in bed with me and told them to go back to sleep.

As I lay across my bed thinking, I got back on my knees for the second time that night. "Lord, I'm sorry for what I've done. I know it wasn't your answer, but I felt like I didn't have a choice. Please watch over us and protect us from all evil. Give me strength to make it through this. I want to...need to do better." I couldn't help but ask. "Why me Lord? What did I do to deserve all of this?" I paused, before asking God to watch over the intruder who almost took my life.

By morning, I wasn't up to going to work, so I called in sick. The twins were in the kitchen already, trying to make me breakfast. I saw the big mess they were making, and I told them we'd make breakfast together. As I looked at them, it was like last night had never happened. They didn't say anything about it and spent the day playing games in their room, painting pictures and watching television downstairs.

With a migraine headache, I laid in bed catching up on one of my favorite soap operas I hadn't seen in a while. The phone rang, and when I answered, it was Dwayne's mother. She got right to the point.

"Brenda, what happened last night? Dwayne came home with blood all over his shirt and I had to take him to the emergency room to get stitches."

"Mrs. Montgomery, it's a long story. Dwayne came here last night high on something, and we started arguing. He pushed me around, threatened me and disrespected me in front of my children.

He keeps coming over here bothering me, and when he spit in my face," I paused, swallowing to clear my aching throat. "I vaguely remember the details but I...I did stab him."

"Dwayne and you have been at this mess for too many years. I'm sick of it! I don't understand why you can't leave each other alone. Last night, I told him he better not ever step foot in your home again. And if he does, his father and I will make sure we deal with him. Be done with it, Brenda, and don't you ever open up that door for him again."

If anybody could get through to Dwayne, it was his mother. She pretty much stayed out of our arguments, but when she did intervene, Dwayne, sometimes, listened.

As I started to feel better about our conversation, Mrs. Montgomery continued. "Brenda, you haven't done Dwayne any favors by supporting him while he's on drugs. You never let him see what it was like to fall flat on his face, and every time you picked him up, he got worse. He knew if I wouldn't be there for him, he'd always have you. If you haven't already, it's time to let go. If you were my daughter, I'd encourage you to wash your hands and never look back. Keep Dwayne away from your children and stop subjecting them to all of this foolishness. They may not understand all of this now, but one day they will. You don't want them to grow up thinking or believing that the kind of relationship you're in with Dwayne is a healthy one."

She was right, but I still tried to justify my actions. "Mrs. Montgomery, a part of me always thought we were destined to be together. We'd been on and off again since high school and I didn't want to let those years go to waste. I thought he'd change. I always felt as if I could help him overcome his habit. I did my best to help him, but Dwayne treated me like his enemy. I don't understand—"

"He will never be what you want him to be. He hasn't fallen yet and his issues are beyond your control. One day, he'll realize all of his mistakes. Until then, you stay away from him. Take care of yourself and your daughters, and I wish you well. If I find out you let him back into your home, for any reason, I'll deal with you myself."

"Yes Ma'am," I said, showing her respect.

"I love my son, Brenda," she said, getting choked up. "I know when he's done wrong. Still, I'm not going to stand by and let another woman take him away from me, as you could have easily done last night. His destiny is not in your hands and you can't pave the way for him. He has to do it for himself, and with you having children, I'm sure you understand."

"Yes, I do. You have my word that I will never involve myself with your son again."

"Thank you," she said.

"Kiss the girls for me, and before you go, Dwayne has something that he wants to say to you. Hold on."

I held my breath as I listened to Dwayne apologize to me for last night. "I know you're tired of hearin' it, but those drugs are fuckin' with me. Bad. I'ma get some help and get myself together. You know I would never do anything to intentionally hurt you or the twins. It would break my heart if they are left with memories of me like this. I'ma step back and let you do your thing. Take care of my girls for me and just pray for me, au'ight?"

I rushed to speak, because no matter what, I still wanted the best for him. "I will pray for you, always. And the twins will always love you, but we both have been reckless parents that they don't deserve. They deserve better, and as their mother, I owe it to them to get this right. You have to get focused on you, and get your life together. It's imperative, because you can't go on living like this. I know that giving up those drugs is easier said than done, but they have turned you into a man that I never thought you would be. Please get help. I'm begging you, before it's too late. Tell your mother I said thanks for calling and I'll be rooting for you."

There was silence, and then Dwayne hung up. Little did I know, it would be the last conversation that we would ever have, but a sudden calm came over me. At that moment, I thanked God for my life, and prayed for Dwayne. I started to feel better, so I made the twins put on some clothes so we could go to the playground. While they played, I sat on the bench writing in a notebook that I had carried to the playground with me. I was hopeful that this was a true turning point in my life: *I hope I'm not fooling myself, again, but for some reason, I feel as though this is the end of me and Dwayne. I'm sad, but glad. I take some responsibility for this ongoing mess and I'm not going to play the victim because I contributed to years of this chaos too. I didn't want to hurt him yesterday, but he left me no choice. If this continues on, one of us will die. I appreciate him being there for the twins, but it's time to let go. They'll be fine, and I'm so glad that they've met some new friends in the neighborhood. I love my babies and it's because of them that I want to live on and do better. I will do better...*

Chapter Twenty-Seven

I hadn't been working in the Member Services department for one month, before rumors started to circulate. Physician's Health Plan was downsizing. Because night school and my job became too much for me to handle, I'd quit school and was now regretting it. However, since my manager, Elaine, and I had developed an excellent work relationship, she called me into her office and shared the information with me firsthand.

"Maybe another month or so with the company," Elaine said. "And after that, many of us will be looking for new jobs. But whatever move I make, I'd love to take you right along with me. You're a hard worker, Brenda, and I love how you are with our customers. What you don't know is many of them call to let me know how helpful you've been to them. That's great and you should feel good about that."

"I do," I said. I was still a bit nervous about losing my job, and I hoped my manager was able to hook up something for me.

On my way back to my desk, I never thought, in a million years, a White lady would be so committed to helping me, but she seemed to genuinely have my back. I had felt that way because of those White police officers in my neighborhood who displayed true racism. I shouldn't have put all White people in one category, and it became obvious that the color of my skin wasn't an issue for everyone. As long as I showed I was capable of doing my job, I earned my respect in the work place.

It wasn't long, actually weeks after I had spoken to Elaine, before the pink slips had been handed down at work and more were on the way. I hadn't gotten mine yet, but it was soon to come. Elaine had already interviewed with a new healthcare company, Health Partners of the Midwest, and she gave me a lead on a position in Sales and Marketing. She said her job was pretty much set in stone, but I definitely had to sell myself in the interview. I called to set it up for the next day.

When the next day came, I put on my dark blue pantsuit and black pumps. My portfolio was in one hand and my short resume was in the other. The company was in Clayton, an elite part of town that was known for having lavish homes and buildings. I took the elevator to the tenth floor of the building and made my exit. Nothing but class hit me, as I walked through the tinted double doors and stood in front of the receptionist.

"My name is Brenda Hampton, and I'm here to see Mr. Joseph Schnieder for the lead administrator position in Marketing."

"I'll let him know you're here." She placed an application on top of her desk. "Please have a seat and fill out this application. Mr. Schnieder will be with you shortly."

I took a seat in the leather comfy chair, breezing through the application—until I came to a question that asked: *Have you ever been convicted of a crime? If so, explain.* I hesitated for a minute, and then checked no.

When I was finished, I gave the clipboard back to the receptionist and she called Mr. Schnieder again. He came out wearing a pin-striped black suit, silver framed round glasses that had a tint, and his hair was a smooth salt-and-pepper gray. He was an older White man, but was very handsome.

"Brenda Hampton?" he asked, holding out his hand.

"Yes, Mr. Schnieder. How are you?" I kept a bright smile on my face while shaking his hand.

"Come this way. You'll have to excuse my office; it's a mess. We're just now getting things moved in and I can't find a darn thing. Have a seat," he said, directing me to the chair in front of his mahogany desk.

He made a ticking sound with his mouth while looking over my application. "So, let's see here. I see most of your background has been with the health insurance industry, particularly in customer service. I assume you can use a computer and you must know how to deal with irate people very well."

"Yes," I laughed, feeling the tightened knot in my stomach loosen. "Very well."

He removed his glasses, placing them on his desk. "First, let me tell you what I'm looking for in the Marketing department, and then you tell me if it sounds like something you would be interested in."

"Okay," I said, sitting back and listening.

Big responsibilities, I thought as he talked. The position sounded interesting, but it was way out of my league. When he started talking bid letters, proposals, quotes, brokers, underwriting and spreadsheets, I figured this job was more than I could handle. But when he mentioned the stunning starting salary, and said they would train me, I had a whole new attitude. *I could do this*, I thought. *Most definitely*. I always caught on pretty quickly, and this job would be no exception.

"So, Ms. Hampton, does this sound like something you would be interested in?"

"Yes, it does, Mr. Schnieder. I truly believe I can be an asset to this company, if given the opportunity."

"Good, because you came highly recommended," he said, writing something on my application. "How soon can you start?"

"As soon as you'd like me to," I said. "But I would ask that you allow me to give my present employer two week's notice."

"Sure, that'll be no problem." He stood, extending his hand to mine. We shook. "Come on, let me show you around," he said, making his way around his desk.

I followed him out the door, thinking about how halfway through the interview, he'd put me at ease with his great sense of humor. The intimidation I'd felt when I first laid eyes on him disappeared.

"Since you're going to be my Lead Administrator for Marketing, I need you close by. Your desk will be right here," he said, pointing to a spacious cubical area close to his office and next to his secretary. "I'm going to fill the rest of this area with your staff. These people will report to you and the Marketing Manager, which you already know will be Elaine. So, if you know of any qualified individuals who would be interested, send them my way."

I told Mr. Schnieder I would, and I quickly learned that Corporate America was all about who you know, not necessarily what you know. After the tour, he gave me directions to take a physical exam, and to bring back a police record check for Human Resources. I damn near fainted. I shook his hand, thanking him before I walked back to the elevator. *I can kiss that job goodbye*, I thought. When he finds out I lied on the application, he was going to find somebody else. I was disappointed—my past had finally caught up with me.

Since the record's building was in the vicinity, I decided to go there to find out what was actually on my police record. I'd heard after a few years, convictions were removed from your record, as long as you stayed out of trouble.

I pulled a number and stood in line. When the woman called my number, I gave her my driver's license so she could search for my information. She hit key after key on the keyboard, frowning as she looked at what was on the computer and sighed.

"I'll have to mail this to you," she said. "There are too many convictions on file."

My heart sank to my stomach and face cracked all at the same time.

I felt so disgusted with myself. I was warned that this mess would come back to haunt me. How did I ever let this happen to me? I wanted that job so bad I could taste it, but there was no way I could tell Mr. Schnieder I'd lied on my application. He would never want to hire someone who was known as a thief, and I knew my police report painted me out to be a serious criminal.

I went home feeling rotten about myself. Earlier, I couldn't wait to get home and break the news, but now there wasn't any sense in me calling anyone. Elaine had left a message, asking how the interview had gone. I knew I had to call her back, at least to thank her for the high recommendation.

"Hi, Elaine," I said in a gloomy mood. "This is Brenda."

"Hello," she said with excitement. "So, how did it go?"

"It went well."

"Well, why do you sound like it didn't? Did he offer the job to you?"

"Yes, he did but—" I paused, taking a moment to gather my thoughts.

"Brenda, sweetie, what's wrong? Are you okay?"

I waited before speaking. This was so damn embarrassing, and to me, my police report did not paint a clear picture of who I really was, or should I say, had become. People changed, but I didn't know how to say that to Elaine. "Yes, I'm okay but there's something I have to tell you. At a time in my life when things weren't going too good for me, I turned to crime. I shoplifted to make money and had to face the judge several times for doing so. I also had a confrontation with an officer and he arrested me for obstruction of justice. Mr. Schnieder asked me for a police report and my convictions are on there. On my application, I checked that I didn't have a criminal history. There's no way I can go back and tell him I lied. What will he think of me?"

"Listen, don't be so upset. We've all done things in our lives we aren't proud of. Tomorrow, call him and tell him exactly what you told me. You're a good person, Brenda, and a darn good employee. Your past should not matter, but you have to be honest with him. I'm sure he made you a good offer, so you call him back and get that offer! By all means, you deserve it."

Speaking to Elaine put me at ease. I thanked her for the support and told her I'd call Mr. Schneider, once I got my report.

After two days, I waited for the mail to come and there it was. I opened the envelope and couldn't believe my eyes. ARRESTS ON FILE stamped big as day, in red, on the front of the paper. On the back it listed three shoplifting charges, one obstruction of justice charge, resisting arrest, and a disturbing the peace charge I got by clowning with Dwayne in front of my apartment one day. They were all misdemeanor charges, but sure as hell didn't look good. I had messed up my life and didn't even know I was doing so. I tossed the paper aside, deciding there was no way in hell I was going to show something like that to Mr. Schnieder.

Later that day, I took the twins to the library, and as they read books, I sat at a table writing. I wrote a letter to Mr. Schnieder, thinking about mailing it to him, but eventually threw it away. My mind was boggled, and in order to clear it, I started all over and began to write about my life. From the beginning...how it all started, as far as I could remember. I wrote for hours, feeling so good and clearing my mind. I had so much inside of me that needed to come out. That day, it did.

After we got home from the library, I turned the lights out in the twins' room, telling them not to stay up late watching TV. I then lay across my bed, looking for answers to my problem with Mr. Schnieder. I got on my knees and held my praying hands together. *Lord, I know it seems like when I come to you I'm always asking you to fix something, but I have nowhere else to turn. I feel this opportunity is a good one and might not ever present itself to me again. Please give me the courage to make the right decision. If this position is for me, open the door and let me walk through it. Any help you can send would be appreciated. And...thank you, thank you for all that you've done for my family and all that you will continue to do. Amen. Oh...one more thing. Please continue to look over my intruder, as he not know better. Dwayne too. Help them and use your power to will them away from the negativity. Amen again.*

While at work the next day, I didn't waste any time calling Mr. Schnieder. When I got his voicemail, I left a message for him to call me back. Shortly thereafter, he did. I made an appointment to go see him at one o'clock, and took my lunch break at twelve-thirty. That gave me plenty of time to make it there, but I knew I wasn't going to make it back within an hour.

When I arrived, Mr. Schnieder was in an interview with another person, so I had to wait. After waiting twenty minutes, he said goodbye to the lady who would, most likely, replace me. He motioned for me to come into his office.

"Have a seat, Ms. Hampton. What can I do for you today?" He leaned back in his leather chair, waiting for a response.

I sighed, shaking my leg and nervous as ever! "Mr. Schnieder, the other day when I interviewed with you, I wasn't completely honest on my application. I checked that I did not have a criminal history, when in fact I did." I gave him the police report and continued to explain my situation. He glanced over the police report, looking very puzzled. A few times, he scratched his head and stared at me as I continued to talk. After my teary-eyed confession, he folded up my report, giving it back to me.

"Brenda," he said, sitting up straight. "It took a lot of courage for you to come here today. In that position out there," he pointed out the door, "I need someone who has courage, who has vigor, who's aggressive, honest, and who isn't afraid to tell me when they've made some mistakes. Someone who's determined to help me run this darn Marketing Department the right way. I don't care what you've done in the past; it's no concern of mine. All I care about is what you can do for this company in the future."

I blinked away the tears in my eyes, but a slow tear had slipped. I in no way wanted to present myself as being weak, but my life had been a true struggle and I was delighted that Mr. Schnieder hadn't judged me, based on that police report. He had no idea where I'd come from or what I'd been through and he offered me a chance. He reached for his box of Kleenex and put it down in front of me. "Now, you go take that physical exam and I'll see you here in about two weeks."

"Thank you, Mr. Schnieder. You will never regret your decision." I shook his hand and he joked about it falling off. Before leaving the building, while on the elevator, I looked up and thanked the Lord out loudly. Another lady on the elevator puzzlingly looked at me, but I didn't care. Tears welled in my eyes and I shook my head. "I'm sorry, but you might not understand."

"Oh, yes I do," she said, patting me on my back. "God is good and he'll never let you down."

I nodded, and when I got off the elevator, I encouraged her to have a good day.

"I got the job!" I screamed to the kids while dancing around in the kitchen. "Mama got the job she wanted!" They hugged me and jumped for joy with me.

As usual, I shared the news with everyone, Mama first.

"I guess you can finally buy me that new car I wanted," she said, knowing darn well that she couldn't drive.

"Only if you learn how to drive, Mama. If you do, I will definitely buy you one."

We laughed, and after speaking to her, I called Jesse and Rita. Rita and I talked about saving money, and Jesse talked to me about buying a house. She was in the process of doing so, and we planned our house search together. Things were falling into place. I was beginning to believe that anything I wanted to do was possible, and at this point, I was starting to realize my own strengths. For so long, I didn't know what they were. My life, however, was never complete without setbacks.

Chapter Twenty-Eight

Things at my new job were moving fast. Mr. Schnieder hired two Italian women I'd recommended from my previous job, and someone else recommended a third lady. On the home-front, the twins had it going on with school and I was extremely proud of them. They gave me no trouble whatsoever. I couldn't have asked for better kids. I was starting to feel at peace, and I knew that with peace, prosperity would soon follow.

As for relationships, I'd gone out to dinner with a young man named Aaron that I'd met at a comedy club one night. He seemed cool, but he had some ex-girlfriend drama that forced me to keep my distance. I had a no tolerance attitude and I simply told him over the phone one day, "Work it out and get back to me when you do."

Other than that, and referring to my job, it was the bomb, but I still felt as if something was missing. I had met all kinds of people; positive people who was all about living large, making money and enjoying life! I found myself at exquisite dinner parties, lavish Marketing functions and five-star restaurants that I didn't even know existed. I was often in the presence of the elite people in St. Louis, but I remained humble as ever. I knew where I'd come from, what I'd been through and never would I forget. I was just happy to get a taste of the other side, and since Mr. Schnieder had put me in charge of many of the marketing responsibilities, nearly everyone in our department came to me to get things done. I was overwhelmed at times, but loved it because I was learning more by the day. The only downside was I didn't have enough time to write—writing was put on the backburner.

I had just finished running a report for Mr. Schnieder, using the Access database. He was expected in a meeting within five minutes, and since his secretary was absent, he asked me to double check the report and print it for him. I did, and then carried the report into his office.

"Thank you," he said, reaching out for the report. He looked at it, while nodding his head. "Can you do me a favor and print off thirty more copies? Once you're done, bring them to the boardroom to me."

"Will do," I said, getting ready to turn and walk away.

"Also," he said, halting my steps. "I would like for you to get your insurance license. Have you thought about it?"

I really hadn't thought about it, and from what I'd heard, the test was pretty tough. "I haven't thought about it, but that doesn't mean it's something I'm not open to."

"Good," he said, rushing out of his seat. "We'll talk more about that later. Just please have those copies in the boardroom as soon as you can."

Mr. Schnieder rushed out the door, trying to make it to his meeting on time. I stood at the copy machine, making copies and thinking about getting my insurance license. That was a big...huge step. I knew many of the brokers who visited our office made a whole lot of money. Even the Account Managers in Marketing did well, and making that kind of money would surely turn things around for me. I mean, things were going good, but I was open to doing whatever to make them better. Seemed like God was lining up angels everywhere, and never, again, would I ask Him, *why me?*

Mr. Schnieder's copies were in my hand, and I hurried to the boardroom to give them to him. As I entered, not many people were there, but several businessmen in suits were trickling in. Mr. Schnieder was standing by the door, talking to a broker who visited the Account Managers from time to time. I knew him well, his name was Chris.

"Brendaaa," he said, giving me a hug. "Good seeing you."

I smiled and gave the copies to Mr. Schnieder. "Same here, Chris. I didn't know you were coming by today. If so, I would have made you another one of those Marketing baskets, filled with goodies."

He looked at his watch. "Well, I won't be leaving until another hour or two. You still have time," he joked.

Mr. Schnieder laid the papers on the round cherry-wood conference table, and asked me to have a seat. "If you don't have anything else to work on right now, please stay and take notes for me. I couldn't get anyone else to cover for Sherry, and I would really appreciate it."

Mr. Schnieder had done so much for me; he didn't have to ask twice. Actually, I enjoyed lending a hand when needed, and while some may have looked at it as being used, I looked at it as seeking knowledge about the business I was in. The brokers were treated like kings and queens, because they were responsible for obtaining companies that purchased health insurance from Health Partners. They made what was called residual income; money that you could make while basically sitting on your ass, doing nothing.

I sat at the table dressed in my mustard colored suit, knowing that I didn't fit in moneywise, but what the hell. More businessmen came in, and then, I got the shock of my life when I looked up and saw Jay Rogers strut through the door. He had stolen my attention that fast. Yet, again, he was the only Black man in the room and everyone gravitated towards him. Why? I didn't know. I sat up straight, hoping that my short hair was intact and not a strand was out of place. Seeing this man just did something to me, and just like the last time I'd seen him, he looked fabulous. His silver-blue crisp shirt with a pointed pressed collar was underneath his black suit, making his grey eyes glisten even more. I sat there visualizing him naked, and there was no doubt that he was doing one hell of a number on me. I didn't even think he remembered who I was, until he came over to me and shook my hand.

"I know this may sound cheesy," he said with his snow white teeth on display. "But haven't I seen you somewhere before?"

I could tell him the date, time, hour, second...as I had written it down. "Physician's Health Plan," I reminded him. "I used to work as the receptionist there."

He snapped his finger, and displayed those dimples I had written about as well. "I remember. So, I take it you're working over here now, right?" he asked.

I nodded, trying to downcast my gaze into his addictive eyes. "Yes, for Mr. Schnieder in Marketing."

"That's what's up. Do you have a business card you can give me? I promise to only use it for business, not pleasure."

He winked and OMG! I wanted to scream. I hoped he couldn't see my heart slamming against my chest, or for that matter, hear it. "I don't have my cards on me, but I will go back to my desk to get you one."

"You do that," he said, then walked away. I damn near broke my neck getting out of my chair and going to get him my business card. When I came back into the room, Jay was sitting at the table, talking to two other men. I excused my interruption and gave my business card to him. He thanked me.

The meeting got on the way, and Mr. Schnieder was at the head of the table, telling the brokers around the room how it would be in their best interest to sell Health Partners of The Midwest Insurance to their clients. He, along with our Executive Account Manager, Dora, shared each plan design we had to offer, and bonuses the brokers would receive for selling our product. Like I'd said…the brokers made hella money and the benefits that came along with it was unbelievable. At that moment, I knew why Mr. Schnieder had asked me to stay. He wanted me to hear, and see for myself, what obtaining an insurance license could possibly do for me.

In knowing so, I jumped on it! Day in and out, I studied my ass off, wanting to pass that test. I didn't allow any distractions in my life, and when out of the blue Jay called me at the office one day, I was skeptical. I truly felt that he would be a setback for me, and as nice looking as he was, his money…I knew there had to be drama. I didn't want him to think I wasn't interested, Lord knows I was, but I wanted to focus on passing that test.

"Dinner," he said. "You can meet me at Morton's, on Bonhomme, right across the street from your building, Friday at six."

He would not take no for an answer, so I agreed to meet him on Friday. My test was scheduled for Thursday, and since it was only Tuesday, I had plenty of time to study. Unfortunately, though, when Thursday came around, and I went to take my test, I failed. I looked at the computer screen, seeing the word FAILED, and hoping that it was incorrect. It wasn't. I had studied so hard, and needless to say, this was a big disappointment.

On Friday, I was in a shitty mood. Failing the test didn't go over well with me, and telling Mr. Schnieder, who had been really pulling for me, it was embarrassing.

"Try again," he said as I stood in his office. "That's all you can do and don't be so hard on yourself."

I guess I was the only person standing in my own way, and I had to start believing in myself a bit more. I had planned to take the test again, soon, hoping that I wouldn't have the same results.

Once I left work, I stopped at home to pick up the twins and we headed to Mama's house. They wouldn't go one weekend without seeing her, and they loved their grandmother to death! I dropped them off, and then headed to Morton's so I could have dinner with Jay. He had definitely been on my mind, maybe so much that my thoughts of him caused me to fail the damn test. So, to be honest, I wasn't too enthused about dinner. That certainly changed, however, when I walked inside of this fabulous restaurant and spotted him sitting at a table. Dressed in a gray blazer and black v-neck ribbed sweater underneath, I felt lucky to be in his presence. The "Why Me?" hit me again, but you know what? Why not me?

I looked at the crystal chandeliers that hung from up above, and at the crisp white table cloths that covered each table. Everything was so orderly and clean, and the staff was extremely polite. What was a young woman like me doing at a place like this, with a man who had to be every bit of a millionaire, or if not, close? Even at my best, I felt as if I had fallen short. The red silk mini-dress I wore clung to my body like a layer of skin, but I felt it was rather plain. My short hair had been whipped together by me, not a beautician, and I was afraid that my conversation wouldn't be up to par. I guess I was being too hard on myself, again, because as I moved in Jay's direction, he was all smiles. He stood, pulling my chair back for me to take a seat. I hesitated for just a second, thinking the chair gesture was totally unnecessary. Little did I know, it was the manly thing to do.

"Thank you for coming," Jay said. "You look nice."

"So do you," I said, crossing my legs so they would stop shaking.

The waiter came over, pouring us glasses of water and handing us menus. When he walked away, Jay snapped his fingers and the waiter returned in a flash.

"Yes, sir," the waiter said, almost bowing to Jay. "What else can I get you?"

Jay rubbed his trimmed goatee that was squared on his mouth and chin to perfection. "Do you mind telling us what the special is for the day?"

"Oh, uh, I'm sorry, sir," the man said, looking around. "Let me find out—"

Jay caught an attitude. "Look, if you don't know what it is, then get me somebody over here who knows what the hell they're doing. Preferably, Joe. My time is precious, and it needs not to be wasted."

My eyes damn near popped out of my head. I couldn't believe Jay's arrogance, or his tone. Obviously, he was irritated by something or someone. The waiter excused himself, and another one returned, telling Jay the special of the day. Before he could finish, Jay cut him off.

"That's alright, Joe. I don't like that. I'll have the usual."

"Filet Mignon, double cut with a baked potato. Would you like the Caesar salad and what can I get for the lady?"

"A Caesar salad will be fine, and the lady will have exactly what I'm having, but make it a single cut, not double."

"Will do. Thank you, Mr. Rogers, and if you need anything else, I'll be delighted to assist you."

Jay ordered a bottle of wine, as I sat there looking clueless. How did he know what I wanted to eat? I hadn't even looked at the menu to see what I wanted. This wasn't working for me right now, but I held back on saying anything.

The waiter walked away, and as soon as Jay opened his mouth, his beeper went off. It was clipped to his black pants and he swung his jacket back to take a look. I noticed that he grunted a little, and then turned off his beeper. Afterward, he placed his hands on the table and clinched them together. The diamonds from his watch glistened and drew my eyes straight to it.

"I see you like my Rolex," he said, turning it to look at the time.

"It's real nice. Looks like it cost a fortune."

"Not really, but, uh, tell me some things about yourself. Who is Brenda Hampton and what kind of mission in life are you on?"

Good question, and truthfully, I didn't know how to answer his question. He'd caught me completely off guard, but I did my best to answer.

"I'm just taking this one day at a time approach. Don't quite know what the future holds for me yet, but I'm open to whatever possibilities swing my way."

"You mentioned that you were taking your insurance test on Thursday. How did you do?"

Oh, God, Jay was making this so difficult. Felt like I was on an interview, instead of a *date.* I dropped my head a little and fumbled with my nails. "I didn't pass it, but I'm going to take it again next week."

"That's all you can do. The only one I failed was my Series 7. Got a ninety percent on my insurance test and the other two Series, but the Series 7 was tough. I retook it, passing with a ninety-five percent. I had a lot going on at the time, and I believe I over-studied for it. That's probably what you did, and my advice would be to not study again. Just go take it and I bet you'll pass it."

A person had to be pretty darn smart to pass those Series tests and to score what Jay had. I was impressed. "Thanks for the advice," I said, lifting the flute glass and clinking it against his. "Here's to me passing my test."

"No doubt."

Dinner was served, and to say the least, the food was outstanding. I had never had a steak so thick and juicy, and the one Jay ordered took up most of his plate.

"So, when am I going to see you again, besides when I come to your office for visits?" he asked.

I shrugged. "When would you like to see me again?"

"In a week, maybe two."

My feelings were bruised. I guess I hadn't made a good impression. I just knew he would say tomorrow or the next day. A week or two seemed way off.

"I need to jet out of town on business. When I get back, I'll check in with you," he said.

"Sounds like a plan," was all I could say.

We continued to talk and I found out some very interesting things about Jay. He was a few years younger than I was, and that came as a total surprise because he seemed very mature for his age. More mature than any man I had ever dated. At such a young age he appeared to have it all together. Yes, he was a millionaire, and then some, with the help of his inheritance and years of working as a broker. According to him, he only worked so he wouldn't get bored. His home was in Chesterfield, Missouri, and for someone who had known the St. Louis area pretty well, I knew that only rich...filthy rich people lived in Chesterfield. I could only imagine what his house looked like, and there was no way in hell I would ever invite him to my townhouse. He shared a lot with me during dinner that night. It appeared that no one was exempt from drama. He was upset about his ex-girlfriend going to Detroit with her new man. The other chick was in Denver trying to escape the fallout from their relationship and had told him she wanted to live there on a regular basis. He felt betrayed and seemed to have a lot going on. I appreciated him telling me about his situation, before I decided to test the waters.

"So, you say you still have love for your ex, but you want the other chick to come back home. If she does, then what Jay? And where do you think I can fit into all of this?"

He was blunt. "You fit where I place you."

"Wrong answer," I hurried to say. I stood up ready to leave, because his comment rubbed me the wrong way. As I tucked my purse underneath my arm, he touched my hand.

"Please, sit back down. I didn't mean it like that, but what I wanted to say is I'm not married to no one. I'm a young man, who is taken time to explore options. Love for me don't come easy, but I have been with my ex, on and off again for a very long time. Right now, I'm just in the mood to have some fun. If you're down with that, let me know what's up."

I hesitated before taking my seat again. Jay was tripping, and even though I liked confident men, this was too much. I knew all too well about on-and, off-again relationships and his situation didn't seem stable. I was, however, interested in having "fun" too, so I told him to be sure to call me when he returned home from his trip. He said he would. I thanked him for the fulfilling meal that set him back a few hundred dollars and we went our separate ways.

During dinner, Jay had inquired about my current and past life too. I only told him so much, but my past was something I really didn't want to run from. It had made me who I was, but there was a time and place to share with Jay all that I wanted him to know. That day was coming soon, but for now, he'd given me a little more to add to the story I had been trying to piece together about him. It was...interesting.

Chapter Twenty-Nine

I took Jay's advice about not studying and I passed the test! I was so excited, until I applied for a promotion within my department and didn't get it. It was a letdown, only because I had been working my ass off and truly felt as if I deserved it. Mr. Schnieder did offer me another pay increase, and for that, I was grateful.

Much of what was going on in Corporate America was political. I had no room to complain; after all, I had benefited from the 'not what you know, but who you know' theory. It was happening throughout our company, and people who definitely had skills could in no way get a foot in the door, unless they knew somebody. That's just the way it was, but with having my insurance license, I was ready for a change. When one door slammed, I would always try another one. I would fall, but you could never count me out. I began to see Health Partners as a stepping stone, not my ultimate destiny. I started making many more connections with the brokers and one broker had offered me a job at his firm, Cutter & Company.

"I really do like where I'm at right now, Robert, but if that ever changes will you still have a position for me?" I asked.

"Of course," he said, walking with me to the elevator.

He waved goodbye, telling me to be sure to call, if anything changed.

While sitting inside of my convertible Mustang, I decided to return Jay's phone call that he'd left earlier that day. I had seen him twice since dinner, once when I visited the brokerage firm he worked for, and another time we'd met at CJ Muggs for drinks. We spent more time on the telephone than anything, and that was understandable because he was truly a busy man. To me, he only made time for people, if he wanted to. I was able to share some of my past with him, and when I told him about my shoplifting days, all he did was laugh. What bothered me didn't even seem to trouble him at all and his words were always on point. "There are some things in life that are beyond your control," he said that day. "But if they are within your control, correct them. Sounds like that's what you did. Now, you're creating an image of success for yourself. You've broken out of your box and you're starting to believe that anything you want or desire is within your reach. That mindset, Brenda, will take you far places in life. It's only when you minimize your vision that you make little progress. Trust me, I know." Jay was so right and his words were encouraging. I appreciated his realness during our conversations, and without him knowing it, his words had given me hope. Even when I belittled myself, saying that I was stupid for staying with Dwayne for as long as I had done, Jay had an interesting reply.

"You're so wrong, Brenda, and you didn't go through that shit just to come out of it feeling stupid. What you need to realize is that many women, even the ones that I deal with, have underling problems that existed, before they entered into relationships. Hell, I got problems, too, but I am far from being stupid. It all stems from things that relate to fathers, mothers, your upbringing...maybe some women have been raped before, who knows? But summing it up as being stupid is a stupid thing for you, or for anyone to do. The ignorance lies only with those who will judge you and act like they ain't been through nothing. There are plenty of people who will shame you because your life experiences have been different from theirs. Let no one dictate the timeline of your life experiences or relationships, and give no explanation for battles that were chosen for you. Accept what you've been through as a learning experience that will take you to new heights. There ain't no other way to look at it, baby, and when you start seeing things from your eyes, instead of through the eyes of others, you will have a better understanding. You feel me?"

Yes, I did feel him, and in no way could I dispute what Jay had said that day, because I wasn't sure if I would be in this position right now, if it weren't for my trials and tribulations.

As I thought more about him, I sat in my car, waiting for him to answer his phone. He finally picked up. "Jay Rogers."

"Hi, Jay," I said with a smile on my face.

"Where are you?" he asked.

"At Cutter & Company, dropping off some insurance proposals."

"So you're in Chesterfield?"

"Yes."

"Then, stop by to see me. My house isn't too far from there."

I looked at my watch. It was a little after one, and I still had a few more proposals to drop off and deliver Christmas cookies to my clients for the holidays. I hadn't had lunch, though, so I told Jay I would stop by. He gave me directions and I headed to his place.

When I got there, it was another very shocking moment for me. I felt like I was pulling up to a red-carpet event and was underdressed. To my right was a humongous castle-like brick house, sitting on acres and acres of land with a lake beside it. I parked my car and walked to the double front doors that viewed the inside of the house. I could see Jay making his way to the door, and it was the first time I'd seen him dressed down in jeans and a v-neck soft cream t-shirt that tightened on his muscles.

Jay opened the door, and I couldn't believe that the first thing he asked was for me to remove my shoes.

"That's if you don't mind," he said with a shrug. "As you can see, my carpet is white and I don't want any dirt on it."

My shoes weren't even dirty, but as I glanced at the plush white carpet, it was a beautiful sight. One speck of dirt would ruin it. Already, the house looked made for a king and it was good to know that, yes, Black people could live like this too. No doubt, I was inspired.

I took off my shoes, and Jay placed them on a shoe-rack that was close by the door. He gave me a tour around his house, leaving me in awe. Had never witnessed anything like it and my mouth was hanging open. *One day*, I thought. *One day I am going to live like this too!*

As the day proceeded with more talks, laughter and drinking, I was completely sold on Jay Rogers and everything about him. If he wanted to have fun, hell, yes, I was all for it! Especially with someone like him...why not? However, what I didn't expect was for us to be in his shower that was big enough for, at least, ten people to stand. There was even a seat inside, and the whole bathroom, including the oval shaped Jacuzzi tub, was bigger than the top level of my townhouse. I felt a little uncomfortable, because I hadn't showered with anyone before. However, Jay made me feel comfortable, and as he washed my body with his lathered strong hands, squeezing in all the right places, my nervousness subsided. The slip of his fingers entering me had me mesmerized. There was something about the way his lips delicately touched mine that made my whole body tremble. I wanted...needed to feel his long hard muscle that had to be the prettiest dick I'd ever seen. Umph...I felt lucky, as our light-skinned bodies left no breathing room in between them.

"See, this feels good, doesn't it?" he whispered while massaging my breasts. "I knew you'd like it in here. Now, open your eyes and tell me who or what you're thinking about."

I slowly opened my eyes to look at Jay, and then smiled. "I'm thinking about Denzel Washington in *Mo Better Blues*."

He snickered and eased his arms around my waist, bringing me even closer to him. My nipples pressing against his soapy buffed chest had my thoughts on no one but him.

"I doubt that you're thinking about Denzel," he said with confidence. "But just in case you are, I'd better figure out a way to change the mood and shake things up in here."

My words were clipped tight, as I held my stare, gazing into his eyes. Denzel was the furthest person from my mind, but Jay didn't have to know it. I was feeling real good, and witnessing him naked in a steam-filled bathroom with hot water dripping down his body...my heart couldn't stop pitter-patting. I lathered my hands to wash him, and as I rubbed all over his body, I was in awe by how well his frame was carved to near perfection. I got a chance to look at every single inch of him and I only wished that my girls could see this, instead of what they had seen with Miles. Again, they wouldn't believe it! Someway...somehow I had to get the word out about this man, and I was already thinking about what to write in my notebook. Jay had definitely given me something more to write about, and much of it stemmed from what had happened only hours later.

I had fallen asleep, and as soon as I walked out of Jay's bedroom, I could see him sitting in the near dark living room while I stood on the balcony above him. There was a humongous Christmas tree in his living room, and as the lights blinked, he stared at the tree as if he were in deep thought. I wasn't sure what was on his mind, but he was holding what looked to be some type of ornament in his hand. He sat back on his couch, and when he closed his eyes, I waited a few minutes before going downstairs. No doubt about it, I could tell Jay was going through something deep.

I slowly made my way down the winding staircase, without Jay hearing me. It was only when I straddled his lap that he opened his eyes and secured his arms around my waist. I kissed down the side of his neck and licked my tongue around his ear, tickling it.

"You're trying to seduce me, aren't you?" he asked.

"No, I just want you to forget about where you've been and think about where you're going?"

He slowly nodded. "Is that with you?"

"I hope so, but you tell me. Is it?"

"No doubt," was all he said, but I wasn't so sure.

Jay held the sides of my face in his hands, as if I were the most precious thing ever. He laid me back on the couch, opening my shirt until it revealed my naked body. With his eyes closed, he pecked down my neck and entered me at the same time. At first, his pace was slow, and the way he grinded to reach the depths of my walls was impressive. Then, his rhythm sped up. His breathing increased and so did mine. A few more minutes into our sex session, our bodies started to sweat. I reached up to hold the back of his head, and ran my fingers through the natural wet curls in his hair. My insides were hurting a bit from his hard thrusts and I became curious as to why he had chosen to indulge himself in such a way. Eventually, he calmed down a little, and as we both observed his nine-plus inches of thick meat disappear inside of me, the moment intensified again.

"How does your pussy feel?" Jay asked in a smooth and sultry voice, as if he genuinely cared for the wellbeing of my pussy. "Am I treating *it* right?"

Before I answered, I thought about Dwayne being the silent lover, Miles being the dirty-talker, and Jay being the sexy, smooth talker that took our intimate moment to a whole new level. He locked his eyes with mine, waiting for an answer, so I gave him one. "If it wasn't filled to capacity with all of your goodness, then it would be able to tell you how spectacular it feels. I hope it's okay that I speak for it, and yes...hell yes you're treating *it* like royalty."

"That's because I respect the pussy, especially when it's this wet and sweet. I don't mind giving it the red carpet treatment."

"*Sweet?* How do you know it's sweet?"

Jay slowed his strokes, and circled his fingers around my clit. He then sucked his fingers into his mouth and licked his lips. "Like I said before...sweet. I'm damn sure gon' find out how sweet, before all is said and done."

Well, get to it and let me know what you find out! I thought. The red carpet treatment was working quite well for me. So well, that as his fingers continued to circle my clit, I was in the midst of having my first orgasm ever. I roared Jay's name, expressing my enthusiasm. The passion that I desired to feel for a man had finally arrived, and I was near tears because being with Jay felt so good! His overall deliverance was an A, triple plus. I could feel his body get tense, so I thought he was on the verge of coming. But his next words shocked me like electricity.

"Daaaamn, Scorpio," he shouted, and then paused to take a deep breath. My eyes shot open and he dropped his wrinkled forehead on my heaving chest. I pulled his hair, lifting his head away from me. There was a blank expression on my face. I narrowed my eyes as I gazed into Jay's agonizing facial expression that displayed shame. All that I had felt for him escaped from every window. My blood was boiling inside, and I couldn't believe he had called me by another woman's name. A woman who was in Colorado, trying to escape the fallout from their relationship. He'd told me a lot about their unstable relationship, but she was obviously the one on his mind, not me.

At that moment, I flashed back to Dwayne being on top of me and thought about what the end result would be, if he'd called me by another woman's name. He would have paid for inflicting this kind of hurt on me. There I was, again, contemplating a fistfight or setting some of Jay's shit on fire, like this house! I could see Jay knocking the hell out of me, him calling the police and us going at it like damn fools. But I couldn't go there again—no, I wouldn't, especially with men who continued to bring out the worst in me. There were two words that came to mind and those words were...walk away. Before I did, I had to be sure that I'd heard Jay say what he did.

"What did you just call me?" I asked. "Did you just say what I think you said?"

He shut his eyes and turned his head to look away. "Brenda, I'm sorry. I just—"

My emotions were about to take over, but I held back on shedding any tears. "You ju...just need to get up off me."

His eyes were back, staring into mine as he continued to lay over me. "Look, I understand how you must feel, but I got caught up in the moment."

"With her, Jay, or with me? I don't think I need an answer, so plea...please, get up."

Jay hesitated for a second, and then he got up. He couldn't say anything else to me, and I was so damn tired of the bullshit with men. I was starting to hate them. Why was it so damn hard for me to find a decent man? More so, where was the man who was capable of bringing out the best in me! I was proud of myself for not cussing, fighting, screaming...basically, acting a fool because someone had done me wrong. Walking away made me feel good, and I wasted no time going upstairs, putting on my clothes and getting the hell out of there. Jay knew not to say one word to me, but when I got home, there was a message from him on my voicemail.

"I'm so sorry," he said, pitifully.

I was sorry, too. Sorry for having to hear those words over and over again. Sorry that I couldn't figure out why men did the shit they did, and sorry that my experience with Jay would go down as another gotdamn lesson learned. Not only that, but I was going to have to immediately dismiss the next man who told me he was fucking sorry!

That night, I got busy. What had happened with Jay hurt me, but it also inspired me, like I had never been inspired to write before. *So much for the red carpet treatment! Respect the pussy, fine, but respect the woman too. Was that so hard to do? I guess so, and for that I take back my A, triple plus and give Jay a big fat B! No, okay...an A, single plus. Double?*

This time while writing, I laughed, instead of crying. My pen was moving fast and I was definitely getting it in. My character's name in my story was Daisha—a name that I thought was pretty cute. I hadn't written to this extent in a long time, but my enthusiasm was back! A sense of true joy came over me and I vowed to never depart with my notebook again—no matter what!

Chapter Thirty

Over the course of one year, so many things had transpired. Many things were good: I moved into my first home, was saving for the twins' college education, was close to completing a whole novel and I had a job that I loved. But life brought about the unexpected too. My cousin, Josh, had died in his sleep and the news devastated me. I was saddened that I hadn't made peace with him, and I vowed to never, again, let another person that I loved leave this earth with bitterness between us.

I had also remained friends with Jay, but eventually, intimacy was left completely off the table. What I appreciated about him the most was he gave me the truth about his relationships with other women, allowing me to decide if I wanted to continue on with a man that I knew would never fully commit to no one. I needed more than a man like Jay in my life, and great sex and being able to grant me multiple orgasms wasn't enough. I realized that every man who crossed paths with me wasn't destined to become my husband. Even Dwayne had taught me some valuable lessons; lessons that made me wiser and unable to let a man ever take me to that level again. I needed peace, and my platonic relationship with Jay enabled me to develop a solid and respectful connection with a man I truly considered my first love. At times, he was my inspiration to keep my eyes on the prize, pertaining to business, and he was doing his best to show me the ropes on how I, too, could make money. His confidence and perspective about so many things had rubbed off on me and my vision about what life could be had grown beyond my expectations.

For him, I was the friend to lend an ear to, when he needed someone to talk to. That was quite often, because even though Jay had it together financially, and could offer some of the best advice to benefit others, his life was filled with everlasting drama. Drama, that when combined with mine, could make one hell of a good story. I couldn't help but think of him, and his business advice, when I received Health Partners of the Midwest Most Valuable Person Award that totally shocked me. Mr. Schnieder watched as they presented the award to me that day, and smiled as I gave my speech commending him for believing in me to begin with and for giving me an opportunity.

Then, less than three months after that, news broke fast: Health Partners was being sold to another insurance company and downsizing happened again! Mr. Schnieder said the final payout would carry us through for about six to eight months and that would be it. I had just about had it with Corporate America, but I'd already had my foot in the door at Cutter & Company in Chesterfield, so I wasn't too worried. The salary that was offered to me was unbelievable and it didn't include the commissions or ongoing residual income I'd receive. I had damn sure made a way out of no way, but in no way had I done it alone. So many things had to fall into place, and timing was everything. Only by my Saviors design did He line up the individuals in my life to help me pull this off.

If I planned everything accordingly, within the next year or so, my own business could be well on its way. I worked countless hours, trying to prepare myself for a rewarding life. Even while I was on welfare and would sell stolen clothes for money, I'd visualized what my current life would look like. I was lazy at times, but deep down, I wanted more. It wasn't until I started trusting and believing that all things were possible that my life took a turn for the better.

As I worked hard on reforming myself, I surrounded myself with people I could learn something from. I was hungry for knowledge, starving for it would be more like it. Many people were encouraging me to someday start my own insurance business, and since I was growing and maintaining Cutter & Company's million-dollar-plus book of business, starting my own business made sense.

My family, however, wanted me to stay committed to writing! Mama had asked to read some of my writings, but they were so salacious that I didn't want her to read them.

"It's too much, Mama. I really don't know how you're going to feel about what I be writing."

"What do you mean by too much?"

"I mean, I kind of talk about sexual stuff and use profanities sometimes. My stories have good messages, though, and I hope people get it."

"I hope so too, but your stories couldn't be any worse than those notebooks you used to keep in that closet. I started to throw those damn things away, and you thought you were so slick, trying to hide them from me."

"Mama!" I shouted. "You read my notebooks? Why didn't you ever say anything?"

Mama laughed. "There are a lot of things I know, that you don't think I know, but remember this. I'm your mother. I know you like the back of my hand. You're very gifted, Brenda, and I'm so glad that you're on a path to finding out who you really are and what you're capable of doing."

Mama always knew the right things to say and when to say them.

As for Jesse, she couldn't get enough of what I had written and was calling me on a daily basis, asking if I had written more so she could read it.

"This shit is the bomb!" she shouted. "I'll be over after work to get the rest of those pages. Have them ready!"

My smile was wide, and she could count on it, as I definitely had more pages ready for her to read. Rita hadn't read any of my writings, but from speaking to Jesse, Rita knew I was on to something.

"My little sister, a writer?" Rita questioned. "Or, are you going to start your own insurance business?"

"I'm going to do both," I replied with confidence. "The sky is the limit."

"I heard that. Do your thing, girl. Hampton Insurance Agency does have a ring to it."

No doubt, it did. Then, there was Jay who I'd let read the first five chapters of my manuscript. I was waiting patiently for his feedback. I had called him several times that day to see what he'd thought, but he promised to get back to me within the hour.

I was in the kitchen washing dishes, while listening to the radio. I snapped my fingers to the beat of Janet Jackson's music, and after the song ended, the radio host chimed in.... *The forecast calls for sunshine in the Show-Me-State and rain, again, for the weekend. So, keep your umbrellas handy, as it looks to be a wet one. In other news, Dwayne Montgomery of the 1100 block of Johanna was arrested this morning for shooting at two police officers...*

My heart dropped to my stomach. I turned up the radio to hear what Dwayne had gotten himself into. I sadly shook my head, and all I could do was say another prayer for the man who had taught me one of my biggest lessons about life, as well as relationships. For that, I had no regrets, because I now knew why Dwayne and I had crossed paths. He was an obstacle...one that I had to overcome. I jumped when the phone rang, startled as the blaring sound knocked me out of my thoughts. When I answered, it was Jay.

"I don't like this," he said straight to the point and referring to the numerous chapters I'd written about him. "Start over."

My heart dropped, again, and my feelings were hurt because he didn't enjoy my story like I thought he would. The only reason his opinion mattered was because I had used him as my main character. My face fell flat and I stuttered, defending my writing. "I...I regret that you didn't like it, but—"

"I said I didn't like it. I loved it!" he shouted. "Damn, Brenda, you did your thing, but the reason why I want you to start over is because you...you got me being a little too weak and...*nice*. That's not me all the time and I think you know that."

I laughed. A huge smile was plastered on my face. "I know it's not, but I tried to be as gentle as possible with your character, because I didn't want to hurt your feelings."

"You only hurt my feelings when you don't tell that shit like it is! I'm a hundred percent satisfied with who I am, and I want my personality to shine on these pages. Put that shit out there, baby. Bring out the real me and don't hold back. You won't regret it, and the women will love me, or hate to love me. Trust me on this."

I hesitated going his route; after all, Jay could be something else! He was too much at times, and putting him out there "as is" would definitely infuriate some readers. Either way, I agreed to it. "I hope I won't regret it, but I'm going all in. Wish me luck."

"You got it. I don't want to read anymore until you're done. Get busy."

Jay hung up and I did just that—got busy.

I was on a roll with writing and it was so funny how every person who had been a part of my life served a purpose for what I was creating. I spent the next several months reworking my story, trying to make sense of it. I laughed and cried with my characters. Each of them had traits of me or resembled someone I had met or known. So, hell, yes, I used my own experiences to write, as I believed most writers did. I added a touch of creativeness to the story, and most of all, made Jay out to be the man who he truly was.

As I neared the end, the first person I called was Jesse. She rushed over to get my manuscript and within a few hours she was done reading. I could hear her laughter over the phone.

"Girrrrrrl," she shouted. "I don't know how you do it, but you are on to something. What's next? What are you going to do next?"

"I'm going to keep on writing, and then find me an editor. Then, I'll do some research on how to publish a book, look for a literary agent and pretty much go from there. Are you sure you liked it, though? You aren't just saying that because you're my sister, are you?"

"I have always been honest with you about everything. I'm not lying when I say, This Is It!"

I was smiling so hard. "You think so, huh?"

"Yes! Did you hear what I said...This Is It!"

I nodded and Jesse was so very right. THIS WAS IT! Writing was my calling...

Epilogue

Now at the age of thirty-three, I was in my home office, reviewing insurance quotes and making cold calls to grow my insurance business even more. It was going well, and under my own company, Hampton Insurance Agency, I had brokered insurance deals for over fifty companies throughout the St. Louis Metro area. That didn't include the hundreds of individual insurance policies I'd sold and I was on a roll! I had plenty of contacts, and during my spare time, I was preparing to write my next book, and then send it to my editor. *Two's Enough Three's A Crowd (Naughty One)* had been out there for three months. I self published it, because I had gotten numerous rejection letters from literary agents. My sales were nothing to brag about, so I started to put together a marketing plan. As I worked on it, I received an instant email on my computer.

Dear Ms. Hampton,

First, let me CONGRATULATE you on a wonderful well put together book, *Two's Enough Three's a Crowd*. I have recommended this book to over 10 PEOPLE at my job already and we are all loving it! Your characters are so lively and I read your book in a day and a half. I am trying to find out when will the sequel, *My Way or No Way*, be released? Can I order from you now? If so, is there a physical address so I can order two books and send your payment overnight? As you can see, I am anxious and you are such an inspiration!

P.S. Me and my girlfriends, especially Sabrina, are going crazy trying to find more copies of this book. We lucked up on your website and I hope you get this message! Please help us so we can help Jaylin and Nokea stay together!

Peace & Blessings
Merry Ann Murphy and Sabrina Hubbard
Los Angeles, CA

As I read the first email I'd gotten from a reader, my heart was overwhelmed with joy. I quickly responded and was surprised that my book had made it into the hands of someone all the way in California. Not only that, but I wondered how someone like me was considered an inspiration to others? I bounced my pen against the notepad in front of me, and couldn't help but think about my past.

The past was exactly what it was—the past. At this point, I hadn't regretted much about it, and whenever posed with the question about taking back anything that occurred in my life, my answer was absolutely not. My experiences, whether good or bad, I learned valuable lessons. My lessons gave me strength, and they provided me with the confidence I may have never had. Each and every person in my past was there to lift me to a higher calling.

I thought about even in my darkest moments, seconds, days and hours...I was being prepared. Prepared to one day stand before those who bullied me, who made fun of me because my family was poor, who said I wouldn't amount to anything, who abused me, who had lost faith in me, and to those who claimed so dearly to love me but didn't. Today, I was the PRODUCT of what many of those people made me. They turned me into a fighter, determined to achieve great things. I was truly grateful for crossing paths. Only by their design, could I provide my testimony through writing.

I took a deep breath and rested back in my chair. More thoughts swam in my head, and I reminisced about the countless times I'd thought about taking my life. What a tragedy and waste of a good life that would have been. All the pain and suffering I'd endured could have ceased sooner, had I paid attention to what God had shown me and what He was trying to tell me. In not doing so, I paid the price. My aspirations were delayed, and two people claiming to love each other, with no direction in life, will make little or no progress. It had taken me a while to realize that, but thankfully, I did.

I sat thinking about how I'd made my transition from a struggling teenage mother, a welfare recipient, a troublemaker, a very confused young woman, and a criminal, to an outstanding mother who was proud of her daughters away at college, an entrepreneur with a sharp business mind, a woman who could afford to pay for what she wanted and a true believer in God. At least by the age of thirty, a broader vision of my life started to come together for me. I knew my purpose, and all I had to do was figure out how to drive it to the next level. The possibilities were endless, and whenever one door closed, I got hyped. Hyped because I knew another door would open soon.

For now, I thought, while clinching my hands in front of me, my storm had settled. I knew it would soon rage, again, because that's just how life was. I wasn't exempt from trials and tribulations. There would always be setbacks that were setups for changes to come. However, this time, I'd be ready, because, over the years, I was being prepared for this thing called life. Faith was my back-up plan, and with it I'd be promoted to what was to come next. I was glad that I hadn't accepted what society had said about me. And believe it or not, a teenage mother can amount to something. I was living proof that she could be whatever her heart desired, and a person without a college degree can be successful as well. Success wasn't determined by the house I lived in, not by the amount of money I had, nor by the kind of car that I drove. For me, it was determined by the struggles and obstacles for which I've had to overcome to get to where I was today. I was successful even when I didn't have a dime in my pocket, but I had the determination to put one there. My struggles continue, and for each and every time I overcome, I become more successful by the day. More than anything, I've put myself in a position to be a possible inspiration to others, and that defined true success for me.

As I continued to gather my thoughts, I'd have to admit that growing up was tougher than what I had revealed. Often, I was upset by the way my mother had raised me. Because of her upbringing, she rarely showed her emotions and had neglected to share important things with her children such as: periods, sex, education...and most importantly, love. It wasn't until I became an adult that I realized she expressed her love by providing for her family, protecting her family and through exemplifying independence. My sisters and I took those values in which Mom taught us and applied them to our everyday lives. In addition, the things in which my mother failed to share, we broke the cycle and took the initiative to share the realities of life with our children. Because of our willingness to change the past, the bond in which we all share as a family can now be passed down to generations to come. Mama would want it to be that way and so would my father.

I lifted a picture of Mama and held it in my hand. I was visiting her one day at home with the twins and we'd finally had our discussion about men. She told me that men were always going to do the things that men do, and there was no need in me wasting my time trying to figure them out. "Continue to see about your children," she said. "And God will take you a long, long way." That was the best advice she could have given me. We continued to talk further and she said that my grandmother always told her, I'd be "the one." Basically, being considered the Black Sheep of the family would turn in my favor. When I asked what she meant, all she would say was, "You'll see. In due time, you will see." Later on in life, I realized what Mama meant. She was called home, leaving behind a legacy to be proud of. I never did get her that car she wanted, but I knew she was riding high in heaven, especially after seeing her daughter become all that she hoped I would be. Mama fulfilled her purpose in life, and even though I used to ask the Lord...*Why? Why did You take my mother?* I now know why. I often see and speak to Mama in my dreams and her answer to me is always the same...*For 65 years, I walked In My Shoes. There were good days, as well as bad days. Days that I'm proud of and some days that I'm not. Situations that I wish I could take back, but I've accepted with little or no regrets. Still, nobody has walked in my shoes better than me, and now, my dear Daughter, you must continue to hold your head up high and faithfully walk in yours.*

With that, I faithfully and so happily do.

I turned to my computer, laughing at what I was about to write for my next book. I'd gotten the hang of this writing thing, and my characters were already causing quite a stir. *I could do this forever,* I thought. *Oh, how I lovvvve my life. What if, in less than ten years, I, Brenda Hampton, could become a household name and my books would be in bookstores all around the country?* I chuckled from the thought, but little did I know, that thought became my reality!

Brenda M. Hampton has dedicated her career to all things literary. She has penned more than twenty-plus bestselling novels and anthologies, and works as a representative for numerous authors on the literary scene. Her career is filled with many accomplishments; none more satisfying than assisting talented writers reach their goals. The Brenda Hampton Honorary Literacy Award, rewarded each year, celebrates writing and acknowledges individuals who put forth every effort to uphold the standards of African American Literature. Additional information regarding this dynamic author can be found at www.brendamhampton.com.

Made in the USA
Charleston, SC
23 August 2012